THE GOOD, THE BAD, AND THE BEAUTIFUL

JOSEPH PEARCE

The Good, the Bad, and the Beautiful

History in Three Dimensions

IGNATIUS PRESS   SAN FRANCISCO

Art credits

(Top panel)
Last Judgement
Fra Angelico, circa 1450
Gemäldegalerie, Berlin
Wikimedia Commons Image

(middle and bottom panel)
Landscape with Crossing of the Styx
(details of Sheol and the Land of the Blessed)
Joachim Patinir, circa 1480–1524
Museo del Prado, Madrid
Wikimedia Commons Image

Cover design by Enrique J. Aguilar

© 2023 by Ignatius Press, San Francisco
All rights reserved
ISBN 978-1-62164-534-4 (PB)
ISBN 978-1-64229-249-7 (eBook)
Library of Congress Catalogue number 2023934924
Printed in the United States of America ∞

CONTENTS

Prologue: The Three Dimensions of History   7

"In the Beginning ..."   11
Life, Death, and Resurrection

First Century   15
"This Is My Body"

Second Century   26
Romans and Catholics

Third Century   36
Mother and Bride

Fourth Century   46
"Upon This Rock"

Fifth Century   56
The City of God

Sixth Century   69
The Resurrection of Rome

Seventh Century   82
Northern Lights

Eighth Century   93
Anglo-Saxons and Saracens

Ninth Century   105
Great Kings and Vikings

Tenth Century   116
Monasteries and Monstrosities

Eleventh Century   126
Ends and Beginnings

Twelfth Century   140
    Charity and Chivalry

Thirteenth Century   154
    The Best and Worst of Times

Fourteenth Century   165
    Holy Women and Divine Poets

Fifteenth Century   179
    Rebirth and Rebellion

Sixteenth Century   193
    Rupture and Reformation

Seventeenth Century   207
    Old and New

Eighteenth Century   220
    Religion and Superstition

Nineteenth Century   236
    Revolution, Revelation, and Revival

Twentieth Century   254
    Wars of Irreligion

Epilogue: The End of History   277

Index   281

PROLOGUE

The Three Dimensions of History

Director Sergio Leone considered his iconic spaghetti Western, *The Good, the Bad, and the Ugly*, to be a satire on the Western genre and a deconstruction of the romanticism surrounding the Old West. His antihero, played by Clint Eastwood, represents the antithesis of the archetypal Western hero, the latter of whom, epitomized by John Wayne, could be seen as a modern-day knight in shining armor, sure-sighted in terms of both virtue and marksmanship, and unswervingly chivalrous in the face of chicanery. In shockingly sardonic contrast, all three of the protagonists in Leone's Western are utterly self-serving, spurning the self-sacrifice that is the very essence of true heroism. It could be argued, therefore, that a more accurate and fitting title for the film, or at least a more accurate depiction of its spirit, would be *The Bad, the Worse, and the Ugly*. In this sense, it can be seen that Leone looks at what he perceives to be New World naiveté from the jaded perspective of Old World cynicism.

And it could be argued that Leone takes his cynicism still further. On a deeper level than the desire to deconstruct and subvert the romance surrounding the "Wild West" is the desire to subvert the traditional transcendental foundation of the Old West, which is wisdom itself. At the heart of all healthy societies and cultures is the presence of the good, the true, and the beautiful. This triune presence is perfected in the Person of Christ, who is, as He tells us, "the way, and the truth, and the life".[1] He is the way of goodness, which is to say that He embodies the fullness of virtue made manifest in love; He is the truth, which is to say that He is the end to which all properly ordered reason points; and He is the very life of beauty, which is to say that He shines forth the glory of creation as the Word-made-flesh, as the poem that perfectly reflects the perfection of the Poet. Since this is so, it can be seen that the more that Christ is present in the soul of a culture or society, the more will such a society or culture truly reflect the goodness, truth, and beauty of His image. Conversely, His absence leads to the way of evil, to the de(con)struction of truth in the living of the lie, and to the killing of life in the culture of death and its cult of ugliness.

Once this is understood, we can see the very pattern of history as a tapestry, time-stitched and weird-woven,[2] of varying threads that are good, bad, or beautiful. These threads reflect the three facets of man, who manifests himself in life and therefore in history as *homo viator*, *homo superbus*, and *anthropos*.[3]

Homo viator is pilgrim man; he is the man on the journey of life, which he sees as the quest for heaven, his ultimate

---

[1] Jn 14:6.

[2] The word *weird* derives from the Old English *wyrd*, which is often erroneously defined as "fate" or "personal destiny". Irrespective of whether such a definition might have applied to earlier Germanic pagan culture, the word, as used in the profoundly Catholic culture of Anglo-Saxon England, meant the mystical presence of divine providence. The idea of the weird-woven web is that all human actions impact others in a way that ultimately expresses God's providential design.

[3] Although scholars differ with respect to the etymology of *anthropos*, the Greek word for *man*, it is being used here according to Plato's definition that it means one who looks up (in wonder or contemplation) as distinct from other animals that do not do so. The animal grazes but man gazes!

and only true purpose. His is the path of virtue, the path of the saints and aspiring saints. He weaves the threads of goodness that we see in history.

Homo superbus is proud man; he is the man who refuses the appointed journey, spurning the quest for heaven so that he can "do his own thing". *Homo superbus* does not sacrifice his life for others; he sacrifices the lives of others for himself. He wanders from the path of virtue in the waywardness of egocentrism and the viciousness that is its cankered fruit. He weaves the bad threads of wickedness that we see in history.

Anthropos is poetic man; he is man who looks up in wonder at the beauty of the cosmos, singing its praises by the making of beautiful things. His is the way of creativity that reflects the presence of the Creator Himself in the creation of beautiful works. He weaves the threads of beauty that illuminate the threads of goodness, offering hope in the midst of evil.

These three threads weave their way through the hearts of each and every person, forming the tapestry that reveals the pattern of their individual lives. In consequence, these same threads weave their way through the collective lives of men, which we call history. They are the three dimensions of history itself.

In every generation, the virtuous find themselves living as exiles in a vale of tears, witnessing to the goodness of love even unto death in a world of sin and sorrow dominated by viciousness. In the midst of this never-ending interwoven battle between good and evil is also woven the indomitable power of beauty, both in the grandeur of God to be seen in the beauty of creation and also in the glory of God's creative presence in the beauty of great art. No one has seen this perennially present three-dimensional pattern in the tapestry of history more clearly than Joseph

Cardinal Ratzinger (the future Pope Benedict XVI). In words of beauty and brilliance, Cardinal Ratzinger speaks of the goodness of the saints and the beauty of art as the only antidote to the dark thread of evil that runs through the whole of human history:

> The only really effective apologia for Christianity comes down to two arguments, namely the saints the Church has produced and the art which has grown in her womb. Better witness is borne to the Lord by the splendor of holiness and art which have arisen in the community of believers than by clever excuses which apologetics has come up with to justify the dark sides which, sadly, are so frequent in the Church's human history. If the Church is to continue to transform and humanize the world, how can she dispense with beauty in her liturgies, that beauty which is so closely linked with love and with the radiance of the Resurrection? No. Christians must not be too easily satisfied. They must make their Church into a place where beauty—and hence truth—is at home. Without this the world will become the first circle of hell.[4]

It is, therefore, the twin threads woven by the goodness of the saints and the beauty of the arts that witness to God's presence, in contrast to the third dark and twisted thread of pride that witnesses to his absence. All three threads are interwoven in the history of man because they are all interwoven in the heart of man. Inspired by this understanding of history and by these words of Cardinal Ratzinger, the present author has sought to present the history of the past two millennia in the light of this three-dimensional pattern of the good, the bad, and the beautiful.

---

[4] Joseph Cardinal Ratzinger with Vittorio Messori, *The Ratzinger Report* (San Francisco: Ignatius Press, 1985), 129–30.

"In the Beginning ..."

Life, Death, and Resurrection

> *In the beginning was the Word, and the Word was with God, and the Word was God.*
>
> —John 1:1

The very first thing that we need to know about history is that it is worded into being. Its pattern preexists it in eternity. It is made manifest in what we call time by the Word of God and the will of God, in whom and in which there is no past and no future, only omnipresence. To the One who patterns it, Alexander the Great and Alfred the Great are equally present, even though, in terms of time, they lived more than a thousand years apart. To our finite and timebound perception this is, of course, a mystery. History is, therefore, a mystery. It needs to be seen in the light by which it exists: "God said, 'Let there be light'; and there was light. And God saw that the light was good."[1]

None of this would be known or indeed knowable unless God Himself had revealed it. This He does in the Person and the Incarnation of Jesus Christ. It is in Christ that God reveals Himself to man, and it is also in Christ that God reveals Man to men. Christ shows us in Himself the perfect man to whose perfection we are called to strive, and He reveals to us in His life, death, and Resurrection

[1] Gen 1:3.

the very template of the pattern of history. "And the Word became flesh and dwelt among us."[2]

In His revelation of Himself as "the way, and the truth, and the life",[3] Christ reveals Himself as the good, the true, and the beautiful. When He commands us to follow Him, He calls us to love one another as He has loved us.[4] When He tells us to take up our cross in order to follow Him,[5] we are shown that love is inseparable from self-sacrifice, demanding the death of the self for the good of the other. He shows us that love comes at a great price, which we must be willing to pay. The way of Christ is, therefore, the way of the cross. There is no other way, except the way of refusal. The acceptance of the cross is the thread of goodness, or sanctity, which weaves its way across the centuries; the refusal of the cross is the evil thread, which, ironically and paradoxically, is the very cause of the suffering that it refuses to accept.

In this sense, the whole of humanity and the whole of human history can be seen to be present at Golgotha, on either side of Christ, in the presence of the good and bad thief.[6] The one is repentant, accepting his suffering; the other is unrepentant, resenting his suffering. One accepts the cross, the other refuses it; but both are crucified. Golgotha shows us that there is no escape from suffering. It is simply what we choose to do with it. This is the pattern of good and evil, which is weird-woven throughout history by the choosers and refusers of the cross.

But what of the third thread? What of beauty? As with the acceptance of the cross, it is inseparable from humility.

[2] Jn 1:14.
[3] Jn 14:6.
[4] See Jn 15:12.
[5] See Mt 16:24.
[6] See Lk 23:39–43.

It is humility that gives us the sense of gratitude that opens the eyes in wonder; and it is only with eyes wide open with wonder that we are moved to the contemplation that leads to the opening of the mind and soul into the fullness of the beauty of God's presence in creation. We will follow Christ only if we see Him as the Son of God and acclaim Him as such. If our eyes are wide open with wonder, we will see that He is not merely a man but also is our Lord and our God. It is the scribes, Pharisees, and hypocrites, with their eyes shut in pride, who refused to believe the Word of God, even when He was in their midst. It was they who saw only the man and not God, and it is they who demanded that the man be crucified, not that God be adored.[7] They were blind to the beauty dwelling among them.

Returning to Christ's revelation of Himself as "the way, and the truth, and the life", we can see that beauty is the *life* of Christ in both the beholder of beauty and in the beauty beheld. Without such life, our pride and prejudice make us blind. This is evident in the way that we perceive the Gospel, which, as we have seen, is the very template of the pattern of history. It is only if we see the ugliness of the Crucifixion from the perspective of the beauty of the Resurrection that we can perceive the fullness of the life of Christ that defeats death itself. Without this Christ-life, we see only death; and if we see only death, it is because we are not alive. Without this Christ-light, we see only darkness; and if we see only darkness, it is because we are blind. The problem is not with the life or the light but with the lifeless blindness of the one who fails to behold it.

In seeing the Crucifixion in the light of the Resurrection, we are also seeing the long defeat of human history,

[7] See Mt 27:22–23; Mk 15:13–14; Lk 23:21–23; Jn 19:15–16.

awash as it is with wickedness, in the light of the final victory that Christ has already won. This is the light and the life that illumines and animates the three dimensions of history.

First Century

"This Is My Body"

The Good

The life, death, and Resurrection of Christ was enacted on a Roman imperial stage, Palestine being part of Rome's burgeoning empire. Such was the pomp and pomposity of imperial Rome that it saw itself as the Eternal City, destined by the gods to rule the world. This was expressed with triumphalist zeal in *The Aeneid*, Virgil's patriotic epic, written twenty or so years before the birth of Christ. *The Aeneid* depicted Rome as being founded by the Trojan warrior Aeneas, who had sailed to Rome on a perilous voyage, via many adventures, having been warned in a dream to escape the fall of Troy. The idea was that Rome, the Eternal City, had risen phoenixlike from the ashes of Troy. Seen in this mythical light, the great historian Christopher Dawson perceived that St. Paul was the real-life Aeneas, introducing the Church to Europe, which, a few centuries later, would rise from the ashes of the fallen Roman Empire:

Now the Virgilian myth became the Christian reality. When St. Paul, in obedience to the warning of a dream, set sail from Troy in A.D. 49 and came to Philippi in Macedonia he did more to change the course of history than the great battle that had decided the fate of the Roman Empire on the same spot nearly a century earlier, for he

brought to Europe the seed of a new life which was ultimately destined to create a new world.[1]

It is largely through St. Paul, along with St. Luke, that
we gain our knowledge of the first century of Christendom, the latter of whom, as author of the Acts of the Apostles, wrote the earliest history of the Church. It is through
their testimony that we know that, within ten years of
Christ's death and Resurrection, Christianity (as it became
known) had spread from Palestine to Antioch, Ephesus,
Corinth, Cyprus, Thessalonica, Crete, and Rome. There
were Christians in Rome before either St. Peter or St. Paul
arrived in the city.

Although St. Paul, as the apostle to the gentiles, seems
to have been the most successful in spreading the Gospel and winning converts, he was never considered the
leader of the early Church, nor the one who spoke with
most authority. That role clearly belonged to St. Peter.
In all three of the synoptic Gospels (Matthew, Mark, and
Luke), Peter's name is always placed first in every list of
the names of the apostles. In all three Gospels, he is the
first of the disciples to be called by Christ. In St. Matthew's Gospel, we are told that it is Christ Himself who
gives Peter his name, which means "rock", declaring that
"on this rock I will build my Church", adding that He
will give to Peter "the keys of the kingdom of heaven",
promising that whatever Peter bound on earth would
be bound in heaven also.[2] St. John, echoing the other
three Evangelists, also gives Peter prominence as the first
of the apostles, telling us that Christ commanded Peter

---

[1] Christopher Dawson, *Religion and the Rise of Western Culture* (New York: Image Books, 1958), 27.

[2] Mt 16:18–19.

three times to "feed my lambs",[3] "tend my sheep",[4] "feed
my sheep."[5] There was, therefore, from the beginning,
no doubt about the apostle to whom Christ had bestowed
the authority to govern and lead the Church. It is also
clear from the Acts of the Apostles, St. Luke's continua-
tion of, or "sequel" to, his Gospel, that Peter is considered
the foremost figure in the newborn Church. It is Peter
who leads the proclamation of the Resurrection at Pentecost; it is he who presides over meetings; it is he who
works miracles; and it is he who is rescued from prison
by an angel.[6] In his baptism of the centurion Cornelius
in obedience to a heavenly vision,[7] which showed that
the reception of the gentile into the Church was God's
will, he precedes and therefore symbolically supersedes St.
Paul's role as apostle to the gentiles.

After his miraculous escape from prison, it seems that
Peter went into exile to escape Herod's persecution of the
Church. All that St. Luke tells us is that "he departed and
went to another place".[8] The next we know of Peter's
whereabouts is given in his First Letter, which was written
in a time of persecution from "Babylon", an early Christian euphemism for Rome.

If St. Peter had escaped from persecution in Jerusalem,
only to find a similar persecution in Rome, moving from
the proverbial frying pan to the fire, St. Paul was similarly dogged on his travels by persecutors of the Church.
In Damascus, he escaped from a garrison of soldiers sent
to arrest him by being let down in a basket through a

[3] Jn 21:15.
[4] Jn 21:16.
[5] Jn 21:17.
[6] See Acts 2–5; 9–12.
[7] See Acts 10:1–33.
[8] Acts 12:17.

window in the wall of the city, and this was by no means the worst of his troubles:

> Five times I have received at the hands of the Jews the forty lashes less one. Three times I have been beaten with rods; once I was stoned. Three times I have been shipwrecked; a night and a day I have been adrift at sea; on frequent journeys, in danger from rivers, danger from robbers, danger from my own people, danger from Gentiles, danger in the city, danger in the wilderness, danger at sea, danger from false brethren; in toil and hardship, through many a sleepless night, in hunger and thirst, often without food, in cold and exposure.[9]

The apostle's courage in the face of these trials and tribulations is breathtaking. He tells the Romans that he reckoned "the sufferings of this present time are not worth comparing with the glory that is to be revealed",[10] and to the Corinthians, who were prone to sensuality and the desire for comfort, he counsels the embrace of the suffering that comes with discipleship:

> We are afflicted in every way, but not crushed; perplexed, but not driven to despair; persecuted, but not forsaken; struck down, but not destroyed; always carrying in the body the death of Jesus, so that the life of Jesus may also be manifested in our bodies. For while we live we are always being given up to death for Jesus' sake, so that the life of Jesus may be manifested in our mortal flesh.[11]

These words of courageous faith, written by an apostle, were also the words of a prophet. St. Paul, along with St.

[9] 2 Cor 11:24–27.
[10] Rom 8:18.
[11] 2 Cor 4:8–11.

Peter, would be put to death in Rome, sometime between A.D. 64 and 68, during the persecutions in the reign of the emperor Nero. According to tradition, St. Peter was crucified upside down on the site of what is now the high altar of St. Peter's Basilica, a tradition that appeared to be confirmed forensically during excavations in the twentieth century in which the remains of a first-century man, who was aged around sixty at the time of death, was discovered beneath the crypt under the altar. St. Paul was beheaded just south of Rome. "The 'Healthful Fountains' still whisper beneath the whispering trees where they beheaded him," wrote the Jesuit C.C. Martindale, "and you may find it easier to pray to him there than in the vast basilica under which still his body lies."[12]

The Bad

Nero's persecution of the Church was one of the earliest manifestations of the secularist intolerance of those who refuse to render unto Caesar the things of God.[13] It is to Caesar that we now turn our attention.

Tiberius Caesar, the ruler of Rome during the time of Christ, was a septuagenarian when Jesus began His public ministry, and died four years after the Crucifixion. It is not known whether he died of natural causes or whether he was murdered on the orders of Caligula, his successor. Caligula would rule for a little under four years before falling victim to a conspiracy of senators and members of the elite Praetorian Guard. He was murdered in what was

---

[12] C.C. Martindale, S.J., "Paul; Apostle, Martyr", in *Great Catholics*, ed. Claude Williamson, O.S.C. (London: Nicholson and Watson, 1938), 49.
[13] See Lk 20:25.

effectively a military coup, the Praetorian Guard proclaiming Claudius, Caligula's uncle, as the new emperor, a fait accompli de facto that was ratified by the Senate de jure. Claudius would reign until A.D. 54, dying at the age of sixty-three, probably being poisoned by his wife Agrippina so that her son, Nero, could rule in his place.

The political culture of endemic treachery and murder, which had characterized the reign of his predecessors, would characterize the reign of Nero, who was only sixteen years old when he became emperor. If anything, Nero took the art of treachery and murder to even more tyrannical extremes. He had his own mother murdered, an act of ingratitude that was fitting recompense for the murderous way she had brought him to power.

According to the second-century Roman historian Suetonius, writing only fifty or sixty years after Nero's reign, "Nero practiced every kind of obscenity",[14] including marrying a boy whom he had castrated specially for the occasion. Many of his other perversions are so obscene that they do not even bear mentioning. His most famous or infamous act, the arson that set Rome ablaze in A.D. 64, is also recounted by Suetonius, who claims that the deranged emperor wanted to destroy "drab old buildings" to make way for the building of a new palace for himself, as well as for the perverse aesthetic pleasure of seeing "the beauty of the flames".[15] Having raised the fury of the people for this act of wanton destruction of their own city, Nero sought to deflect blame through the use of a scapegoat. According to another Roman historian, Tacitus, who was also writing only fifty or sixty years after the

---

[14] Gaius Tranquillus Suetonius, *The Twelve Caesars*, trans. Robert Graves (London: Folio Society, 1994), 225.

[15] Ibid., 232.

events he describes, Nero chose the followers of Christ as the scapegoat he needed. According to Tacitus, the killing of Christians "was made a matter of sport: some were sewn up in the skins of wild beasts and savaged to death by dogs; others were fastened to crosses as living torches, to serve as lights when daylight failed."[16] As we have seen, it was during this period of intense persecution that SS. Peter and Paul were martyred.

In A.D. 68, four years after the Great Fire, Nero fled Rome to escape the military and civil authorities who had risen against him. Learning that he had been tried in absentia and sentenced to death as a public enemy, Nero committed suicide, thus ending one of the most tyrannical episodes in history.

Two years after the death of Nero, and over a thousand miles to the east of Rome, another major historical event would prove crucial to the future of Christianity and there-fore to the future of the world. This was the destruction of Jerusalem and its temple by the Romans in retribu-tion for the Jewish revolt against Roman rule. According to Eusebius, the historian of the early Church—writing in the early fourth century, about 250 years later—the destruction of Jerusalem and its temple was not merely retribution by the Roman Empire for the Jewish revolt against Roman rule but divine retribution for the Jewish revolt against the rule of Christ:

After the Ascension of our Saviour, the Jews had followed up their crime against Him by devising plot after plot against His disciples. First they stoned Stephen to death; then James the son of Zebedee and brother of John was

---

[16] Tacitus, *Annals* 44, 3–7, quoted in H. W. Crocker III, *Triumph: The Power and the Glory of the Catholic Church* (New York: Three Rivers Press, 2001), 25.

beheaded; and finally James, the first after our Saviour's Ascension to be raised to the bishop's throne there, lost his life in the way described [by being clubbed to death], while the remaining apostles in constant danger from murderous plots were driven out of Judaea.[17]

Ironically, the first-century Jewish historian Josephus also ascribed the destruction of Jerusalem and its temple to divine retribution, though he points the finger at the wickedness of the Jewish mobs who preyed on their fellow Jews during the famine that accompanied the siege of Jerusalem, prior to its destruction:

I cannot refrain from saying what my feelings dictate. I think that if the Romans had delayed their attack on these sacrilegious ruffians, either the ground would have opened and swallowed up the city, or a flood would have overwhelmed it, or lightning would have destroyed it like Sodom. For it produced a generation far more godless than those who perished thus, a generation whose mad folly involved the nation in ruin.[18]

Irrespective of the natural or supernatural reasons for the destruction of Jerusalem, its impact would be seismic with respect to the growth and spread of Christianity and the subsequent and consequent history of Christendom. This impact and its importance were summarized with succinct and evocative eloquence by H. W. Crocker:

Whether [the destruction of Jerusalem] was with divine sanction or not, Roman swords forever severed any continuing Jewish influence over the development of

---

[17] Eusebius, *The History of the Church from Christ to Constantine*, trans. G. A. Williamson (London: Penguin Classics, 1989), 68.

[18] Josephus, *The Jewish War*, quoted in ibid., 71.

the Christian Church. With Jerusalem and its temple destroyed, Christianity was now, more than ever, a missionary Church to the Gentiles, traveling on Roman roads, sailing in Roman waters ... and communicating in the language of the Greeks. There was no danger that Christianity would be a hermetic religion of a single people. Instead, it was a cosmopolitan religion spreading to all the lands covered by Roman law and garrisoned by Roman soldiers.[19]

The Beautiful

If Christ's self-revelation as "the way, and the truth, and the life"[20] is a manifestation of the transcendental trinity of the good, the true, and the beautiful, we are able to see beauty itself as the *life* of Christ in both the beholder of beauty and in the beauty beheld. In this light, we can see that the beauty of Christ is made manifest most especially in the sacraments that He instituted. Since it is through sacramental grace that the life of Christ becomes present to His followers in all ages, we can see the sacraments as the spiritual conduit through which the beauty of Christ becomes present in history. Without them, the world would be bereft of all true beauty and all true goodness, or, at any rate, it would be bereft of those able to behold such beauty. The Christ-life made present in the sacraments is, therefore, the very light by which we see and the life by which we live.

Such sacramental beauty is present preeminently in the Eucharist, through which the Church is revealed in the

[19] H. W. Crocker III, *Triumph: The Power and the Glory of the Catholic Church* (New York: Three Rivers Press, 2001), 29.

[20] Jn 14:6.

New Testament as the "body of Christ".[21] As Cardinal Ratzinger reminds us, "One is Church and one is a member thereof, not through a sociological adherence, but precisely through incorporation in this Body of the Lord through baptism and the Eucharist."[22] Furthermore, as Ratzinger explains, it is through this eucharistic presence that Christ is present in His Church:

> So let no one say, "The Eucharist is for eating, not looking at." It is not "ordinary bread", as the most ancient of traditions constantly emphasize. Eating it—as we have just said—is a spiritual process, involving the whole man. "Eating" it means worshipping it. Eating it means letting it come into me, so that my "I" is transformed and opens up into the great "we", so that we become "one" in him (cf. Gal 3:16). Thus adoration is not opposed to Communion, nor is it merely added to it. No, Communion only reaches its true depths when it is supported and surrounded by adoration. The Eucharistic Presence in the tabernacle does not set another view of the Eucharist alongside or against the Eucharistic celebration, but simply signifies its complete fulfillment. For this Presence has the effect, of course, of keeping the Eucharist forever in church. The church never becomes a lifeless space but is always filled with the presence of the Lord, which comes out of the celebration, leads us into it, and always makes us participants in the cosmic Eucharist. What man of faith has not experienced this? A church without the Eucharistic Presence is somehow dead, even when it invites people to pray. But a church in which the eternal light is burning before the tabernacle is always alive, is always something more than a building made of stones. In this place the Lord is always waiting for me, calling me, wanting to

---

[21] I Cor 12:27; Eph 4:12.

[22] Joseph Cardinal Ratzinger with Vittorio Messori, *The Ratzinger Report* (San Francisco: Ignatius Press, 1985), 47.

make me "Eucharistic". In this way, he prepares me for the Eucharist, sets me in motion toward his return.[23]

Although Cardinal Ratzinger's words refer to the presence of the Eucharist in individual tabernacles in individual churches, they apply of course to the eucharistic presence in the Church herself throughout all the centuries, from the first to the last. Taking the cardinal's words and applying them to history, we can say that history "never becomes a lifeless space" as long as the Eucharist is present "but is always filled with the presence of the Lord". The presence of the Eucharist in history makes history itself and all those participating in it, "participants in the cosmic Eucharist". It makes time a participant in eternity. It makes the past and the future coeval with God's omnipresence. History "without the Eucharistic Presence is somehow dead". It is Christ, present in the Blessed Sacrament, who gives life. It is He who makes all things new—and all things beautiful. It is his eucharistic presence in all ages that, as J. R. R. Tolkien proclaimed, is "the one great thing to love on earth":

> Out of the darkness of my life ... I put before you the one great thing to love on earth: the Blessed Sacrament.... There you will find romance, glory, honour, fidelity, and the true way of all your loves upon earth, and more than that: death: by the divine paradox, that which ends life, and demands the surrender of all, and yet by the taste (or foretaste) of which alone can what you seek in your earthly relationships (love, faithfulness, joy) be maintained, or take on that complexion of reality, of eternal endurance, that every man's heart desires.[24]

[23] Joseph Cardinal Ratzinger, *The Spirit of the Liturgy* (San Francisco: Ignatius Press, 2000), 90.

[24] *The Letters of J. R. R. Tolkien*, ed. Humphrey Carpenter (London: George Allen and Unwin, 1981), 53–54.

Second Century

Romans and Catholics

The Good

The writing of the Gospels and the other books of the New Testament was concluded by around the year A.D. 100, at the end of the first century of the Christian era. It was the Church, whose authority was already in place institutionally, that decided on which books were bona fide doctrinal and could consequently be considered canonical and part of Sacred Scripture. It was, therefore, the Church that canonized Scripture, stamping it with the permanence her authority bestows.

This ecclesial authority had been defended by the second-century theologian St. Irenaeus in his book *Adversus Hereses (Against Heresies)*:

> We must obey the elders in the Church, who hold the succession from the Apostles ... who with the episcopal succession have received the sure gift of truth. As for the rest, who are divorced from the principal succession and gather where they will, they are to be held in suspicion, as heretics and evil-thinkers, faction makers, swelled-headed, self-pleasing.[1]

---

[1] St. Irenaeus, *Adversus Hereses* IV, 26, 2, quoted in Philip Hughes, *A History of the Church: An Introductory Study*, vol. 1, *The World in Which the Church Was Founded* (New York: Sheed and Ward, 1937), 117.

26

Even earlier, in A.D. 107, St. Ignatius of Antioch had instructed Christians to respect the authority of the Church and to "abjure all factions", which were "the beginning of evils": "Follow your bishop, every one of you, as obediently as Jesus Christ followed the Father."[2] He also insisted that receiving valid Communion was under the jurisdiction of the Church: "The sole Eucharist you should consider valid is one that is celebrated by the bishop Himself, or by some person authorized by him. Where the bishop is to be seen, there let all his people be; just as wherever Christ is present, we have the catholic Church."[3] These words of St. Ignatius, written as he was being dragged off to Rome from his see in Antioch to be martyred, are the earliest surviving record of the Church being called "catholic", though it is of course possible that the word had been used freely prior to that without any records of such use surviving. It is intriguing, therefore, as Fr. Meconi states in *Christ Unfurled*, his history of the early Church, that followers of Christ were called "Christian" for the first time in Antioch[4] and that it was also in Antioch, apparently, that they were first called "Catholic".[5]

At the center of all "Christian" and "Catholic" worship, as St. Ignatius stressed, was the holy sacrifice of the Mass: "Make certain ... that you all observe one common Eucharist; for there is but one Body of our Lord Jesus Christ, and but one cup of union with his Blood, and one single altar of sacrifice."[6] In his teaching on the Eucharist,

---

[2] St. Ignatius of Antioch, *Letter to the Smyrnaeans*, quoted in Fr. David Vincent Meconi, S.J., *Christ Unfurled: The First 500 Years of Jesus's Life* (Gastonia, N.C.: TAN Books, 2021), 41.

[3] Ibid.

[4] Acts 11:26.

[5] Meconi, *Christ Unfurled*, 41.

[6] Quoted in ibid., 43.

St. Ignatius was following what was already customary belief and practice. This is evident from an anonymously authored text known as the *Didache*, the Greek word for "teaching", which is believed to date from the late first century. Central to this early Church teaching was the proper celebration of the Eucharist: "No one is to eat or drink of your Eucharist but those who have been baptized in the Name of the Lord; for the Lord's own saying applies here, 'Give not that which is holy unto dogs'."[7]

A major figure in the Church of the second century was St. Polycarp, Bishop of Smyrna, who had been consecrated by St. John the Evangelist, the last surviving apostle, in the late first century, and who was bishop when St. Ignatius passed through Smyrna on his way to martyrdom in A.D. 107. This holy bishop would serve the Church faithfully throughout a long and fruitful life, finally suffering martyrdom himself in Rome in around A.D. 160, at the ripe old age of eighty-six.

Martyrdoms continued throughout the second century as the secular power of Rome sought to crush the early Church. Eusebius, quoting a text from the reign of the emperor Verus, who ruled from A.D. 161 to A.D. 169, gives a graphic depiction of the brutal suffering of Christians in Vienne, near Lyons, in what is now southeastern France:

> From that time on, their martyrdoms embraced death in all its forms. From flowers of every shape and colour they wove a crown to offer to the Father; and so it was fitting that the valiant champions should endure an everchanging conflict, and having triumphed gloriously should win the mighty crown of immortality. Maturus, Sanctus, Blandina, and Attalus were taken into the amphitheatre to face the wild beasts, and to furnish open proof of the inhumanity

[7] Ibid., 39.

of the heathen.... There, before the eyes of all, Maturus and Sanctus were again taken through the whole series of punishments.... Again they ran the gauntlet of whips, in accordance with local custom; they were mauled by the beasts, and endured every torment that the frenzied mob on one side or the other demanded and howled for, culminating in the iron chair which roasted their flesh and suffocated them with the reek. Nor even then were their tormentors satisfied: they grew more and more frenzied in their desire to overwhelm the resistance of the martyrs, but do what they might they heard nothing from Sanctus beyond the words he had repeated from the beginning— the declaration of his faith.[8]

Far from succeeding, this secularist persecution served only to fan the flames of faith. In the words of Tertullian, the second-century Christian apologist, the blood of the martyrs was the seed of the Church: "Nor does your cruelty, however exquisite, avail you; it is rather a temptation to us. The oftener we are mown down by you, the more in number we grow; *the blood of Christians is seed.*"[9]

Then, as now, however, the greater threat to the Church did not come from Caesar but from Judas, from the enemies within, preaching heresy. Then, as now, it was the heirs of Judas Iscariot who proved to be the most destructive of Christian unity. It was, therefore, to the problem of heresy within the Church that Pope Victor, who reigned in the final decade of the second century,

[8] Eusebius, *The History of the Church from Christ to Constantine*, trans. G. A. Williamson (London: Penguin Classics, 1989), 144.

[9] Tertullian, *Apology* 50, trans. S. Thelwall, in *Ante-Nicene Fathers*, vol. 3, ed. Alexander Roberts, James Donaldson, and A. Cleveland Coxe (Buffalo, N.Y.: Christian Literature Publishing, 1885), revised and edited for New Advent by Kevin Knight, 2021, https://www.newadvent.org/fathers/0301.htm. Italics in original.

turned his attention. He excommunicated the Theodotians, who denied the divinity of Christ, and disciplined
members of the clergy who were spreading Gnostic ideas.
It is to these heretics that we will now turn our attention.

The Bad

It was during the second century that the Gnostic heresy
began to gain ground among those professing themselves
to be Christians. Its influence waned, however, almost as
soon as it had waxed, because of the robust response of
orthodox theologians, most especially St. Irenaeus, whose
seminal defense of the faith, *Against Heresies*, was a devas-
tatingly effective denunciation of Gnosticism's dogmatic
and moral errors. In writing this work, St. Irenaeus laid the
rational foundations of the science of Christian apologetics. According to the Church historian Philip Hughes, Irenaeus had produced "a model line of reasoning applicable
to test the truth of all theories that call themselves Christian, a line of argument that has, necessarily, been followed
ever since by the Church in its contests with doctrinal rebels".[10] Essentially, St. Irenaeus argued that knowledge of
the bona fide truth was dependent on the deposit of faith
as taught by the Church in the continuum of her apostolic
succession, as handed down since the time of Christ's apostles. Anything that contradicts these truths, handed down
from the apostles, is necessarily false. Specifically, St. Irenaeus taught that the test of Christian orthodoxy resided in
the authoritative teaching of the Roman Church, which
had been founded by SS. Peter and Paul. "For with this
Church all other churches must bring themselves in line,

[10] Philip Hughes, *A Popular History of the Catholic Church* (New York: Macmillan, 1962), 18.

on account of its superior authority."[11] In this provision of the classic and perennial test of Christian orthodoxy, Hughes asserts that "St. Irenaeus of Lyons must rank as one of the leading figures in the Church's history."[12] In a more general sense, as Hughes states, "Christianity ... shows itself, in its first meeting with doctrinal controversy, as a religion that is, essentially, strictly traditionalist."[13]

Gnosticism was not the only doctrinal controversy to plague the Church in the second century. Two other heresies, Marcionism and Montanism, would lure many away from the practice of the true faith. Drawing parallels with more contemporary controversies, Philip Hughes likens the Gnostics of the second century to the modernists of the twentieth century, whereas he sees similarities between the second-century Marcionists and the sixteenth-century Protestants. Marcion, like Luther, left the Church, calling others to follow him, in the quest for what he perceived to be the primitive purity of the Gospel. According to Marcion's dualistic misreading of the Gospel, there were two Gods, a greater God and a lesser God. The lesser God, the Demiurge, had created the visible or physical world. It was this lesser God who had expelled Adam and Eve from paradise, in an act of jealousy, thereby causing the world of sin and misery that man had inherited. This lesser God was the God of the Jews, who were his Chosen People. Man is delivered from the bondage of this lesser God by the greater God, who sent Jesus Christ, who was truly God but could not be truly man because all physical matter, created by the Demiurge, is essentially evil.

In order to justify his warped theology, Marcion issued a revised version of the New Testament in which he had

---

[11] St. Irenaeus, *Adversus Hereses*, quoted in ibid., 19.

[12] Hughes, *Popular History of the Church*, 18.

[13] Ibid.

simply excised anything that did not conform to his teaching. He made many disciples, luring Christians from the true fold, and established his own institutional church, which spread across the Roman Empire. The Marcionist "church" had its own rituals and its own moral code, the latter of which was puritanically strict, rooted in a belief that all matter was evil and was, therefore, to be spurned as far as possible.

Protestantism, another major heresy, which appeared in the latter half of the second century, could be likened to the Jehovah's Witnesses or to en-"raptured" fundamentalism. The Montanists, followers of Montanus, believed in the imminent Second Coming of Christ, prophesying and awaiting the end times with zealous fanaticism. According to the self-styled prophet, Montanus, who claimed to have had a private revelation, the Second Coming of Christ would happen on a certain date at Pepuza, in what is now modern-day Turkey. His followers flocked to the area to await the coming of Christ in His glory, settling in such numbers that a whole new city arose. Even after Christ failed to materialize at the appointed hour, the Montanists continued to prosper. Their members claimed to have a privileged and personal relationship with the Holy Spirit, rejecting the authority of the Church. This heresy lingered until the middle of the sixth century, illustrating how error can persist for many generations of men, acquiring an air of durability and even perceived "permanence" before finally fading from the historical landscape.

From the perspective of posterity, the greatest achievement of Montanism was its winning of the great Tertullian as a convert to its creed. This was a coup of the first order, the great writer proving a thorn in the side of the Church as he unleashed his polemical gifts against the orthodoxy that he had previously proclaimed so powerfully. In the estimation of Philip Hughes, Tertullian was "a polemicist of the first order, gifted with the clear ferocity of Swift and a literary style that recalls Tacitus".[14] As the first great Latin theologian, his loss to the Church was considerable. "The secession of his gigantic personality must have been a frightful blow to the Church," wrote Hughes, "which henceforth he attacked with all the savage skill he had for years put forth against her foes."[15]

Marcion and Montanus were perhaps the most influential and therefore the most destructive of the heretics to beset the Church of the second century, but they were by no means the only powerful disseminators of error. Tatian, a philosopher from Syria, rejected the whole of Hellenic civilization as being incompatible with the Gospel, advocating what we might call a "cancel culture" in which the heritage of the past is abandoned as being systemically evil. Valentinus, a Gnostic of a singular sort, taught that God pours forth his power in male and female couplings, Christ and the Holy Spirit being one such example. Finally, there was the Ebionite sect that revered Christ as a righteous man who was chosen by God as a prophet but who was not Himself divine, prefiguring the humanist "nice guy" Jesus of our own dumbed-down culture.

The Beautiful

There is an enigmatic connection between the earliest Christians and the earliest pagans in the sense that both had to resort to living in caves. G. K. Chesterton began his "outline of history", *The Everlasting Man*, with a chapter

[14] Ibid., 20.
[15] Ibid., 21.

entitled "The Man in the Cave", in which he illustrated that the only solid, factual evidence we have of our earliest ancestors is that they were artists. "Art is the signature of man," Chesterton says.[16] It is art that unites the cave man to the modern man. The paintings on the walls of the cave indicate the kinship of all humanity across the abyss of the ages in our shared love of beauty and our shared desire to depict that beauty through the God-given creative talents bestowed on us. In similar fashion, the earliest Christian art is also to be found on the walls of a cave, or more specifically on the walls of the catacombs.

During times of persecution, the Christians of Rome were quite literally forced underground, taking refuge in the catacombs, which were burial chambers arranged along miles of labyrinthine passages, built under the city and on its outskirts. As with the caves of our Neolithic ancestors, these caves of our Christian ancestors also bear evidence of art, the earliest examples of which are truly primitive, being hardly more than what might be considered holy graffiti. Yet even these have a true beauty of their own. The symbol of the fish, known as the ichthys (the Greek word for "fish"), is probably the oldest emblem used by Christians to signify their creed. Apart from the obvious allusive connections to the Gospel and Christ's call for Christians to be fishers of men, the word *ichthys*, employed as an acronym, becomes a prayer, each letter representing the first letter of the phrase "Jesus Christ, Son of God, Savior". Another early symbol found on the walls of the catacombs is the Chi-Rho, a symbol composed of the first two Greek letters of the name *Christos*, one superimposed upon the other.

---

[16] G. K. Chesterton, *The Everlasting Man* (San Francisco: Ignatius Press, 1993), 34.

Although the symbolic simplicity of the ichthys and Chi-Rho predominated, the first fully fledged religious paintings also date from the late second or early third centuries. In the Catacomb of Priscilla is a painting known as *The Banquet Scene*, depicting men and women gathered round a table with platters and a large drinking vessel. Its religious significance is unclear, but it is likely to have been drawn to decorate a sacred space in which the Christians, in times of intense persecution, gathered for prayer and, in all probability, for the celebration of the Eucharist.

Chesterton began the second part of *The Everlasting Man* with a chapter entitled "The God in the Cave". Alluding to the stable in Bethlehem, Chesterton wrote that "the second half of human history, which was like a new creation of the world, also begins in a cave.... God also was a Cave-Man, and had also traced strange shapes of creatures, curiously coloured, upon the wall of the world; but the pictures that he made had come to life."[17] There is, as Chesterton implies, a delightful and divine symmetry in the history of the world that God has made and the history of the creativity with which He has made it. Human art began in a cave. The Incarnation also began in a cave, in the womb of the Blessed Virgin at the Annunciation, that other "cave" which Gerard Manley Hopkins described as the "warm-laid grave of a womb-life grey",[18] and is shown forth at the birth of Christ in the cave of Bethlehem. And then, a couple of centuries later, Christian art also began in a cave. "In the riddle of Bethlehem it was heaven that was under the earth," wrote Chesterton.[19] The same was true of the riddle of imperial Rome.

[17] Ibid., 169.
[18] Gerard Manley Hopkins, "The Wreck of the Deutschland".
[19] Chesterton, *Everlasting Man*, 173.

Third Century

Mother and Bride

The Good

The third century of the Christian era is washed with the blood of the martyrs. In the first years of that century, in the year 202 or 203, two holy women from North Africa, Perpetua, a noblewoman, and Felicity, her slave, were condemned to death for refusing to deny their Catholic faith, in defiance of an edict by the emperor Septimus Severus that had mandated that all Christians must publicly recant. Felicity was heavily pregnant, giving birth to a child two days before her martyrdom. According to an anonymous witness, Perpetua showed such defiant courage and resolute faith that she "took the trembling hand of the young gladiator and guided it to her throat".[1] Such courage and resolute faith was also displayed by the Christians who attended these public martyrdoms who would chant *salvum lotum, salvum lotum* (Saved and washed! Saved and washed!) as the blood of the saints was poured forth as an oblation to the Lamb who had poured forth His blood for them.

Apart from the persecution during the reign of Septimus Severus, the first fifty years of the third century were a

---

[1] *Martyrial Act of Perpetua and Felicity*, in *The Acts of the Christian Martyrs*, trans. and ed. Herbert Musurillo (Oxford: Clarendon Press, 1972), 131.

time of relative peace in which the seeds of faith were sown throughout the empire, from Persia to England. By the middle of the century, St. Gregory the Wonder-Worker was preaching the Gospel so successfully in Armenia that it would become the first nation to adopt Christianity as its official religion. Other Christian missionaries penetrated into the hinterlands on the edge of the empire and beyond, bringing Christianity to the peoples of what is now Romania and the southern parts of Russia. In Syria and Asia Minor, almost half the population was probably Christian by this time, eclipsing the old pagan religions, and Christianity was spreading beyond the Middle East into Africa.

If Christianity was spreading far and wide, it was also spreading upward to the highest echelons of society. Alexander Severus, who was emperor of Rome from 233 to 235, and Philip the Arab, who was emperor from 244 to 249, were both sympathetic to Christianity. By around the year 250, it is estimated that around 7 percent of the population of the Roman Empire was Christian. As for Rome itself, the Church was so well established in the city that it owned much property and was solidifying its institutional structure. In 251, the Church employed forty-six elders, seven deacons, seven subdeacons, forty-two acolytes, and fifty-two lesser clerics, readers, and doorkeepers. These served an estimated fifty thousand practicing believers, of which there were over fifteen hundred widows and others receiving poor relief.[2]

The early third century also saw the rise to prominence of Origen, whom the Church historian Philip Hughes considered possibly "the greatest mind [the Church] has

[2] Eamon Duffy, *Saints and Sinners: A History of the Popes* (New Haven: Yale University Press, 2014), 19.

ever known".[3] As a pioneering and painstaking scholar in theology, philosophy, and apologetics, Origen helped to clarify Christian doctrine, while at the same time, some of his speculations, though not contrary to the Church's defined dogma at the time, were later condemned. In spite of his virtuous life and heroic death, some of his ideas, considered heterodox after his death, would lead to many heated controversies and would preclude any possibility of his ever being canonized. Origen would fall victim to the renewed persecution of the Church following the edict of Emperor Decius in 250. Imprisoned and tortured for two years, refusing to deny his faith, he died in 252.

The edict of Decius brought an abrupt end to the period of relative peace that preceded it. Not that the Church was ever entirely free from danger. Pope Callistus had been lynched in 222 by an anti-Catholic mob. Nonetheless, the state had largely left its Christian citizens alone until Decius' edict brought the full weight of the empire down on them. Now, as Christians were rounded up and forced to offer sacrifices to the pagan gods on pain of death, all hell broke loose and all heaven responded.

Pope Fabian was one of the first to be arrested and was killed by his torturers. A few years later, in 258, Pope Sixtus II was arrested while celebrating Mass in the catacombs. He was beheaded. Six weeks later, Cyprian, the leading African bishop, was martyred in Carthage.

As with earlier periods of persecution, the Church seemed to emerge stronger than ever, at least in terms of her understanding of herself as being both the Mother of the faithful and the Bride of Christ. It was the martyred Cyprian who had said that "you cannot have God for your

[3] Philip Hughes, *A Popular History of the Catholic Church* (New York: Macmillan, 1962), 28.

Father if you have not the Church for your mother".[4] As Fr. Meconi explained, the renewal of persecution would actually result in a renewal of the Church:

> A fruit of this renewed bloodshed and the widespread attacks on the Church was a new spirituality devoted to defending the Church as the Bride of Christ, the mother of all who bear Christ's name. Cyprian stands at the head of this movement, writing eloquently about the need to love the Church as one does one's own mother, the mother who gave birth to you, fed you, cared for you and instructed you, just as the Church does. Another North African theologian, Tertullian, described the Church as *domina mater ecclesia*, our matron and mother Church, while Origen of Alexandria highlighted her as the *sponsa Christi*, the bride of Christ.[5]

If there is one lesson that emerges from the Church's experience of persecution, it is that true faith, like true love, is never stronger than when it is tested. If the blood of the martyrs is indeed the seed of the Church, it can also be said that the sword of orthodoxy is forged in the fiery furnace of hell's attacks upon it.

The Bad

If the Catholic faithful refused to render unto Caesar the things that were God's, Caesar was struggling to keep the things that he considered rightfully his for himself, especially the empire he nominally ruled. The aging Septimus

---

[4] Fr. David Vincent Meconi, S.J., *Christ Unfurled: The First 500 Years of Jesus's Life* (Gastonia, N.C.: TAN Books, 2021), 69.
[5] Ibid.

Severus, the emperor in whose reign Perpetua and Felicity had been martyred, was forced to travel to the far-flung northern reaches of his empire to put down an uprising in that part of northern Britain that is now called Scotland. He would never return to Rome, dying in the Roman city of Eboracum, modern-day York, in 211. He was succeeded by his two sons, Caracalla and Geta, the one murdering the other soon afterward in true Caesarian fashion.

Having committed fratricide, it was hardly surprising that Caracalla should prove to be a tyrannical ruler, ordering a massacre of the citizens of Alexandria in 215 for reasons that do not seem clear. Dying in the same treacherous fashion in which he had lived, Caracalla was murdered on the orders of Opellius Macrinus, who was then declared emperor by the army in what was effectively a military coup. Losing support, Macrinus fled to Cappadocia, in modern-day Turkey, in 218, being murdered himself three years later. In the following year, 222, the emperor who had succeeded Macrinus, Elagabalus, was also murdered, the thirteen-year-old Alexander Severus being named emperor in his place. There followed a brief period of rare and relative stability until Alexander Severus and his mother were murdered in 235 by mutinous members of the army. This put an end to the Severus dynasty and ushered in a period of military anarchy in which the army proclaimed new emperors from their own ranks, who were soon killed and replaced by others.

With such political chaos prevailing, it was hardly surprising that enemies of the empire, most notably Germanic tribes, began to flex their military muscle, invading Italy itself in 260. In the same year, Marcus Postumous declared himself ruler of what became known as the Gallic Empire, which included what is now Spain and Portugal, France, England, and parts of Germany, effectively severing the whole northwestern part of the empire from Rome. In time-honored fashion, Postumous was murdered in 269 by his own troops and the Gallic Empire was reabsorbed into the Roman Empire five years later.

The tragedy of terrors continued. The emperor Aurelian was murdered in 275. Two other short-lived emperors followed before Probus took power in 276. In spite of military successes against the Goths and the Franks, he was murdered by his own troops in 282. Two years later, Diocletian became emperor. He would rule for over twenty years, ending his reign with anti-Christian edicts ordering the destruction of churches, the burning of Christian books, and the killing of all Christians who refused to offer sacrifices to the pagan gods.

So much for Caesar. Within the Church, the problem was one of weakness in the face of persecution. Whereas the saints witnessed to their faith with the laying down of their lives for their friends and enemies, that "greater love" which Christ had proclaimed and modeled,[6] their weaker brethren apostatized to save their bodies, making sacrifice to the gods as the edicts demanded.

After the ending of the persecution under the emperor Decius in 250, the question arose within the Church with respect to what should be done with those Christians seeking readmittance to Christian Communion after their apostasy in the time of trial. Pope Cornelius and the Bishop of Carthage, Cyprian, taught that bishops could absolve repentant Christians of their sin of apostasy, though penances for such grievous sin were severe. Hardliners, such as Novatian, disagreed vociferously, demanding that none of those who had betrayed the Church in times of persecution should be readmitted to Communion. Novatian

[6]Jn 15:13.

split from the Church in protest, endeavoring to establish a breakaway church of like-minded "purists".

Then, as now, the life of the Church has been buffeted by the tragedy of terrors imposed by the rulers of the secular world, and the comedy of errors of those within her own ranks. Through it all, in Chesterton's memorable words, the Church resembles a "heavenly chariot ... thundering through the ages, the dull heresies sprawling and prostrate, the wild truth reeling but erect".[7]

The Beautiful

The Christian art that has survived from the third century, as with that which had survived from the previous century, is to be found on the walls of the catacombs. In the Catacomb of the Jordani, there are third-century tomb paintings depicting scenes from salvation history, signifying Christ's triumph over death. One of these murals depicts Daniel in the lion's den; another shows Abraham and Isaac, a story from Genesis that is considered a typological prefiguring of God's offering of His own Son for the sins of men, the symbolic scapegoat being transfigured into the spotless Lamb.

In the Catacomb of Priscilla, which contains the *Banquet Scene* mentioned in the previous chapter, there is a mural known as *The Three Men in the Fiery Furnace*, which is clearly a presentation of the story of Shadrach, Meshach, and Abednego from the Book of Daniel.[8] In this story from the Old Testament, these three holy men were thrown into the furnace after they had refused to bow before

---

[7] G. K. Chesterton, *Orthodoxy* (New York: John Lane, 1909), 187.
[8] See Dan 3:8–30.

an image of the Babylonian king, Nebuchadnezzar II, but were preserved from the flames and saved from death by God. It is easy to see how such a story would prove inspirational and would provide encouragement at a time when Christians were being martyred for refusing to bow before images of Caesar or the pagan gods. As for the quality of the image as art, the art historian E. H. Gombrich wrote that the artists who painted *The Three Men in the Fiery Furnace* "were familiar with the methods of Hellenistic painting used in Pompeii".[9] Also in the Catacomb of Priscilla, specifically in what is known as the Crypt of the Veiled Lady, there is a female figure with hands held aloft in prayer, flanked by disciples and by a woman with a child in her lap. Although the meaning of the image is disputed, it is possible that the figure in the center represents Mother Church in her magisterial role as intercessor and teacher, and that the woman and child is an early representation of the Madonna and Child.

It was easier to practice the faith more freely and without fear of retribution, as a general rule, the further one was from the cauldron of persecution in the city of Rome. At Duro-Europos, in modern-day Syria, there is (or was until it was desecrated and largely destroyed by ISIS) a house church, in which Christian worship took place from the earliest centuries. Religious paintings in this ancient shrine date from as early as the third century. They depict a woman bearing myrrh and approaching the empty tomb of the risen Christ, and other scenes from the Gospel, such as Christ's healing of the paralytic and His meeting with the Samaritan woman at the well.

If the beauty of Christ and His Church is made manifest in these early examples of Christian art, there are

[9] E. H. Gombrich, *The Story of Art* (London: Phaidon Press, 1989), 90.

also examples of the beauty of music as a manifestation of the divine mystery. St. Clement of Alexandria, writing in the late second or early third century, describes Christ, the Logos, as the "New Song" who controls the music of the cosmos: "[The New Song] ordered the universe concordantly and tuned the discord of the elements in a harmonious arrangement, so that the entire cosmos might become through its agency a consonance."[10] As early as the first century, an earlier Clement, Pope St. Clement I, had separated sacred music from its profane counterpart: "In the pagan festivals, let us not sing the psalms ... for fear of seeming like the wandering minstrels, singers and tellers of tales of high adventure, who perform their art for a mouthful of bread. It is not fitting that we sing the canticles of the Lord in a strange land."[11]

It would be remiss to discuss the beauty of music in the third century without paying due deference and reverence to the beauty of the third-century martyr St. Cecilia, the patron saint of music and musicians. Cecilia, who was martyred sometime between 222 and 235, is said to have sung in her heart to her true Bridegroom, Jesus Christ, as the musicians played at the celebration of her forced marriage to Valerian, a pagan nobleman. Her husband would eventually embrace the faith and would also attain the glory of martyrdom. The present-day Basilica of Santa Cecilia in Trastevere is said to have been built on the site of the house in which Cecilia lived during the reign of

[10] Clement of Alexandria, *Protrepticus* I, 5, 1, trans. James McKinnon, in *Music in Early Christian Literature*, ed. James McKinnon (Cambridge: Cambridge University Press, 1988), 30.

[11] J. P. Migne, ed., *Patrologiae cursus completus: Patrologiae Graecae*, 167 vols. (Paris: J. P. Migne, 1844–1855), I, p. 432, trans. Robert F. Hayburn, quoted in Robert F. Hayburn, *Papal Legislation on Sacred Music: 95 A.D. to 1977 A.D.* (Harrison, N.Y.: Roman Catholic Books, 2005), 2.

her contemporary Pope Urban I, signifying that the site of Cecilia's martyrdom had become a shrine and place of worship from the moment of her death. In the ninth century, Pope Paschal I moved the relics of Cecilia from the Catacombs of St. Callixtus to the church in Trastevere, where they remain to this day.

As the patron saint of music and musicians, she has played a major role in the history of music, proving inspirational to some of the greatest composers and some of the finest poets. Those composers who have written music in her honor include Marc-Antoine Charpentier, Henry Purcell, Alessandro Scarlatti, George Frideric Handel, Joseph Haydn, Charles Gounod, Benjamin Britten, and Arvo Pärt. Those poets who have paid her homage include Geoffrey Chaucer, John Dryden, Alexander Pope, Edmund Blunden, and W. H. Auden. In the case of St. Cecilia, the blood of the martyrs did prove to be not only the seed of the Church but also the inspirational seed of some of the greatest musical and literary works of Christendom.

Armed with Sacred Scripture, the greatest literature ever written, and assisted with the goodness of the saints and the beauty of religious art and sacred music, the Church of the third century had taken its place in the long and linked line of centuries through which Christ has vanquished the darkness of evil with the light of His love and the life of His creative presence. As the third century ended, Christians looked upon the Church as the Bride of Christ, the Bride and Bridegroom becoming one flesh in His Mystical Body. In addition, the Bride was seen by Christians as their holy Mother and teacher (mater et magistra), to whom they would cling doggedly and dogmatically in the midst of the maelstrom of the world's darkness and rage, its error and terror.

Fourth Century

"Upon This Rock"

The Good

The intermittent persecution of the previous century had done nothing to curtail the dissemination of the Gospel or the growth of the Church. By the year 300, it is estimated that there were about five million Christians, which constituted about 10 percent of the population of the Roman Empire.[1] Such growth alarmed the emperor Diocletian, who issued his first *Edict against the Christians* in February 303, instigating a period of trial for the Church that would last for eight years. As with the previous efforts to crush Christianity through the tyrannical use of state-sponsored terror, Diocletian's assault upon the Church, known as the Great Persecution, failed to achieve its goal of eradicating the presence of Christ from the empire. By 311, when Diocletian's successor, Galerius, rescinded the anti-Christian edict and restored religious liberty to Christians, it was evident that the followers of Christ could not be bullied into abandoning their faith. Such grudging toleration was the best that Christians could expect from an avowedly pagan empire, or so any observer would have thought at the time. None could have foreseen that, ten years after Diocletian's anti-Christian edict, a Roman

[1] Alan Schreck, *The Compact History of the Catholic Church* (Ann Arbor, Mich.: Servant Books, 1987), 22.

46

emperor would issue an edict that would effectively make Christianity the official religion of the empire itself.

According to two contemporary accounts, by Eusebius and Lactantius, the emperor Constantine had seen a vision in the sky prior to the decisive Battle of the Milvian Bridge in 312. Eusebius, who claimed to have heard the account from Constantine himself, recorded in his *Life of Constantine* that the emperor had seen a cross of light in the sky with the words "Through this sign you shall conquer." From this moment, Constantine owed his allegiance to the God of the Christians. In 313, the famous Edict of Milan granted "free and absolute permission to practice their religion to the Christians" and to "every man ... free opportunity to worship according to his own wish".[2] From this moment, in the words of the historian Eamon Duffy, "the fortunes of Christianity throughout the empire changed forever."[3] Property that had been confiscated during the previous decade's anti-Christian pogrom was returned, and public funds were made available to the Church. From being a persecuted sect, Christianity was now actively favored by the secular state and even pampered. Such comforts could themselves be a danger, as we shall see, but one can only imagine the exhilarating sense of relief that must have accompanied the onset of authentic religious liberty.

In spite of his active support for the Church and his tacit acceptance of the Christian creed, nobody would claim that Constantine was a saint. His sordid personal life and his acts of tyranny were a source of scandal. He had political rivals and even his own wife executed, the latter

[2] Quoted in Diane Moczar, *Ten Dates Every Catholic Should Know* (Manchester, N.H.: Sophia Institute Press, 2005), 9.

[3] Eamon Duffy, *Saints and Sinners: A History of the Popes* (New Haven: Yale University Press, 2014), 25.

for her alleged adultery. If, however, the emperor was a disgrace, his mother, St. Helena, exemplified the life of a true Christian. In her old age, she went on a pilgrimage to the Holy Land and ordered the excavation of the sites associated with the life of Christ. She ordered the building of churches, including the Church of the Holy Sepulchre on the site of the tomb in which Christ had been buried and from which He rose from the dead.

At the other end of the saintly spectrum from the pomp of imperial power, which St. Helena enjoyed, were the Desert Fathers. These hermits, who lived lives of solitude in remote places, were the original monks, the word *monk* deriving from the Latin *monos*, which means "alone". As radical practitioners of the Gospel, these hermits answered Christ's counsel of perfection literally: "If you would be perfect, go, sell what you possess and give to the poor, and you will have treasure in heaven; and come, follow me."[4]

In 305, St. Anthony of Egypt emerged after thirty-five years in the desert, becoming a great spiritual master. St. Pachomius, another Egyptian, founded a community of ascetics near the River Nile and is considered the founder of monasticism. This revolutionary vision of the Christian life, rooted in radical asceticism, spread far and wide throughout fourth-century Christendom. In Cappadocia, in what is now Turkey, the new monastic way of life produced three great saints: Basil the Great, Gregory of Nyssa, and Gregory of Nazianzus, known collectively as the Cappadocian Fathers. Each would become a great theological defender of the faith against the heresy of Arianism. St. John Chrysostom was another great saint of this time who began his spiritual journey

[4] Mt 19:21.

as a monk, as was St. Martin of Tours, who founded a monastery in Gaul (France) in 371 and is considered the father of Western monasticism.

Two of the greatest saints in the history of the Church, St. Jerome and St. Augustine, embraced the monastic life following their respective conversions to Christianity, Jerome as a hermit and Augustine in community. St. Jerome would translate the Bible into Latin in the final decade of the fourth century, his translation, known as the Vulgate, becoming the standard text for centuries. At the same time, between 397 and 400, St. Augustine was writing his masterful *Confessions*, one of the truly Great Books of civilization.

The fourth century would also see the solidifying and clarifying of the doctrinal understanding of the papacy as the rock upon which Christ builds His Church.[5] Pope St. Damasus I, who was Bishop of Rome from 366 until 384, declared that papal authority did not come from any council of the Church, and still less from the emperor, but from Christ Himself as made manifest in His words to Peter. St. Damasus had a powerful ally in St. Ambrose, Bishop of Milan from 374 until his death in 397, who asserted that "where Peter is, there is the Church" ("Ubi Petrus, ibi ergo Ecclesia").[6] St. Jerome, writing to Pope Damasus, concurred: "I follow no one as leader except Christ alone, and therefore I want to remain in union in the Church with you, that is, with the chair (office) of Peter. I know that on this rock the Church is founded."[7]

---

[5] The doctrinal understanding is based on the Church's interpretation of Jesus' words to Peter in Matthew's Gospel: "Upon this rock I will build my church" (16:18; KJV).

[6] Ambrose, "Explanatio psalmi 40", in *Corpus Scriptorum Ecclesiasticorum Latinorum*, vol. 64 (1919; repr., New York: Johnson Reprint Corporation, 1962).

[7] St. Jerome, *Letter* 15, 2, quoted in Michael Schmaus, *Dogma 4: The Church* (Westminster, Md.: Christian Classics, 1984), 184.

Upon this rock, the Church had stood secure for four centuries against wave after wave of Roman imperial might. In the following century, it would remain secure even as the empire itself crashed and crumbled.

The Bad

Having withstood the Great Persecution under Diocletian at the start of the century, the Church would need to guard herself during the remainder of the century against the danger of corruption that her increasingly privileged position within the empire presented. All of a sudden, from the Edict of Milan onward, it was socially respectable to be a Christian. In consequence, many people would become Christian for worldly reasons without really being bona fide believers. Their faith was weak, confused, and tainted with pagan superstition. Many were nominally Christian while continuing to practice the hedonistic life-styles that had become increasingly prevalent as the empire succumbed to cultural decadence. Having withstood the power of the world when the world had sought to take it by force, the Church faced the danger of being seduced by worldliness from within. Yet, in spite of these very real dangers, the Barque of Peter would never surrender to the ship of state. The new spirit of asceticism and monasticism that characterized the leadership of the Church would keep her on an even keel in the midst of these new and unusual challenges.

A greater threat was posed by heresy, especially in the form of Arianism. Taking its name from Arius, a priest in Egypt who taught that Christ was not divine but merely a creature who was highly favored by God, Arianism spread through the Church like a virulent virus. The Arian heresy was condemned by the Church at the Council of Nicaea in 325, the Council teaching definitively that God the Son was "consubstantial" with the Father. In plain terms, this affirmed that whatever the Father is, so is the Son. This should have been the end of the matter, except that several bishops refused to accept the teaching of the Council and continued to teach Arianism. These bishops then convinced the emperor that Arianism was correct, persuading him to use his political power to force Arianism upon the Church. A succession of emperors embraced Arianism and sought to crush all opposition to it within the Church. Pressure was placed upon those bishops who continued to proclaim the teaching of the Council of Nicaea, and several were forcefully removed from their dioceses. It seemed as though the Arian heretics, aided and abetted by the secular power of Rome, would succeed. St. Jerome lamented in 361 that "the entire world awoke and groaned to find that it had become Arian".[8]

Thankfully, the "entire world" was no match for the holy theologians who came to the defense of orthodoxy. St. Athanasius, who was exiled five times by Arian emperors for his defense of the Council of Nicaea, was at the forefront of this successful rearguard action, as were the aforementioned Cappadocian Fathers—Basil the Great, Gregory of Nyssa, and Gregory of Nazianzen. These great minds argued so forcefully for the divinity of Christ that the tide turned against the Arians. In 381, the Council of Constantinople reaffirmed that the Son is "consubstantial" with the Father, adding that the Holy Spirit was also fully God. Such was the triumph of this orthodox understanding of the Trinity that Catholics affirm it every Sunday at Mass with the recitation of the Nicene Creed.

[8] Quoted in Schreck, *Compact History of the Church*, 24.

Although the emperors who supported Arianism would have called themselves Christian, there was one fourth-century emperor who sought to return Rome to its former paganism. This was Julian the Apostate, who, having been raised an Arian, was not really an apostate in the fullest sense of the word. As emperor, he declared his own brand of paganism, which was a sort of Neoplatonic mysticism, to be the state religion. His farcical efforts to enforce this pagan restoration came to a sudden and ignominious end in 363, when he was killed in battle only eighteen months after becoming emperor. It was said that his last words, "Vicisti, Galilaee", were a cry of fatalistic despair to the Christ he had willfully denied and defied: "Thou hast triumphed, Galilean."

Julian's words would seem apposite. In spite of the paleo-paganism of Diocletian in 303 and the neo-paganism of Julian sixty years later, and in spite of a succession of heretical and truly apostate emperors, the Galilean had emerged triumphant.

The Beautiful

The immediate consequence of the Edict of Milan was the emergence of the Church from the catacombs into the full light of Roman day. Churches began to be built throughout the empire, none of which was more important historically or symbolically than St. Peter's Basilica in Rome. Dedicated in 326, St. Peter's was built over the very place at which St. Peter himself had been buried, with the altar being placed over his tomb. The symbolic significance of a basilica, presided over by the Bishop of Rome, St. Peter's successor, built on the relics of the rock himself upon whom Christ had promised to build His Church, speaks more loudly and clearly than any words. In a real sense, therefore, St. Peter's is a symbolic presentation of St. Peter himself.

By any criteria, the old St. Peter's was an impressive edifice. The nave was "as long, as high, and twice as wide as the nave of a great Gothic cathedral" of the Middle Ages,[9] and its interior was "one of the most spacious, most imposing, and most harmonious ... ever built, imperially rich in its marbles and mosaics, grandiose yet forthright and large in the best Roman sense of the word".[10] Such was the sheer scale of St. Peter's that it could hold at least fourteen thousand worshipers and remained the largest church in Christendom until the eleventh century. Construction on such a scale was made possible by the financial patronage of the emperor himself or, as in the case of the Church of the Holy Sepulchre in Jerusalem, by the patronage of the emperor's mother, though the church in Jerusalem would not be completed until around 345, fifteen years after St. Helena's death.

In 326, the same year in which St. Peter's was dedicated, Pope Sylvester I also dedicated a smaller basilica on the site of the tomb of St. Paul, the other great apostle martyred in Rome. Almost sixty years later, in 385, construction began on a much larger church on the same site, the Papal Basilica of St. Paul Outside the Walls. The two apostles are united with each other and with Christ in the crypt of St. Peter's Basilica in a fourth-century sculpture carved on the sarcophagus of Junius Bassus, who died in 359.

If the fourth century marked the beginning of church architecture, it also marked the early flowering of liturgical chant. Ambrosian chant is named in honor of St. Ambrose,

---

[9] Helen Gardner, *Art through the Ages* (New York: Harcourt, Brace & World, 1970), 239.

[10] Kenneth Conant, *Early Medieval Church Architecture* (Baltimore: Johns Hopkins Press, 1942), 6.

who championed the use of music in the liturgy, introducing Eastern hymnody into the Western liturgy and composing several original hymns of his own, four of which survive with music that may be similar to the original late fourth-century melodies. Perhaps the best known of Ambrose's hymns is *Veni redemptor gentium*, an Advent or Christmas hymn that is assigned to the Office of Readings for Advent, from December 17 until Christmas Eve, in the Liturgy of the Hours. John Mason Neale, the nineteenth-century Anglo-Catholic hymn writer, translated it into English and set it to music, with the title *Come, Thou Redeemer of the Earth*, which is usually sung as a Christmas carol.

In his writings, St. Ambrose refers to the singing of the Psalms in the liturgy by a solo cantor, who alternates with the congregational singing of a refrain or antiphon. He is also credited with the composition of the famous Latin hymn *Te Deum*, which he is said to have written for the baptism of his most famous convert, St. Augustine of Hippo.

As for St. Augustine himself, the magnitude of his contribution to literature can hardly be overstressed. Apart from the magisterial splendor of his *Confessions*, written in the last years of the fourth century, and his *City of God*, written in the first years of the following century, his groundbreaking work, *De doctrina Christiana*, begun shortly after he became Bishop of Hippo in around 396, has been credited with providing "the fundamental plan of Christian culture".[11] In his analysis of the language of signs and symbols in Scripture, Augustine provides the analogical and typological keys for unlocking the allegorical dimension of Christian art and literature.

---

[11] Translator's note in St. Augustine, *On Christian Doctrine*, trans. D. W. Robertson, Jr. (Upper Saddle River, N.J.: Prentice Hall, 1997), ix.

In terms of his inspirational impact on the history of art, St. Anthony of Egypt has proved as influential on the visual arts as his third-century counterpart, St. Cecilia, had proved with respect to music and poetry. The temptation of St. Anthony in the desert, first recounted by his contemporary St. Athanasius, has borne fruit in memorable masterpieces by artists as diverse as Michelangelo in the fifteenth century, Hieronymus Bosch and Matthias Grünewald in the sixteenth century, and Paul Cézanne and Salvador Dali in the nineteenth and twentieth centuries. As for literature, Gustave Flaubert considered his prose poem, *The Temptation of Saint Anthony*, published in 1874, to be his magnum opus.

Fifth Century

The City of God

The Good

The fifth century, one of the most chaotic and cataclysmic in terms of political conflict, would be a time in which the Church would rise from the ashes of empire. In 400, the Roman Empire held dominion over most of Europe, the north of Africa, and swathes of Asia; by 500, it lay in ruins. "The world is perishing," wrote St. Augustine, "the world is aging, the world is going to pieces, with the labored, wheezy breathing of old age. Don't be afraid, *your youth shall be renewed.*"[1]

In his seminal work, *The City of God*, St. Augustine made the crucial distinction between the pomp and power of the secular world, under the dominion of pride (the City of Man), and the eternal dominion of Christ, in which the humble are exalted (the City of God):

One sort [persisted] resolutely in that Good which is common to all—which for them is God himself—and in his eternity, truth, and love, while the others were delighted rather with their own power, as though they themselves were their own Good. Thus they have fallen away from

[1] Saint Augustine, *Sermons* 81, 8, *Sermons: The Works of Saint Augustine: A Translation for the 21st Century*, ed. John E. Rotelle, trans. Edmund Hill, vol. 3, *Sermons 51–94* (Brooklyn, N.Y.: New City Press, 1991), 365.

that Supreme Good which is common to all, which brings felicity, and they have devoted themselves to their own ends. They have chosen pride in their own elevation in exchange for the true exaltation of eternity; empty cleverness in exchange for the certainty of truth; the spirit of faction instead of unity in love; and so they have become arrogant, deceitful, and envious.[2]

Certain of her own divinely instituted authority, the Church spoke definitively as the very embodiment of the City of God. It was appropriate, therefore, that the Council of Chalcedon in 451 should proclaim that the earlier Council of Nicaea in 325 had been "ecumenical". This was hugely significant. The word *ecumenical*, from the Greek *oikoumene*, means "the inhabited (world)", or more generally "the whole world" or, in any event, the whole civilized world, that part of the world which is encompassed by a common and universally accepted creed and culture. It was in this sense that it was used by the Church to signify Christendom (the City of God) and the administration of it; hence, an ecumenical council was a council convened by the authority of the Church to discuss and define disputed matters of doctrine, which would then be binding on all of Christendom. The Council of Chalcedon's affirmation that the earlier Council of Nicaea was "ecumenical" was confirmation that the doctrines defined at Nicea were binding on all Christians.

The ecumenical power of the Church was executed at the Council of Ephesus in 431 in the Council's dogmatic declaration that the Blessed Virgin could be addressed in prayer as *Theotokos*, meaning "God-bearer", or Mother of God. This was necessary theologically as a consequence

---

[2] Saint Augustine, *The City of God*, 12, 1, trans. Henry Bettenson (London: Penguin Classics, 1984), 471.

of the doctrine that Jesus Christ was both fully God and fully man. Mary was the mother of God in his human nature, not of course in his divine nature. She was the mother of Jesus Christ, the God-Man. This understanding of Christ was clarified still further at the Council of Chalcedon, which declared that Jesus exists in two natures, the divine and the human, in the one undivided Person, the incarnate Son of God.

Such cohering of the Church's teaching was the fruit of the coming together of theology and philosophy, a cohesive union that would characterize the teachings of the Church throughout the future centuries. Henceforth, faith and reason (*fides et ratio*) would be joined in an indissoluble marriage, enabling the Church to respond to the changing fads and fashions of the world with the timeless touchstone of truth.

Once again, it was the great and indomitable Augustine who blazed the trail by introducing the great Greek philosophers into the conversation. Although he insisted that theology was the most important of the sciences since it is the means "by which that most wholesome faith, which leads to true blessedness, is begotten, nourished, defended, strengthened",[3] he also insisted that philosophy was the friend of faith. In his work on the Trinity (*De Trinitate*), he employed the reasoning of Plato, Aristotle, and the Neoplatonists to enlighten the discussion of foundational Christian doctrines, forging the union of faith and philosophy. Reason brings us to the threshold of faith. After the threshold is crossed, faith enlightens reason.

---

[3] Saint Augustine, *De Trinitate* 14, 1, 3, *Nicene and Post-Nicene Fathers, First Series*, vol. 3, ed. Philip Schaff, trans. Arthur West Haddan (Buffalo, N.Y.: Christian Literature Publishing Co., 1887), rev. and ed. for New Advent by Kevin Knight.

The teaching authority of the Church, rooted in reason and reaching to "the whole world", was further
strengthened by the primacy of the See of Peter. "It has
been decreed by a divine, not a human authority," wrote
Pope Innocent I (401–417), "that whatever action is taken
in any of the provinces, however distant or remote, it
should not be brought to a conclusion before it comes
to the knowledge of this See, so that every decision may
be affirmed by our authority."[4] Such authority was not
absolute, however, but was subject to the teaching Magis-
terium of the Church. A pope could not contradict or ride
roughshod over doctrines previously defined solemnly by
the Church. "The rules rule us," declared Pope Celestine I
(422–432). "We do not stand over the rules: let us be subject to the canons."[5]

Pope Leo the Great (440–461) was not merely the
greatest pope of the fifth century but one of the greatest
popes of all time. For this holy and courageous leader of
the Church, the power of the See of Peter lay in the mystical presence of St. Peter himself: "And so if anything is
rightly done and rightly decreed by us, if anything is won
from the mercy of God by our daily supplications, it is of
his work and merit whose power lives and whose authority prevails in his See."[6]

Toward the end of the century, Pope Gelasius (492–
496) wrote to Anastasius I, emperor of the Eastern Roman
Empire, delineating the limits of secular authority. In terms
that reflected Augustine's reasoning, the pope proclaimed
the primacy of the City of God over the City of Man:

---

[4] Quoted in R. B. Eno, *The Rise of the Papacy* (Wilmington, Del.: M. Glazier,
1990), 94.
[5] Ibid., 100.
[6] Ibid., 109.

There are, most august Emperor, two powers by which this world is chiefly ruled: the sacred authority of bishops and the royal power. Of these the priestly power is much more important because it has to render account for the kings of men themselves at the judgement seat of God. For you know, most gracious son, that though you hold the chief place of dignity over the human race, yet you must submit yourself in faith to those who have charge of divine things, and look to them for the means of your salvation. You know that it behoves you, in matters concerning the reception and reverent administration of the sacraments, to be obedient to ecclesiastical authority, instead of seeking to bend it to your will.... And if the hearts of the faithful ought to be submitted to priests in general ... how much more ought assent be given to him who presides over that See which the most high God himself desired to be preeminent over all priests, and which the pious judgement of the whole Church has honoured ever since?[7]

Meanwhile, far from the Eternal City, missionary monks were preaching and spreading the Gospel. The Abbey of Lérins, on an island off the coast of what is now the French Riviera, became the center of a monastic-inspired religious revival. St. Hilary of Arles, a monk of Lérins who served as bishop-apostle in the south of Gaul, won many souls to Christ at a time of great and increasing political turmoil. Far to the north, on the very fringes of the farthest flung reaches of the empire, a British monk named Patrick was preaching the Word of God to the people of Ireland. The zealous labors of these two tireless servants of Christ and His Church would bear the finest fruits of grace.

Last but not least was an unknown and newly professed monk who was still in his teens when the century ended.

[7] Quoted in Eamon Duffy, *Saints and Sinners: A History of the Popes* (New Haven: Yale University Press, 2014), 50.

This was St. Benedict. In a world descending into a dark age of barbarism, he would prove a light in the darkness.

The Bad

At the dawn of the fifth century, few would have predicted the fall of the seemingly impregnable and "eternal" Roman Empire, the epitome of the power and glory of the City of Man. Yet its collapse, when it came, was shockingly sudden.

In 401 and 405, Gothic barbarians raided northern Italy, a foretaste of the violence to come. In 406, hordes of Vandals crossed the frozen River Rhine, joined by two other barbarian tribes, the Alans and Sueves. Finding little resistance from the demoralized and weakened Roman army, they sacked Treveri (modern-day Trier in Germany) and Remi (modern-day Reims in France), sweeping across Europe until they reached the Pyrenees. Adding to the chaos, the Roman army in Britain declared one of their own number to be the new emperor of Rome, naming him Constantine III. They then deserted their posts in Britain, crossing the channel and marching across Gaul intent on seizing the throne from the emperor Honorius. To all intents and purposes, this was the end of the Roman occupation of Britain, which had lasted 350 years, leaving the largely Christian country defenseless against the various pagan tribes that would begin to move in.

In 408, the Visigoths, led by Alaric, invaded Italy. Two years later, Rome itself was sacked, the unthinkable act sending seismic shockwaves throughout the civilized world. St. Jerome had just finished his commentary on the prophet Isaiah when news of Rome's fall reached him in his grotto at Bethlehem. "An ancient city has collapsed," he lamented, "she who was for so many centuries mistress of the world." Later, he would say that "the whole world was decapitated when Rome fell" and, upon hearing from refugees of the rape, pillage, and massacres, he felt that "the universe had collapsed".[8]

It was the fall of Rome that prompted St. Augustine to commence the writing of *The City of God*, inspired, no doubt, by St. Paul's words in the Letter to the Hebrews that "here we have no lasting city, but we seek the city which is to come."[9] By the time of Augustine's death in 430, the barbarians were besieging his own city of Hippo, the Vandals having crossed into North Africa from Spain. Shortly after his death, the barbarians would sack Hippo as they had sacked Rome.

The middle of the century saw an even worse barbaric scourge as Attila the Hun swept through Europe. Advancing through Italy, taking city after city, Rome lay defenseless in his path. Then, in 452, showing remarkable courage, Pope Leo the Great rode out to meet the fearless leader who had struck terror in the hearts of all his foes. The pope and the barbarian met face-to-face. Nobody knows what Pope Leo said, but somehow he persuaded Attila to withdraw his army from Italy, saving the city of Rome and its people from the raping and pillaging horde.

Even as the City of Man was being assailed by men, the City of God was being assailed by heretics. In the fifth century, the prevailing heresy in the West was Pelagianism, which took its name from a British monk, Pelagius, who denied the doctrine of Original Sin, believing that man was incorrupt in his nature. Pelagius taught that the believer in

---

[8] Quoted in Guy Bedouelle, *An Illustrated History of the Church* (Milan: Editoriale Jaca Book, 2004), 33.

[9] Heb 13:14.

Christ could earn the reward of heaven through the triumph of the will by simply doing what Christ commanded. There was no need for supernatural assistance and, in consequence, no need for the sacraments of the Church and the grace they bestow. Although Pelagianism was countered and condemned by the Church, it has proved resilient. As the progenitor of the self-help "spirituality" so prevalent today, it continues to lead souls astray.

If Pelagianism was the major error impacting the Church in the West, the Church in the East was beset by the Monophysite heresy, which denied that Christ was fully human, arguing that he possessed a divine but not a human nature. In 484, Acacius, Patriarch of Constantinople, proclaimed a pro-Monophysite theology, in defiance of the teaching of the Council of Chalcedon. The pope responded by excommunicating him, prompting a schism between East and West that would last for thirty-five years.

If the fifth century must have seemed the end of civilization as people knew it, or even the end of the world, there were signs at the century's end that all might yet be well. Theodoric the Great, who became the Ostrogothic ruler of Italy in 493, was showing signs of wanting to be civilized, adopting Roman dress and retaining the political infrastructure of Rome, including the Senate. "Any Goth who can, wants to be a Roman," Theodoric declared. "No Roman wants to be a Goth."[10] The assimilation of the conqueror to the ways of the conquered was similar, ironically, to the way that the Romans who had conquered Greece were themselves conquered culturally by the Greeks, adopting their religion, their philosophy, their architecture, their art, and their literature. The Romans had conquered the Greeks militarily but had

[10] Quoted in Duffy, *Saints and Sinners*, 48.

been conquered by them culturally. The same was now the case with the Gothic invaders of Rome. The historian Guy Bedouelle sees this as something which the Church actively encouraged:

> The Church consciously and effectively facilitated this reconciliation of conquerors and conquered. Thus, like Rome, "victoriously vanquished" by Greece, the conquering barbarians would themselves be conquered by all that made up the soul of Rome. Was it not true that their conversion would be a sign of their becoming civilized ...? By entering the Church they inserted themselves, psychologically and culturally, into a life regulated by a coherent organization based on monarchy and hierarchy and unified by the prestigious Latin language. The barbarians were peoples without a past, without any other justice than the right of might, and without stability. Now Rome's privileges, culture, history, and written tradition, all those social acquisitions so cruelly lacking to them before, could be theirs.[11]

It is in this light that the conversion of Clovis, the pagan king of the Franks, should be understood and judged. Sometime between 496 and 499, he was baptized by Remigius, Bishop of Reims, together with three thousand warriors. This was seen as being so significant to the future of Christendom that Gregory of Tours called Clovis the "new Constantine".[12] He is also considered the first king of what would become France, a fact that has led many patriotic Frenchmen, including Hilaire Belloc, to call their homeland "the eldest daughter of the Church". Since, however, Armenia had made Christianity the official state

---

[11] Bedouelle, *Illustrated History of the Church*, 35.
[12] Ibid., 37.

religion in 301, almost two hundred years earlier, the grandiose title does not quite fit.

Christopher Dawson remarked that the baptism of Clovis, coupled with the baptism of Ethelbert of Kent a hundred years later, marked "the real beginnings of a new age in Western Europe".[13]

It is a truism, all too easily uttered, that God writes straight with crooked lines, but the fall of Rome at the hands of barbarians, followed so soon by the conversion of the barbarians to the religion of Rome, must be seen as the bringing of great good from barbaric evil. It might also be seen as one of many examples of the Church, as the Mystical Body of Christ, dying and rising from the dead.

The Beautiful

In the fifth century, the city of Ravenna rivalled Rome in terms of its political importance, becoming the de facto capital of the northern part of Italy following the besieging of Milan by the barbarians in 402. One consequence of Ravenna's rise to prominence was the erection of beautiful Christian edifices, the oldest surviving example of which is the funerary chapel attached to the church of the imperial palace, which was built in around 425. A small unimposing cruciform building on the outside, its interior is strikingly beautiful, making the crossing of the threshold a breathtaking and awe-inspiring experience. For the pilgrim, the transition from drabness to splendor as he enters the chapel accentuates the sense in which he has stepped out of the worldliness of the City of Man into the transfiguring

[13] Christopher Dawson, *Religion and the Rise of Western Culture* (New York: Image Books, 1958), 31.

transcendence of the City of God. The seemingly abstract pattern of mosaic overhead is seen to represent a starry heaven, beneath which figures of mosaic apostles gesture rhetorically. Another mosaic over the west entrance depicts the Good Shepherd surrounded by sheep, while the mosaic on the opposite wall shows a martyr, probably St. Vincent of Saragossa but possibly St. Lawrence.

Another ancient building in Ravenna, resplendent with breathtaking mosaics, is the Baptistery of the Orthodox, dating from the early fourth century but renovated between 450 and 460, at around the time of the Council of Chalcedon. The baptistery is so named to denote that it was built by those who accepted the Church's teaching on the two natures in Christ, affirmed at the Council, as opposed to the Monophysites, who did not.

The oldest surviving apse mosaic in Rome is to be found in the Basilica of Santa Pudenziana (dedicated to St. Pudentiana), the oldest place of Christian worship in the city. The church itself dates back to the second century, whereas the mosaic dates from the reign of Pope Innocent I in the early fifth century. It depicts Christ enthroned, surrounded by apostles, beneath a cross, mounted with precious stones. On a much smaller scale is the panel of an ivory diptych, found in Rome and dating from around 400, which shows the Resurrection with an angel and holy women at the tomb.

The final example of a fifth-century work of beauty is St. Patrick's Breastplate, which, according to tradition, was written by the saint in 433 for divine assistance and protection as he prepared to preach to the Irish king Leoghaire and his subjects. Evidently, the prayer was answered because Patrick was successful in converting the king and his people from paganism to Christianity. The prayer is one of the most beautiful ever written, a work of great literary as well as spiritual merit. The section that invokes the beauty of creation as a means of seeing and experiencing the beauty of the Creator, prefigures St. Francis' "Canticle of Brother Sun":

> I arise today, through
> The strength of heaven,
> The light of the sun,
> The radiance of the moon,
> The splendor of fire,
> The speed of lightning,
> The swiftness of wind,
> The depth of the sea,
> The stability of the earth,
> The firmness of rock.

[It is, however, the sublime Christocentrism of the prayer that is most memorable:]

Christ with me,
Christ before me,
Christ behind me,
Christ in me,
Christ beneath me,
Christ above me,
Christ on my right,
Christ on my left,
Christ when I lie down,
Christ when I sit down,
Christ when I arise,
Christ in the heart of every man who thinks of me,
Christ in the mouth of everyone who speaks of me,
Christ in every eye that sees me,
Christ in every ear that hears me.

Let us end this reflection on the good, bad, and beautiful in the fifth century as we began it, with the great St.

Augustine. In his *Confessions*, he praised beauty by praising Beauty Himself:

> Too late did I love You, O Fairness, so ancient, and yet so new! Too late did I love You! ... You gleamed and shine, and chase away my blindness. You exhaled odours, and I drew in my breath and do pant after you. I tasted, and do hunger and thirst. You touched me, and I burned for Your peace.[14]

[14] Saint Augustine, *Confessions* 10, 27, *Nicene and Post-Nicene Fathers, First Series*, vol. 1, ed. Philip Schaff, trans. J.G. Pilkington (Buffalo, N.Y.: Christian Literature Publishing Co., 1887), rev. and ed. for New Advent by Kevin Knight.

Sixth Century

The Resurrection of Rome

The Good

The great Catholic historian Christopher Dawson was claiming too much when he wrote that "the beginnings of Western culture are to be found in the new spiritual community which arose from the ruins of the Roman Empire."[1] The beginnings of Western culture are to be found much earlier in Athens and Jerusalem. Just as Christ could not fulfill the Law unless there had been a Law to fulfill, so St. Augustine and others could not have adopted and baptized Greek philosophy unless there had been a philosophy that could be adopted and baptized. Similarly, the edifices of Christian literature, such as Dante's *Divine Comedy* and Shakespeare's tragedies, could not have been written unless the epics of Homer and Virgil, and the tragedies of Sophocles, had been written first. Nonetheless, Dawson's principal argument that Western culture would be forged by "the new spiritual community which arose from the ruins of the Roman Empire", shaping it into the civilization known as Christendom, is most certainly correct. Since this is so, there is no better way of raising the curtain on the sixth century than the words of Dawson himself:

---

[1] Christopher Dawson, *Religion and the Rise of Western Culture* (New York: Image Books, 1958), 26.

The Christian Church inherited the traditions of the Empire. It came to the barbarians as the bearer of a higher civilization, endowed with the prestige of Roman law and the authority of the Roman name. The breakdown of the political organization of the Roman Empire had left a great void which no barbarian king or general could fill, and this void was filled by the Church as the teacher and law-giver of the new peoples.... It was only in so far as the different peoples of the West were incorporated in the spiritual community of Christendom that they acquired a common culture.... Primitive Europe outside the Mediterranean lands preserved no common centre and no unified tradition of spiritual culture. The people of the North possessed no written literature, no cities, no stone architecture. They were, in short, "barbarians"; and it was only by Christianity and the elements of a higher culture transmitted to them by the Church that Western Europe acquired unity and form.[2]

Seen in this light, it is evident that the sixth century represents a critical and crucial phase in human history. The previous century had seen the collapse of the Roman Empire, the epitome and pinnacle of the power of the City of Man; the sixth century saw the rise of the Roman Church, the manifestation in time of the City of God, from the ruins of the Roman Empire. The key events that brought about the mystical resurrection of Rome were the conversion of the barbarian tribes that had ravaged Europe during the previous century, the rise of monasticism that would sow the seeds of spiritual and cultural renewal, and the election to the See of Peter of one of the greatest popes in the Church's tempestuous and illustrious history.

The century began with the conversion of Sigismund, king of the Burgundians, who was baptized in 500, four years after the baptism of Clovis, king of the Franks. Later

[2] Ibid., 26–27.

in the century, sometime around 570, one of the most vicious of the Germanic pagan tribes, the Suevi, converted en masse. In 589, Reccared I, king of the Visigoths, became a Catholic; ten years later, at the century's very end, King Ethelbert of Kent also converted to Catholicism, opening the way for the conversion of England in the following century.

If the conversion of kings signified the transformation of Europe from the top down, the founding of a monastic community by St. Benedict at Monte Cassino in Italy in 529 would transform the spirit and culture of Europe from the grassroots up. New monasteries, following the Rule of St. Benedict, rooted in the Benedictine motto *ora et labora* (pray and work), spread across Europe, becoming centers of faith, culture, and economic renewal. The impact of the Benedictines was summarized succinctly by the German historian Alfred Läpple: "The achievement of the Benedictine monks can be summarized by three symbols: the Cross (they were messengers of the Christian faith), the book (pioneers and preservers of Western culture), and the plow (promoters of civilization and new settlements)."[3] Edward Gibbon, author of *The History of the Rise and Fall of the Roman Empire* and no friend of the Catholic Church, stated candidly that "a single Benedictine monastery may have done more for the cause of knowledge than Oxford and Cambridge combined."[4]

Apart from the spread of Benedictine monasticism from its beginnings in Italy to its flowering throughout the length and breadth of Christendom, Irish monasticism, the fruits of the evangelical seeds planted by St. Patrick in the previous century, would also flourish at this time.

---

[3] Alfred Läpple, *The Catholic Church: A Brief History* (New York: Paulist Press, 1982), 34.

[4] Quoted in ibid., 34.

Having spread across Ireland, Celtic monasticism would overspill to other countries. St. Columba founded an abbey at Iona, off the coast of Scotland, in 565, from whence Celtic Christianity would spread to the mainland and, in 585, St. Columbanus founded an abbey at Luxeuil in Burgundy and, early in the seventh century, at Bobbio in Lombardy (present-day Italy).

The astonishing proliferation of monasteries across Europe was assisted by St. Gregory the Great, who succeeded to the See of Peter in 590. Having become a monk himself following his conversion to Catholicism, he was a champion of St. Benedict, writing the saint's life and actively encouraging the founding of new monasteries throughout Christendom. He was truly a "consul of God", as his epitaph states, a true statesman as well as being a true saint who succeeded in harnessing the vitality of the barbarians to the traditions of Rome. "Gregory succeeded in making the papacy the veritable axis of the barbarian West," wrote Guy Bedouelle.[5] In 592, he concluded a peace with the Lombards, the latest tribe to invade Italy, doing so without consultation with the emperor in the East, who was the sovereign of Italy, albeit in name only and not in terms of realpolitik. Such was the influence of this truly great and holy pope that, in the judgment of Guy Bedouelle, "he stands out in history as the most important of the popularizers of Christian thought."[6]

The Bad

If the sixth century was a time in which the Church made great strides in the conversion of the multifarious pagan

[5] Guy Bedouelle, *An Illustrated History of the Church* (Milan: Editoriale Jaca Book, 2004), 39.

[6] Ibid., 40.

tribes, it did not, and of course it could not, turn the barbarians into saints overnight. The Franks, who had been Christians from the time of Clovis' conversion at the end of the previous century, became the dominant force throughout the whole of what is now known as France. They defeated the Burgundians and the Visigoths, freeing Gaul of its Arian kings and bringing these lesser tribes under their dominion. In doing so, they often behaved as brutally and barbarically as their pagan ancestors.

St. Gregory of Tours, in his *Historia Francorum* (History of the Franks), gives blood-curdling accounts of murder, treachery, and plunder that rival the worst such excesses in history. Nor was the barbarism of the Franks restricted to their treatment of other barbarian tribes; it also characterized their treatment of each other in a succession of civil wars fought between Clovis' descendants. Since Gregory was writing his history at the end of the sixth century, he is a contemporary witness to the events that he relates, and since he was also well-connected with the kings and other Frankish leaders of whom he writes, we might almost say that he was an eyewitness.

The chaos caused by the barbarous brutality of the Franks was matched by Theodoric, ruler of the Ostrogothic kingdom of Italy in the opening decades of the century. As an adherent of the Arian heresy, Theodoric saw himself as the protector of Arian "Christianity" against the Catholicism of the pope in Rome and the emperor Justin in Constantinople. Anything considered pro-Byzantine was treated as treason. One victim of this intolerance of dissident opinion was Boethius, who had been Theodoric's trusted adviser until the king accused him of treasonable correspondence with Constantinople. It was while awaiting execution for his alleged treachery that Boethius wrote his masterful *Consolation of Philosophy*, one of the Great Books of Western civilization. It is surely a sign of the presence of a

Providential hand in the unfolding of history that Boethius would be destined to have a far greater impact on the future of civilization than the seemingly all-powerful ruler who had ordered his execution.

Theodoric's war on Christian orthodoxy took a further twist when he ordered Pope John I to go to Constantinople on a mission to persuade the emperor to end the persecution of the Arians. Weak-willed and cowardly, the pope agreed to Theodoric's demands. Imagine the darkly comic and deeply tragic scenario. The pope of Rome, the heir of Peter, had become a tyrant's tool, sent on a fool's mission to defend heresy.

As is often the case with the best laid schemes of the proud, Theodoric's plans backfired. The pope's visit to Constantinople, the first time in the history of the Church that the Bishop of Rome had visited the capital of the Eastern Roman Empire, was a triumph for the papacy. Upon John I's arrival, the emperor prostrated himself on the ground before him, a mark of his reverence for the papacy and a token of his gratitude and that of his people for being able "to receive in glory the vicar of St Peter the Apostle".[7] On Easter Sunday, Pope John was installed in Hagia Sophia on a throne higher than that of the patriarch. He celebrated Mass before the emperor in Latin, according to the Roman Rite, not Greek, and it was he, not the patriarch, who placed the Easter crown on the emperor's head.

Although the emperor acceded to the pope's request, at Theodoric's behest, to temper his hostilities against the Arians, there was a feeling that Pope John had been lackluster in his efforts to do the king's bidding. Upon his return to Theodoric's court at Ravenna, the king berated him for failing to secure meaningful concessions, maddened still further, no doubt, by the pope's triumphal reception by the king's own enemies. Thrown in prison by the furious king for allegedly conspiring with the emperor, as Boethius had been only two years earlier, the frail and exhausted pope died on May 18, 526, less than a month after his celebration of Easter Mass in Constantinople. In spite of his apparent weakness in kowtowing to the demands of the king to act as an ambassador on behalf of heresy, Pope John's death in prison at the hands of a heretic made him a quasi-martyr in the eyes of his contemporaries. His body was carried in state back to Rome for burial in St. Peter's, and there were reports of miraculous healings following his death.

The weakness of John I was as nothing compared with the outright corruption of Pope Vigilius, who became pope in 537. As the papal ambassador to Constantinople, Vigilius had ingratiated himself with the notoriously corrupt empress Theodora. Feigning sympathy with the empress' own Monophysite beliefs, he won her support for his own candidacy for the papacy, promising that he would repudiate the "two-nature" Christological teaching of the Council of Chalcedon, should he become pope. Armed with bags of Theodora's gold, his plan was to pave his way to the papacy with well-placed bribes. Unfortunately for him, a new pope had already been elected by the time he arrived in Rome.

Vigilius was not to be denied. In December 536, Rome was "liberated" by Flavius Belisarius, military commander of the Byzantine Empire, on behalf of the emperor Justinian I. Belisarius' wife, Antonina, was the empress Theodora's closest friend and confidante. She and Vigilius persuaded Belisarius to arrest Silverius, the recently elected pope, on the ludicrous charge that he had conspired with the Gothic army in a plot to take Rome. Stripped of his papacy, Silverius was banished to Anatolia. The frightened clergy, effectively at the point of a sword, then elected Vigilius as pope. There was a further twist, however, because one courageous bishop took up Pope Silverius' cause, appealing to the emperor Justinian and securing a personal audience with him. At this meeting, the bishop seems to have put the fear of God into the emperor, making him see the enormity of the act of deposing the pope on a trumped-up charge and no doubt suggesting that there would be hell to pay unless the emperor ensured that justice and the will of God were done. Justinian ordered that Silverius be returned to Rome for a fair trial and that he be reinstated as pope were he to be found innocent. Vigilius had too much to lose, ultimately almost certainly his own life, were Silverius to be cleared of the trumped-up charges. Feeling secure in his position, Vigilius defied the emperor and had the hapless Silverius arrested as soon as he arrived in Rome. He was once more sent into exile, this time to the island of Palmaria, where he was starved to death. To all intents and purposes, one pope had been murdered by another. One is now venerated as a saint, whereas the other's name has become a byword for iniquity. Then, as now and as always, the enemy within the gates is much more dangerous than the enemy without. Judas, like Caesar, is always with us, but Judas is the greater enemy.

God is not to be defeated by the things that are Caesar's, nor by the treachery of Judas, in the sixth or any other century. At the end of the century, a few short decades after Vigilius, he sent his Church a saint who would be a true servant of the servants of God. In the letters and homilies of St. Gregory the Great, we see the voice of

Christian conscience in a world that had been decimated by the bubonic plague, which had cast its shadow over the middle of the century, depopulating town and country alike, and by a world in which prisoners were "tied by the neck like dogs and led away to slavery".[8] We will let this saintly pope, Gregory the Great, have the last word on the wickedness of the age in which he found himself:

> What is there to please us in this world? Everywhere we see sorrow and lamentation. The cities and towns are destroyed, the fields are laid waste and the land returns to solitude. No peasant is left to till the fields, there are few inhabitants left in the cities, and yet even these scanty remnants of humanity are still subject to ceaseless sufferings.... Some are led away captive, others are mutilated and still more slain before our eyes. What is there then to please us in this world? If we still love such a world as this, it is plain that we love not pleasure but misery.[9]

The Beautiful

For all its political intrigue and promotion of heresy, Constantinople, during the reign of the emperor Justinian, was a place at which the patronage of the arts bore great fruit. Most notably was the rebuilding of the great cathedral, known as Hagia Sophia (Holy or Divine Wisdom), after rioters had set fire to the original fourth-century church in 532, only six years after Pope John I's triumphant visit. The magnificent new church, which remains one of the architectural wonders of the world, was built in only five years, being consecrated in 537. Such was its splendor and

[8] Dawson, *Religion and the Rise of Western Culture*, 36.
[9] Quoted in ibid., 36–37.

its sheer size that the emperor, with a customary show of hubris, declared that he had outdone Solomon himself in the building of a temple to the Lord.

More modest in scale but as sublime as art is the icon of Christ Pantocrator (Christ, All Powerful), dating from the mid-sixth century, at St. Catherine's Monastery on Mount Sinai in Egypt. The monastery was built on the orders of the emperor Justinian on the very site at which Moses was believed to have encountered God in the burning bush and where he would later receive the Ten Commandments. The orthodoxy of the image is made manifest in the raised right hand of Christ. The thumb and two of the fingers meet to signify the Trinity, while the other two fingers, joined together, symbolize Christ's divine and human natures.

Parallel with the development of iconography and equally rooted in monastic life is the development of the illuminated manuscript. One of the oldest extant examples is what is known as the *Vienna Genesis*, which is written in silver (now turned black with age) on purple vellum. The brilliantly colored illustrations, depicting scenes from Scripture, were described by the art historian H. W. Janson as being reminiscent in their "sumptuous effect" to the mosaics in the churches of Ravenna.[10]

As for Ravenna itself, it remained a major center of power in the sixth century. This is reflected in the magnificent churches, resplendent with mosaics that were built around this time, especially the Basilica of San Vitale and the Basilica of Sant'Apollinare Nuovo, the latter of which was originally built by Theodoric for the Arians, whom he favored, before subsequently being given over to Catholic worship.

---

[10] H. W. Janson and Anthony F. Janson, *A Basic History of Art*, 4th ed. (New York: Harry N. Abrams, 1992), 114–15.

Ravenna was also the place at which the great Boethius was imprisoned, awaiting execution, as we have seen. It was during his imprisonment that he wrote his master-work, *The Consolation of Philosophy*, a major philosophical work but also a work of great literary merit with its employment of Lady Philosophy as a personified abstraction who comforts the narrator in his time of desolation.

Apart from his seminal *Consolatio*, Boethius was the author of a book on music, *De Musica*, which remained unfinished at the time of his death. Boethius' understanding of music is rooted in Greek philosophy, especially the teaching of Pythagoras and Plato, encapsulated in Plato's dictum, which Boethius cites that "the soul of the universe was composed according to a musical harmony".[11] This harmony is, therefore, ultimately divine, dwelling in the mind of the Maker and expressive of the intrinsic goodness, truth, and beauty of the Godhead, which pours forth though creation in the *musica mundana*, the music of the spheres (or the world), the inner harmony of the cosmos itself. In this sense, music is united with arithmetic or mathematics, following the rules of order and proportion. Boethius also speaks of the *musica humana*, the inner harmony of the human person, body and soul, as well as the *musica instrumentalis*, the physical manifestation of music in an audible sense.

De Musica would become the standard music theory textbook throughout the Middle Ages and beyond, as the *Consolatio* would become a standard philosophical text. Boethius' enduring influence is made manifest in the words of Lorenzo in *The Merchant of Venice*, written more than a thousand years later, in which Lorenzo's words echo

---

[11] Quoted in Susan Treacy, *The Music of Christendom: A History* (San Francisco: Ignatius Press, 2021), 10–11.

Boethius' understanding of the *musica mundana*, the *musica humana*, and the *musica instrumentalis*, alluding to each in the order in which Boethius writes of them:

> How sweet the moonlight sleeps upon this bank!
> Here will we sit and let the sounds of music
> Creep in our ears. Soft stillness and the night
> Become the touches of sweet harmony.
> Sit, Jessica. Look how the floor of heaven
> Is thick inlaid with patens of bright gold.
> There's not the smallest orb which thou behold'st
> But in his motion like an angel sings,
> Still quiring to the young-ey'd cherubins;
> Such harmony is in immortal souls,
> But whilst this muddy vesture of decay
> Doth grossly close it in, we cannot hear it.
> Come ho, and wake Diana with a hymn,
> With sweetest touches pierce your mistress' ear,
> And draw her home with music.[12]

As for the *musica instrumentalis*, it is indisputably Gregorian chant that has a place of prominence and preeminence in the history and culture of Christendom. According to the musicologist and music historian Susan Treacy, "Gregorian chant is a totally humble art that also happens to be sublime prayer. There is no other reason for which it was composed than the praise of God."[13] It is also, she argues, "the foundation of all Western music".[14]

Although it bears his name, it is unlikely that Gregory the Great was responsible for the birth of chant, which

---

[12] William Shakespeare, *The Merchant of Venice*, ed. Joseph Pearce, Ignatius Critical Editions (San Francisco: Ignatius Press, 2009), act 5, scene 1, lines 54–68.

[13] Treacy, *Music of Christendom*, 19.

[14] Ibid., 13.

probably developed from chants used in the early Church and, prior to that, in the Jewish Temple. It is, however, reasonably certain that he did much to encourage its use and popularize it, thereby having his name associated with it so inseparably.

Gregorian chant is, of course, also inseparable from the beauty of the liturgy, which it exists to serve. "The preservation and development of ... liturgical tradition was one of the main preoccupations of the Church in the dark age that followed the barbarian conquest," wrote Christopher Dawson, "since it was in this way that the vitality and continuity of the inner life of Christendom which was the seed of the new order were preserved."[15] Putting the matter more bluntly, John Senior observed that "Christendom, what secularists call Western Civilization, is the Mass."[16] Specifically, and returning to Christopher Dawson, it was the Mass celebrated according to "the ancient and conservative Roman tradition, which from the time of St. Gregory the Great came to exercise a far-reaching normative influence on all the Western Churches".[17]

---

[15] Dawson, *Religion and the Rise of Western Culture*, 43.

[16] John Senior, *The Restoration of Christian Culture* (San Francisco: Ignatius Press, 1983), 15–16.

[17] Dawson, *Religion and the Rise of Western Culture*, 43.

Seventh Century

Northern Lights

The Good

Commencing the discussion of the seventh century, it seems appropriate to reprise what has already been said about the previous century. The key events that brought about the mystical resurrection of Rome in the sixth century were the conversion of the barbarian tribes, the rise of monasticism, and the pontificate of St. Gregory the Great. These three events would also characterize the seventh century, especially in the spreading of the Gospel to the farthest northern reaches of what had been the Roman Empire.

In 595, Gregory the Great selected Augustine, the prior of a monastery in Rome, to lead an evangelical mission to England to convert the pagan tribes that had settled there following the withdrawal of the Romans almost two hundred years earlier. Two years later, Augustine, with a company of monks, arrived in the Kingdom of Kent, in the southeast of England. He was immediately successful in converting King Ethelbert to the practice of the faith, the king granting him land to build a monastery. Augustine was consecrated as a bishop and, on Christmas Day in 597, he received thousands into the Church during a mass baptism.

It would be wrong, however, to assume that England was entirely pagan at the time of Augustine's arrival because a considerable Christian presence remained from the time of the Roman occupation. Having established their own traditions during the two centuries of relative isolation, these native-born Christians were understandably suspicious of the new arrivals from Rome. The native British bishops refused to recognize Augustine's authority, irrespective of such authority being bestowed by the pope himself. This division of the Church in England would remain until the Synod of Whitby in 664 definitively established papal authority throughout the country.

In 601, Pope Gregory sent further missionaries to assist Augustine's apostolate and, in the following year, with the king's assistance, Augustine repaired and then consecrated a church that had been established centuries earlier by Roman Christians. Two years later, Pope Gregory appointed Mellitus as Bishop of London, thereby reestablishing a see that had existed under the Romans since at least three hundred years earlier. Mellitus' first major act as bishop was to build St. Paul's Cathedral, probably on the site of a previous church.

In 627, King Edwin of Northumbria converted to the faith. With all the zeal of a new convert, King Edwin persuaded King Earpwald of East Anglia to accept Christ in baptism, also in 627, so that in one glorious year the east and the north of England embraced the faith. In that same year, a veritable *annus mirabilis*, St. Honorius became Archbishop of Canterbury. During his twenty-five years as primate, he would oversee the transformation of England into an avowedly Christian country and a land of saints. He sent St. Felix to evangelize East Anglia and lived to see the apostolate of St. Aidan in Northumbria; he replaced St. Birinus of Wessex with another saint, Agilbert, as Bishop of Dorchester, and had the joy of seeing the conversion of King Peada and the kingdom of the Middle Angles. It was also during St. Honorius' time that the first English convent of Benedictine nuns was founded, in 630, by St. Eanswith at Folkestone in Kent, beginning a monastic tradition of religious sisters in England that would span nine hundred years until Henry VIII's dissolution of the monasteries in the sixteenth century.

In 642, St. Oswald, the king of Northumbria, fell in battle against the pagans of Mercia. Bede reports miracles at the site of his death, including the healing of a paralytic girl. Miracles were also reported nine years later after the death of St. Aidan, the Irish monk who was the first bishop and abbot of Lindisfarne (Holy Island), off the coast of Northumbria.

Two of Aidan's students, St. Cedd and St. Chad, who had received their education at Lindisfarne, would become great evangelists for the faith in the struggle to wrest the soul of England from the grip of paganism. St. Cedd preached to the East Saxons, in what is now Essex, and proved so successful that he was appointed bishop and subsequently founded monasteries. St. Chad, his brother, would become the first bishop of Mercia, in the English midlands.

Perhaps the most important event with respect to the spread of Christianity throughout England was the aforementioned Synod of Whitby, which conformed the practice of the faith in England with that of the universal Church. At this time, those parts of England still under the influence of the remnant of the Romano-British Church, which had been influenced in turn by the teaching of Irish monks, were celebrating Easter at a different time from that celebrated by Rome. This anomaly was resolved at the synod, ensuring a unified practice of the Church's liturgy thereafter.

One of the most colorful characters of the mid-seventh century was St. Etheldreda, a queen who would become the foundress and abbess of Ely, on the fens of what is now Cambridgeshire. A princess by birth, the daughter of the king of East Anglia, she became a nun and founded a monastery in 673 on the site of what is now the magnificent Ely Cathedral. She also restored an old church that had been reputedly destroyed by Penda, the pagan king of Mercia, and lived an austere and holy life of penance and prayer. She ate only one meal a day and wore clothes of coarse wool instead of linen. Dying in 679, her body was discovered seventeen years later to be incorrupt and the tumor on her neck, the presumed cause of her death, was found to be healed. According to those who witnessed the exhumation of her body, the linen cloths in which her body had been wrapped were as fresh as they were on the day of her burial. Her shrine at Ely became a popular place of pilgrimage, and devotion to her was flourishing many centuries later.

Another great abbess of the Church and contemporary of St. Etheldreda was St. Ethelburga, foundress of Barking Abbey in Essex, to the east of London, which would become one of the most prominent religious houses in England, surviving until its destruction by Henry VIII. The abbey had been founded for St. Ethelburga by her brother, St. Erkenwald, sometime before the latter had become Bishop of the East Saxons in 675. Such was the rise to prominence of Barking Abbey and such was the reputation for holiness of its foundress that St. Bede, writing only a few decades after St. Ethelburga's death, spends several chapters on the events of her life, including accounts of several miracles, such as visions of the afterlife and the healing of a blind woman while praying in the convent burial ground.

A saint of an altogether different sort was Caedwalla, a pagan king of Wessex, who had a reputation for ruthlessness and violence until he fell under the benign and holy influence of St. Wilfrid. Experiencing a dramatic conversion, he abdicated in 688 and traveled to Rome on penitential pilgrimage, desiring to be received into the Church. He was baptized on Holy Saturday 689 by Pope Sergius and given the name of Peter. Although he was only thirty years old, he was taken ill suddenly and died. He was buried in the crypt of St. Peter's, and his epitaph, written by Crispus, Archbishop of Milan, is quoted by Bede. Caedwalla would be the first of four Anglo-Saxon kings to end his days in Rome, two of whom became monks upon their arrival in the Eternal City.

The late seventh century was also a time of great scholarship and culture. St. Adrian of Canterbury established a school, teaching Greek, Latin, Scripture, theology, law, and astronomy, at which many future bishops and abbots were educated. St. Adrian had a reputation for sanctity as well as scholarship, and when his body was exhumed in 1091, almost four hundred years after his death, it was found to be incorrupt. Similarly, the body of St. Cuthbert, the Bishop of Lindisfarne, was found to be incorrupt in 698, eleven years after his death, and miraculous healings were reported at his tomb and in association with his relics.

Even as monks from Rome were heading north to reevangelize England, monks from Ireland were heading south, north, and east, spreading the faith far and wide. St. Columbanus established monasteries as far south as Bobbio in Lombardy, where he died in 615. His presence and preaching in Lombardy helped to convert the Lombard kingdom from the paganism and Arianism with which its people were infected. Columbanus' influence would bear fruit after his death in the evangelical zeal of his followers. In the words of Christopher Dawson, "Almost all the great monastic founders and missionaries of the seventh century … were his disciples, or the heirs of his tradition and his rule."[1] These included St. Gall, St. Wandrille, St. Ouen, St. Philibert, St. Fara, St. Omer, St. Bertin, St. Valery, and St. Romaric. Irish missionaries, such as St. Kilian, journeyed as far east as Würzburg in Germany, whereas other pioneering Irish evangelists established monasteries in the wildest north and west, in places as remote as the Faroe Islands and Iceland. "The rush of missionaries from Ireland," wrote G. K. Chesterton, had "all the air of an unexpected onslaught of young men on an old world, and even on a Church that showed signs of growing old."[2]

This renewal of the Church by Benedictine and Irish monasticism was, in the words of John Henry Newman, "a restoration":

> Silent men were observed about the country, or discovered in the forest, digging, clearing and building; and other silent men, not seen, were sitting in the cold cloister, tiring their eyes and keeping their attention on the stretch, while they painfully copied and recopied the manuscripts which they had saved. There was no one who contended or cried out, or drew attention to what was going on, but by degrees the woody swamp became a hermitage, a religious house, a farm, an abbey, a village, a seminary, a school of learning and a city.[3]

Taking up Newman's theme of the role of the monasteries in conserving the culture of civilization in the wake of the fall of the Roman Empire and ultimately restoring it so that civilization itself could be resuscitated and

[1] Christopher Dawson, *Religion and the Rise of Western Culture* (New York: Image Books, 1958), 58.

[2] G. K. Chesterton, *The Everlasting Man* (San Francisco: Ignatius Press, 1993), 251.

[3] John Henry Newman, *Historical Studies*, vol. 2, quoted in Dawson, *Religion and the Rise of Western Culture*, 53–54.

resurrected, G. K. Chesterton spoke of the Church as the bridge across a barbarian abyss: "Christianity, so far from belonging to the Dark Ages, was the one path across the Dark Ages that was not dark. It was the shining bridge connecting two shining civilizations."[4]

The Bad

Paradoxically, the seventh century was a time when the Christian sun was rising in the West as it was setting in the East. As the people of England embraced the faith and the missionaries of Ireland spread it, the eastern parts of Christendom were under increasing threat. In 614, the very year in which St. Columbanus was founding his monastery in Lombardy, the Persians were invading the Holy Land, taking Jerusalem. H. W. Crocker described the fall of Jerusalem as "the worst symbolic geopolitical disaster for Christianity since the fall of Rome",[5] but much worse was to follow. Even the siege of Constantinople by the Persians twelve years later was of relatively minor importance compared with the imminent rise of Islam and its militaristic ambition. Within a few years of the death of Mohammed, the new religion's prophet, his followers were embarked on relentless campaigns of military conquest. The ancient Christian city of Antioch fell to the Muslims in 637, and by 643, they had conquered Syria, Palestine, Persia, and Egypt. By the beginning of the following century, the whole of Christian North Africa would be in Muslim hands. Alexandria fell in 642 and Carthage in 698. For those along the

[4] G. K. Chesterton, *Orthodoxy* (San Francisco: Ignatius Press, 1995), 154.

[5] H. W. Crocker III, *Triumph: The Power and the Glory of the Catholic Church* (New York: Three Rivers Press, 2001), 108.

southern rim of the Mediterranean, it was literally the end of civilization as they had known it.

As ever, however, the enemies within the fold could be more menacing than the enemies without. Even as the forces of Islam were laying waste to swathes of Christendom, a civil war was being waged between Christians. The emperor of Constantinople, Constans II, endeavored to enforce by law a heresy known as Monothelitism, which denied that Christ had a human will. The papacy condemned this error as being effectively a modified version of the earlier Monophysite heresy, thereby incurring the emperor's wrath. His troops attacked and looted the Lateran Palace, and the pope's ambassador in Constantinople was imprisoned. Tensions were heightened still further with the election to the papacy of St. Martin I in 649. With commendable courage, the new pope called a synod of Western bishops that definitively refuted the Monothelite heresy. The emperor responded by having the pope arrested and taken to Constantinople. Following a political show trial, during which the pope was accused of plotting rebellion and even with conspiring with the forces of Islam, he was exiled to Crimea in May 655, where he died a few months later. As for the emperor, he would live for another thirteen tyrannical years, having his political rivals murdered and becoming increasingly unpopular. Having murdered and martyred his enemies, he would be murdered himself by his own chamberlain while he was taking a bath.

It was ironic that Pope St. Martin I, the last pope to be designated a martyr, should have been killed by the emperor of Constantinople who was, ostensibly at least, the secular ruler of Christendom. It was a Christian Caesar who had sentenced to death the successor of Peter. Such treachery was not unusual. It was often the lukewarm "cafeteria" Christians who put the saints to death, preferring their own worldliness and their own interpretations of Church teaching to the sanctity and orthodoxy of the true disciples of Christ. Such was the fate of a group of Irish missionaries martyred on the coast of Cornwall, as recounted by G. K. Chesterton: "The chief authority on Cornish antiquities told me that he did not believe for a moment that they were martyred by heathens but (as he expressed it with some humour) 'by rather slack Christians'."[6] As often as not, then as now, it is not the infidels who pose the greatest threat to Christendom and the life of the Church but those of little faith.

The Beautiful

One of the most widespread forms of Christian art, from the seventh century and earlier, are the intricately carved stone monuments known as steles. These were common in Armenia and other countries in the Christian east but most were destroyed by the ravages of Islam's "cancel culture". It is, therefore, in countries that remained beyond Islam's reach that the oldest surviving Christian steles are found. The Fahan stele in County Donegal, the northernmost county in Ireland, where St. Mura founded a monastery in the seventh century, shows two intertwining crosses, with two human figures, presumably saints, and a Trinitarian inscription. Just across the Irish Sea in Cumberland in northwest England is the Cross of St. Cuthbert, named after the seventh-century Anglo-Saxon saint. It is a stele in the Irish style, depicting the Cross as the tree of life sheltering God's creatures. In Metz, in northeastern France,

---

[6] Chesterton, *Everlasting Man*, 251.

are seventh-century steles depicting animals, plants, and geometric forms encapsulating classical Eastern and Germanic influences. Another stele from this period is to be found near Bonn in Germany. It shows a victorious Christ holding a lance.

The crypt of St. Paul in the seventh-century Abbey Notre-Dame de Jouarre in France has two elaborately inscribed sarcophagi, one of which shows a group of people surrounding Christ, their hands raised to heaven as they await the Resurrection, and the other decorated with what appear to be scallop shells, which would become the universal symbol of pilgrimage. On the wall of the crypt is a curious image of a beardless Christ, the Book of the Gospels resting on his lap, surrounded by symbolic representations of the four Evangelists.

A marble slab from this period, produced in Brescia in Lombardy, appears to combine pre-Christian pagan influences with the modern (at the time) Irish influence brought to the region by St. Columbanus. Depicting a peacock, traditionally the bird associated with the goddess Juno, it is also symbolic of the resurrection of the dead insofar as the peacock's flesh was said to be incorruptible. The framing of the bird in engraved foliage is Byzantine in style, whereas the interlace at the base is clearly of Irish inspiration.

Apart from steles and other sacred art engraved in stone, the developing monastic tradition also bore creative fruit in calligraphy and the production of illuminated manuscripts. One of the most celebrated examples of such illumination is *The Book of Lindisfarne*, which was said to have been made by the monks of Lindisfarne in the late seventh century for St. Cuthbert himself.

A further blessed consequence of the spread of the monasteries across Europe was not merely the widespread use of Gregorian chant in the daily lives of the monks but the cataloguing of the various chants through the development of musical notation. As with their recording of religious texts in illuminated manuscripts, the monks began what could be called the first recording of music through the use of such notation.

In a very real sense, the monastic communities were practicing tradition in the Chestertonian sense in which it is considered to be "democracy extended through time", the proxy of the dead and the enfranchisement of the unborn: "Tradition may be defined as the extension of the franchise," wrote Chesterton. "Tradition means giving votes to our ancestors. It is the democracy of the dead."[7] In faithfully copying ancient texts, the monks were custodians of the past who were enriching the future. They were saving a priceless heritage from being lost and cancelled by barbarians, thereby ensuring the transmission of civilized culture to future generations who would otherwise have been condemned to ignorance. Once again, since Chesterton says it best, the last word shall be his:

> The Christian Church was the last life of the old society and was also the first life of the new. She took the people who were forgetting how to make an arch and she taught them to invent the Gothic arch. In a word, the most absurd thing that could be said of the Church is the thing we have all heard said of it. How can we say that the Church wishes to bring us back into the Dark Ages? The Church was the only thing that ever brought us out of them.[8]

[7] Chesterton, *Orthodoxy*, 52–53.
[8] Ibid., 154.

Eighth Century

Anglo-Saxons and Saracens

The Good

The seeds of faith that were sown in England by St. Gregory the Great and St. Augustine of Canterbury at the end of the sixth century and the dawn of the seventh would bear great fruit throughout the eighth century. This period of English history would prove to be a golden age in which great Anglo-Saxon scholars, such as St. Bede the Venerable and Alcuin of York, would strengthen Christendom with the fruits of their great learning, while Anglo-Saxon missionaries, such as St. Boniface, would spread the faith into the far-flung regions of the German-speaking pagan east.

St. Bede was described by the Church historian Philip Hughes as "not only the great scholar of his age, but one of the greatest of all time".[1] Leading an uneventful and quiet life of prayer and study in a monastery in Northumbria in northern England, from which he hardly ever traveled, Bede wrote commentaries on Holy Scripture, as well as works on astronomy and mathematics.

The Dominican scholar Gervase Matthew described Bede as "the first of the English Platonists"[2] for the manner

---

[1] Philip Hughes, *A Popular History of the Catholic Church* (New York: Macmillan, 1962), 89.

[2] Maisie Ward, ed., *The English Way: Studies in English Sanctity from Bede to Newman* (Tacoma, Wash.: Cluny Media, 2016), 6.

in which his biblical exegesis followed the reasoning in St. Augustine's *City of God* that the Israel of the Old Testament was "a kind of shadow and prophetic image" of the Church.[3] Bede "studied the shadow world in which he lived preoccupied by the world it shadowed" in the knowledge that "the literal meaning is to the allegorical as water is to wine".[4]

Bede is best known, however, as the great chronicler of Anglo-Saxon history, completing the writing of his celebrated and seminal *Ecclesiastical History of the English People* in 731. The knowledge that we now have of Roman Britain and Anglo-Saxon England is largely dependent on Bede's scholarship, and there is no doubt that he deserves the accolade of being the father of English history as well as the accolade of being declared a Doctor of the Church by Pope Leo XIII in 1899. In his works of theology and his great work of history, "he was conscious that he was the heir of a great tradition, a tradition that it was his life-work to perpetuate in the north."[5] His influence was considerable in his own time and in the centuries that followed. Notker the Stammerer, a monk of the Abbey of St. Gall in Switzerland, wrote in the late ninth century that "God, the orderer of natures, who raised the Sun from the East on the fourth day of Creation, in the sixth day of the world has made Bede rise from the West as a new Sun to illuminate the whole Earth."[6]

If Bede hardly left the monastery in which he spent almost the whole of his life, the same could not be said of his great English contemporary St. Boniface, the great

---

[3] St. Augustine, *The City of God*, 15, 2, trans. Henry Bettenson (London: Penguin Classics, 1984), 597.

[4] Ward, *English Way*, 6.

[5] Ibid., 7.

[6] Quoted in the introduction to Bede, *The Reckoning of Time*, trans. Faith Wallis (Liverpool: Liverpool University Press, 2004), lxxxv.

missionary Apostle of Germany. Born in around 675, about two years after Bede but at the other end of England, at Crediton in Devon, Boniface would be tireless in the first half of the eighth century in his mission to convert the pagan Germanic tribes to the Gospel of Christ. According to Christopher Dawson, "The work of St. Boniface did more than any other factor to lay the foundations of medieval Christendom":

> His mission to Germany was not an isolated spiritual adventure like the achievements of his Celtic predecessors; it was part of a far-sighted programme of construction and reform planned with all the method and statesmanship of the Roman tradition. It involved a triple alliance between the Anglo-Saxon missionaries, the Papacy, and the family of Charles Martel, the de facto rulers of the Frankish kingdom.[7]

In a series of councils supported by both the pope and by Pepin and Carloman, the sons of Charles Martel, held between 740 and 747, Boniface enacted a thoroughgoing reform of the Frankish Church. His personal prestige and the weight of his moral authority were exemplified in 752, when he solemnly consecrated Pepin as king of the Franks, a ceremony that was repeated by Pope Stephen II two years later.

With the assistance of Anglo-Saxon monks and missionaries, Boniface succeeded in converting German barbarian tribes, such as the Hessians, Saxons, and Frisians, establishing monasteries as he ventured further into the German-speaking territories, especially at Fulda in 744 and St. Gall in Switzerland about six years later. "It was in these Anglo-Saxon colonies," wrote Dawson, "that the new type

[7] Christopher Dawson, *Religion and the Rise of Western Culture* (New York: Image Books, 1958), 62.

of Christian culture, which had been developed in Northumbria in the seventh century, was adapted and transmitted to the Germanic peoples of the Continent, and a new generation was trained which provided for the re-education and spiritual leadership of the Frankish Church."[8]

St. Boniface's death would be as heroic as his life. Failing in health and almost eighty years old, Boniface put his affairs in order and made plans for one final mission into enemy territory. Journeying into the marshlands beyond Utrecht, he enjoyed initial success, converting many. In June 755, he and his fellow missionaries were ambushed by pagans and the elderly saint was killed, a sword slicing through his skull. His body was taken in triumph to Fulda, where he lies to this day among the people whose ancestors he had evangelized and brought to the faith.

In 735, the same year in which Bede died, another great English scholar, Alcuin, was born in the north of England. Destined to become the most influential scholar of the eighth century and one of the foundational scholars of Christian civilization, he was educated by men whom Bede had taught. This passing of the baton of knowledge from one generation to the next exemplifies the continuum of accumulated wisdom across the ages that rightly bears the name of civilization.

Writing of the flowering of knowledge and scholarship in Anglo-Saxon England, Fr. Aelfric Manson illustrates the connection between the revival of the liberal arts and the Church's insistence on the marriage of faith and reason. "To Alcuin, as to Alfred the Great, study and the pursuit of knowledge was part of the Christian life, and the liberal arts were not practiced as ends in themselves but as sub-serving, in one way or another, the great end

[8] Ibid., 62–63.

of enriching the Christian life and advancing in the understanding of revelation."[9]

Having spent the first forty years of his life building the great library at York, thereby gaining a reputation for scholarship that was known from one end of Christendom to the other, Alcuin answered the call of Charlemagne to help spread Christian learning to the Franks. Immigrating in 782 to Aachen, in what is now Germany, he became master of the Palace School at Charlemagne's court.

Charlemagne bestowed three abbeys upon Alcuin that became great centers of learning. Alcuin set about raising the standards for the copying of manuscripts, which was such a crucial task in the days before printing, as well as increasing the amount of copying being done. Handpicked scribes would make copies under Alcuin's supervision that were then distributed to other monasteries for further copies to be made. In this way, libraries gradually grew up all over the realms that Charlemagne ruled, all of which had Alcuin's own labor as their fount and source.

Charlemagne was himself a student of Alcuin, considering the learned Englishman to be his mentor. In becoming Alcuin's student, Charlemagne was showing his own people that nobody should consider himself above the pursuit of knowledge. As one whom Charlemagne trusted, Alcuin became what the historian William J. Slattery has described as the empire's unofficial "Minister of Culture". He was, wrote Slattery, "a man for whom Charlemagne held deep admiration, whose friendship he cherished, and to whom he gave an important role in formulating policy and in drafting official documents".[10]

[9] Quoted in Ward, *English Way*, 39.

[10] William J. Slattery, *Heroism and Genius: How Catholic Priests Helped to Build—and Can Help Rebuild—Western Civilization* (San Francisco: Ignatius Press, 2017), 106–7.

As with all rulers, Charlemagne was far from perfect and often abused his great power. Yet, he did far more good than harm and, in this alone, was far better than most other rulers. "Charlemagne is the Christian prince in a far truer sense than could ever be asserted of Constantine or Justinian," wrote Philip Hughes. "It was through the common faith of his peoples that he ruled, and upon that faith that he built, and it was to promote the well-being of that faith, and the extension of its empire, that he toiled for forty years."[11]

The Bad

Even as the Anglo-Saxons were helping to spread the Gospel to the pagan tribes on the eastern fringes of civilized Europe, the Saracens were threatening to lay waste to the ancient heartlands of Christendom, conquering in the name of the new religion of Islam. Having overrun the Holy Land and conquering the whole of North Africa, they crossed into Spain in 711 and soon had possession of the entire Iberian Peninsula. Nor did they stop there. Crossing the Pyrenees, they advanced seemingly inexorably into the very heart of Christian Europe. All the monasteries in their path were sacked and pillaged, including the important monastic centers of culture at Lérins and Luxeuil, the latter of which had been founded by the Irish missionary St. Columban. The Muslim advance was finally stopped in 732 near Tours by a Christian army led by Charles Martel, a military victory that probably saved the whole of Christendom from Islamic conquest. This crucial victory having been won, the Saracens were forced back over the mountains to Spain, from whence they remained in easy

---

[11] Hughes, *Popular History of the Church*, 98.

striking distance of the Christians to the north. "The siege of Christendom had begun," wrote Philip Hughes, "and in every generation, for another nine hundred years, there was made upon it, from some quarter of the Mahometan world, a violent assault."[12]

As always, however, the enemies within the Church were as much of a danger to Christendom as were the infidels without. Besieged by Islam militarily, having almost fallen to Muslim forces in the siege of 717, Constantinople was now succumbing to the theological and cultural influence of the enemy on its doorstep. In 726, the Eastern emperor Leo III banned the use and veneration of icons, ushering in a puritanical iconoclasm that mirrored the iconoclasm of Islam itself. Religious images were destroyed on the orders of the ostensibly Christian emperor, matching the destruction and desecration of such images that had accompanied the Muslim conquest of Christian lands.

There was much popular opposition to the emperor's enforcement of his decree. When imperial soldiers tried to remove a famous and much venerated image of Christ from the gates of Constantinople, the people resisted, riots breaking out across the city in protest. In Ravenna, the emperor's representative was lynched by an angry mob when he endeavored to enforce the imperial edict.

In 731, Pope Gregory III condemned the imperial edict, declaring that anyone who defiled a sacred image was immediately excommunicated. The battle lines being drawn, tensions were once again at breaking point between the emperor of Constantinople and the pope of Rome.

After Leo's death, the imperial policy of iconoclasm was continued by his son, Constantine V, who had the Patriarch of Constantinople publicly blinded and flogged

[12] Ibid., 93.

in the street until he agreed to offer slavish support to the emperor's sacrilegious decrees. Seeking pseudo-ecclesial authority for his iconoclasm, Constantine called a council of cowardly and compliant bishops, pointedly excluding any representatives from the West who might have had the tenacity and temerity to oppose his will. Having received episcopal "sanction" for his policy, the emperor made the monasteries the principal target of his wrath. Monastic buildings were seized, and the monks were either exiled or executed. The patriarch himself would eventually be beheaded for failing to be sufficiently compliant to the emperor's reign of terror.

It was not until after the death of Constantine V and his successor Leo IV that reconciliation with Rome was sought by the empress Irene, who was serving as regent for her nine-year-old son, Constantine VI. A council of bishops was called in 787 that formally condemned the heresy of iconoclasm, which had wrought so much destruction to both life and art in those eastern parts of Christendom that had not already fallen to the iconoclastic forces of Islam.

The Beautiful

In his *Popular History of the Catholic Church*, Philip Hughes claimed that Bede's *Ecclesiastical History of the English People* was "the one production of his time that is as fresh and living to-day as when it was written, twelve hundred years ago".[13] Such a statement, spoken like a true historian, pays no heed to the great works of literature written during the golden age of Anglo-Saxondom, not least of which is

---

[13] Ibid., 90.

the great epic poem *Beowulf*, written by a monk who was
probably a contemporary of Bede himself.

The late seventh and early eighth centuries heralded the
birth of English literature, therefore, much as it had also
heralded, in the work of Bede, the birth of English history. Caedmon, the earliest known of all English poets,
was a monk at Whitby Abbey, and it is to this period that
Beowulf belongs. A profoundly Catholic work, it shows
the same preoccupation as does Bede's *History* with the
continued presence of the heresy of Pelagianism, which
had been condemned as recently as 634 by Pope Honorius
for the growth of its influence, especially in Ireland.

Beowulf warns against Pelagianism in the narrative's
depiction of its eponymous protagonist as the strongest
man alive who believes he can defeat all evil through the
power of his own strength, reflecting the heretical teaching of Pelagius that men could get to heaven through the
power of their own will, without the need of God's grace.
Beowulf discovers, in spite of his great strength, that he
is unable to defeat the supernatural power of Grendel's
Mother without the supernatural assistance of a miraculous
sword, signifying grace. The last part of *Beowulf*, which
tells of the hero's defeat of the dragon, employs numerical
allegory in a manner that would prove very influential to
J. R. R. Tolkien, who was a great scholar of the Anglo-
Saxon language (Old English) and who translated *Beowulf*
and lectured on it.

Structurally, the poem is divided sequentially by Beowulf's fighting with three monsters: Grendel, Grendel's
Mother, and the dragon.

The poet begins by telling us that Beowulf is the might-
iest warrior in the world. He can defeat any foe by the
brute power of his own strength. He proves as much by
spurning all weapons and defeating Grendel through the

strength of his own mighty arm. Beowulf seems to epitomize the Pelagian Man, who can defeat evil through the
power of his own will and strength without the necessity of any outside assistance, natural or supernatural. He
then faces Grendel's Mother, this time carrying the most
powerful sword known to man. The sword proves to
be powerless against the supernatural power of this new
monster, as does Beowulf's own strength. He would most
certainly have been killed had not a magical sword miraculously appeared within his grasp. It is through this supernatural assistance that Beowulf prevails, without which
he would have perished. "If God had not helped me,"
Beowulf says, "the outcome would have been quick and
fatal."[14] As for the supernatural sword, we discover that
its hilt is engraved with biblical images of God's defeat of
evil in salvation history. The moral and theological message is clear enough. No human person, however strong,
can defeat the power of evil without supernatural assistance (grace), nor can the most powerful works of human
ingenuity (the man-made sword signifying what we would
now call technology) save us from evil. Our triumph over
evil is possible only with divine assistance.

This brings us to the final section in which Beowulf,
as an old man, faces the dragon. In this section, numerical allegorical signifiers are employed to connect Beowulf's struggle with the Passion of Christ. We are told
that Beowulf selected twelve "hand-picked" companions,
one of whom was the thief who had raised the dragon's
wrath through the stealing of the "precious cup" from the
dragon's horde. On the eve of the battle with the dragon,
Beowulf is "sad at heart, unsettled yet ready, sensing his

---

[14] Seamus Heaney, trans., *Beowulf: A New Verse Translation* (New York:
W. W. Norton, 2000), 115.

death".[15] At the key moment, when Beowulf goes to face the dragon, eleven of his hand-picked followers "broke ranks and ran for their lives to the safety of the wood".[16] Only one of the twelve had the courage to remain by his Lord's side. After Beowulf is himself slain in his slaying of the dragon, his hand-picked company come skulking from the woods to join the one who had remained at the Lord's side, but only ten of them; the eleventh, the Judas figure, is not with them.

At the poem's conclusion, the people erect a huge burial mound for Beowulf "on a headland, high and imposing, a marker that sailors could see from far away".[17] Then we are told that *twelve* warriors rode around the tomb, mourning the loss of Beowulf as both a man and a king. The traitor, the Judas-figure among the hand-picked troop, has evidently been replaced. The twelve are clearly signifiers of the apostles, which makes Beowulf, in the final part of the poem, in some limited but very real allegorical sense, a Christ figure.

Other great Anglo-Saxon poems written at around this time are "The Dream of the Rood", "The Ruin", "The Wanderer", and "The Seafarer". It is intriguing that lines from one of these poems, "The Dream of the Rood", which tells of a dream in which the Cross itself worships the God who embraced it in death, are carved in runic characters on an ancient eighteen-foot-high stone cross, standing in the chancel of a church in Ruthwell in Dumfriesshire, Scotland. The Ruthwell Cross, arguably the most famous of all Anglo-Saxon monuments, was probably made shortly after Coelfrith, Abbot of Wearmouth and

[15] Ibid., 165.
[16] Ibid., 175.
[17] Ibid., 213.

Jarrow, had returned from a visit to Rome in 701, during which there had been much excitement about the recent discovery of a fragment of the True Cross. Although the inscription of the lines from the poem proves its existence in the early eighth century, the oldest extant version of the full poem is in a manuscript that probably dates from the tenth century.

These poems from the Anglo-Saxon golden age are all profoundly beautiful Christian works that withstand the test of translation, defying Bede's claim, when discussing his own translation of Caedmon's English verse into Latin, that "verses, however masterly, cannot be translated literally from one language into another without losing much of their beauty and dignity".[18] Bede's adage, echoing T. S. Eliot's claim that a shadow falls "between the potency and the existence",[19] is indubitably true; yet it says a great deal about the potency of these wonderful Old English poems that they retain great beauty even after the shadow is cast by translation. As with the wonderful saints of Anglo-Saxon England in the eighth century, these wonderful works of literature shine forth the good, true, and beautiful in an epiphany of praise.

[18] Bede, *Ecclesiastical History of the English People*, trans. Leo Sherley-Price, revised by Ronald Latham, introduction and notes by D. H. Farmer (London: Penguin Classics, 1991), 249.

[19] T. S. Eliot, "The Hollow Men" (1925).

Ninth Century

Great Kings and Vikings

The Good

The ninth century began auspiciously and ostentatiously with the crowning of King Charles the Great, better known as Charlemagne, as the first Holy Roman Emperor. The form of the coronation, on Christmas Day 800, symbolized and encapsulated the core principles of Christian political philosophy. The secular ruler was solemnly crowned by the pope, who was himself the ordained representative of Christ as St. Peter's successor. In essence, the coronation was an affirmation on the part of Caesar that all political authority had its ultimate source in the authority of God. In this sense, in principle if not always in practice, the western half of Christendom was now one nation, or one empire, under God.

Such was the importance of Pope Leo III's crowning of Charlemagne that the historian Diane Moczar named Christmas Day 800 as one of the "ten dates every Catholic should know", an event "that shaped the Church and changed the world". In Moczar's estimation, Charlemagne was "a great warrior, a great king and emperor, a great champion of the Church, a great patron of learning, a great promoter of economic revival":

He is the Great Charles—protector of Rome, unifier of Europe, and Father of Western Christendom. It is hard

to think how Catholic Europe would have emerged from
the Dark Ages without him.[1]

In truth, Charles' reign was full of the fruits of restoration. The enemies of Christendom were defeated in battle, schools were established across the length and breadth
of his dominion, and ecclesiastical institutions were reformed. It seemed that every aspect of life, both sacred
and profane, were placed under the state's protection, for
better or worse. "Church and State seemed at last fused
into one thing," wrote Philip Hughes, "bishops and popes
were the Frankish king's enthusiastic assistants. When, on
Christmas Day, 800, Leo III solemnly crowned Charles as
emperor, restoring the empire of the West in his person,
the gesture seemed to seal divinely the great successes of
his life."[2]

The danger inherent in such a fusion of church and
state is the likelihood that the state will seek to control
the Church. It is indeed a paradox that the spiritual power
of the papacy limits the secular power of the state. This is
the very reason that secular rulers have often found themselves in conflict with the papacy and have sought to sub-
jugate the authority of the pope to the secular authority.
This danger was inherent in the way in which Charles
sidestepped papal authority in the passing of his imperial
title to his son Louis. The coronation ceremony, which
was presumably devised by Charles himself without consultation with the pope, consisted of his placing his imperial crown onto the altar of his palace chapel in Aachen.
Louis then took the crown from the altar, placing it on his

[1] Diane Moczar, *Ten Dates Every Catholic Should Know* (Manchester, N.H.:
Sophia Institute Press, 2005), 47.
[2] Philip Hughes, *A Popular History of the Catholic Church* (New York: Macmillan, 1962), 99.

own head. This do-it-yourself ritual, with a priestless and popeless altar as the religious focus, boded ill for the future of church-state relations. Such was the potency of papal authority, however, that Louis himself sought to legitimize his imperial title by inviting the pope to Rheims in 816, two years after Charlemagne's death, to anoint and crown him as emperor.

The strength of the papacy took many forms, such as that exhibited by St. Leo IV, a warrior pope who turned Rome into a fortress following the sacking of the city by the Saracens in 846. Overseeing the building of the Leonine Wall around the Vatican Hill to protect the city from future Islamic attacks, he also organized a league of Italian cities to fight and defeat the Saracens at the Battle of Ostia in 849.

A warrior pope of an altogether different ilk was St. Nicholas I, whose courageous stand for the indissolubility of Christian marriage, the dignity of women, and the authority of the papacy won the day in the face of secular tyranny and its clerical collaborators. The original standoff was between Pope Nicholas and King Lothair of Lorraine, the latter of whom had divorced his wife, who had failed to give him an heir, and then had married his concubine with whom he had already had three children. A synod of Frankish bishops, meeting in the imperial capital of Aachen, had slavishly recognized the divorce, on the basis of a trumped-up charge of incest. Lothair's wife, Theutberga, appealed to the pope. With characteristic courage and decisiveness, Pope Nicholas ruled in favor of Theutberga, ordering Lothair to return to his wife. Presumably at the king's behest, the archbishops of Cologne and Trier went to Rome to deliver the decrees of a Frankish council recognizing Lothair's divorce and remarriage. The pope responded by excommunicating them for being accessories to the sin and crime of bigamy. In February 864, the emperor Louis II, Lothair's brother, marched on Rome and laid siege to the pope. Even in the face of the military might of the empire, Pope Nicholas refused to back down. He was clearly willing to die in defense of Christian marriage and the legitimate authority of the papacy, refusing to render unto Caesar that which was God's. Faced with the choice of making a martyr of a clearly holy pope or backing down, the emperor withdrew his forces, licking his wounds. With imperial might being defeated and the moral weight of the papal office affirmed, Lothair acknowledged Theutberga as his legitimate wife and the rebellious archbishops submitted to the authority of Rome. The saint had won the day.

Considering St. Nicholas I's courageous stand for the indissolubility of marriage, the dignity of women, and the primacy of the papal office, even unto death, it is no wonder that he is one of only three popes to whom posterity has bestowed the name of "the Great", the other two being his illustrious predecessors, St. Leo I (440–461) and St. Gregory I (590–604).

In the mission field, SS. Cyril and Methodius converted the Slavs of Bulgaria to Christianity. In order to evangelize more effectively, they invented a script to translate Scripture into the Slavic tongue. Becoming known as Cyrillic script, it forms the alphabet used by Slavic languages to this day, including Russian.

If the ninth century had dawned with the coronation of Charles the Great as the Holy Roman Emperor, it would end with the kingly presence of another great Christian monarch, Alfred the Great.

With respect to Alfred's historical importance, Hilaire Belloc insisted that it was crucial not merely to the survival of the faith in England but perhaps to the survival of the whole of Christendom. When Alfred became king of England in 871, Christendom was under siege. Barbarian hordes were pressing Christian Europe from the north and east, and Islam was threatening conquest from the south. By the mid-ninth century, Belloc wrote, "Western Christendom had become a sort of fortress, besieged on all sides." If, in Christendom's weakened state, "the British islands had been swept away the shock would have been severe and might have been final."[3]

If Belloc's assessment of Alfred's importance is to be believed, and it certainly seems credible enough, every Christian owes Alfred the Great a great debt of gratitude.

The first seven years of Alfred's reign were perilous in the extreme, the future of Anglo-Saxondom hanging by a thread that the ever-advancing Danes threatened to sever forever. By 877, Alfred and his court had become exiles in their own land, retreating to fortified positions in the marshes of Somerset, on the very southwestern edge of the kingdom. It was from this isolated refuge that Alfred set forth in the spring of 878, gathering an army on the Feast of Pentecost and then advancing to the Danish host stationed at Chippenham. With the future of Christendom balanced on a knife edge, Alfred's army won the day at the Battle of Eddington, or what Chesterton, in *The Ballad of the White Horse*, calls Ethandune, in conformity to the name used in the primary historical sources. As for the battle's significance, it is encapsulated brilliantly in Chesterton's epic poem by the words that the poet places on the lips of the king: "The high tide!" King Alfred cried. "The high tide and the turn!"[4] Alfred's victory turned the

[3] Hilaire Belloc, *A Shorter History of England* (London: George G. Harrap, 1934), 87.

[4] G. K. Chesterton, *The Ballad of the White Horse* (London, Methuen & Co., 1911), 147.

tide, ensuring that Anglo-Saxon England would survive, as would the faith that animated it.

Chesterton, perceiving the legendary truth that transcends the historical facts, wrote that "Alfred has come down to us in the best way (that is by national legends) solely for the same reason as Arthur and Roland and the other giants of that darkness, because he fought for the Christian civilization against the heathen nihilism."[5] If this is so, it is indeed a fortunate or providential coincidence that Alfred's victory at Eddington came on the centenary of Roland's heroic death at the Battle of Roncevaux Pass in 778, the legendary battle that inspired the medieval French epic *The Song of Roland*, in much the same manner as the legendary Battle of Eddington had inspired Chesterton's epic. As for whether we should consider the coincidence that one battle could be seen as a mystical celebration of the hundredth anniversary of the previous one, we need only hearken to the words of Alfred the Great, in the "Addition" to his translation of Boethius: "I say, as do all Christian men, that it is a divine purpose that rules them, and not Fate."[6]

There is much more that could and should be said about the achievement and legacy of Alfred the Great: his scholarship, as exhibited in the aforementioned translation of Boethius; his unification of England as a nation, and his elevation of English as an official language, alongside a revival and restoration of Latin; his establishment of a navy, enabling better defense of England's ravaged coast; his reform of the legal system; and his establishment of a court school in emulation of Charlemagne's and Alcuin's example. Such is his enduring reputation that Chesterton

[5] Prefatory note in ibid., viii.

[6] *King Alfred's Modern English Version of Boethius De consolatione philosophiae*, ed. Walter John Sedgefield (Oxford: Clarendon Press, 1900), 153.

could refer to "a chiming unanimity, a chain of polite or popular compliment" that had stretched unbroken from the *Anglo-Saxon Chronicle*, dating from Alfred's own day, until the present day.[7]

King Alfred died at the end of the ninth century, bequeathing to his successors a time of relative peace and political stability, radically different from the perilous and anarchic England that he had himself inherited less than thirty years earlier. His death in 899 brought to an end a century that, for all its darkness and debauchery, had brought forth two truly great kings and one truly great pope.

The Bad

Reiterating Belloc's words, by the mid-ninth century, "Western Christendom had become a sort of fortress, besieged on all sides." Sicily had been invaded by the Muslims in the 820s, and by 838, Islamic forces had established a military presence on the Italian mainland. In 846, as we have seen, the Saracens sacked Rome, desecrating the graves of SS. Peter and Paul. To the north, it was the pagan Norsemen, or Vikings, from Scandinavia that were laying waste to the bastions of Christendom. In 793, the Vikings attacked the monastic settlement at Lindisfarne, an island off the coast of northern England, beginning a century of piratical raids along the coast of the British Isles and beyond. In 841, after numerous raids on the monastic settlements in Ireland, the Vikings established a trading settlement, which would become the city of Dublin. In 866, venturing farther inland to the very heart of England, the Vikings captured

---

[7] Maisie Ward, ed., *The English Way: Studies in English Sanctity from Bede to Newman* (Tacoma, Wash.: Cluny Media, 2016), 53.

the ancient northern city that the Romans had called Eboracum, renaming it Jorvik, now known as York, making it their northern English capital as the Romans had done before them. In 885, a large Viking army besieged Paris for several months, weakening the control of the Holy Roman Emperor in the western part of his empire.

The threat that the Vikings posed to Christendom was accentuated and exacerbated by their destruction of the monasteries in the British Isles that had been the very heart and hub of Christian culture and scholarship. The great monastic centers of Northumbrian, East Anglian, and Celtic culture in England and Ireland, from which monks had set forth to spread the faith and the monastic way of life to the far-flung reaches of pagan Europe, were utterly destroyed, never to recover their former greatness and bringing to an end the golden age of Celtic Christian culture. Christopher Dawson quotes a contemporary chronicler's description of the death, desolation, and desecration that the Vikings left in their wake:

> The Northmen cease not to slay and carry into captivity the Christian people, to destroy the churches and to burn the towns. Everywhere there is nothing but dead bodies—clergy and laymen, nobles and common people, women and children. There is no road or place where the ground is not covered with corpses. We live in distress and anguish before this spectacle of the destruction of the Christian people.[8]

The very survival of Christendom might have been secured by Alfred the Great's victory, as Belloc had suggested, or it might have been secured by the great

[8] Christopher Dawson, *Religion and the Rise of Western Culture* (New York: Image Books, 1958), 87.

Christian victory over the Vikings at the Battle of Louvain in 891. Either way, the Christendom that survived
was bruised and battered, bearing the scars of the Scandinavian scourge and onslaught. Never had the Church
faced such a test as that posed by this pagan plague since
the age of Roman imperial persecution had ended four
centuries earlier. As Philip Hughes noted:

> By the end of the ninth century western Europe presented
> a scene of indescribable chaos, an immense waste, with
> only a few islets of security and ordered life scattered about
> it here and there. And for another generation what was
> left of Christendom had barely strength to breathe.[9]

The Beautiful

Although as much beauty was doubtless destroyed by the
pillaging pagans of the ninth century as had been destroyed
by the iconoclasts of the eighth and the Muslims of the
seventh centuries, posterity has been blessed by the beauty
that has survived.

The Book of Kells, a beautiful Gospel book that dates
from the beginning of the ninth century, represents the last
glorious flowering of the flourishing Celtic monastic tradition that was destroyed by the Vikings. Comprising 340
leaves, or folios, it is illustrated with iconographic figures of
Christ, saints, and angels, flanked and framed by ornamental decoration, such as swirling motifs and knots, typical
of the Celtic monastic tradition, as well as the interlacing of
elongated animals more typical of Anglo-Saxon monastic
art. The vibrant use of color accentuates the epiphanous

---

[9] Philip Hughes, *Popular History of the Church*, 100.

purpose of the art itself as does the ubiquitous presence of traditional Christian iconographic symbolism. This is art that is beautiful in its own right but that serves its purpose of preaching and teaching. Taking but one example, the figure of Christ enthroned, holding a book of the Gospel, is flanked by four figures, usually described as angels, but only two of which seem to have discernible wings. Perhaps the other two are saints, or perhaps all four signify, in some sense, the four Evangelists. Christ's head is flanked by a pair of peacocks, which symbolize resurrection and the immortality of the soul. Each peacock is shown with a eucharistic Host on its wing, and the feet of each are interwoven with grapevines emerging from a chalice. Christ enthroned, Christ the King, is also the True Vine.

The ninth century can truly be considered the golden age of the illuminated Gospel book. Styles vary from place to place, and those which were made on the continent are significantly different from Celtic and Anglo-Saxon illuminated manuscripts. *The Gospel Book of Charlemagne*, dating from the early years of the century, contains an image of St. Matthew, which differs from traditional iconography in the sense that the apostle is shown in profile, writing his Gospel, and does not meet the viewer's eye. By contrast, the depiction of St. Luke, from the *Lorsch Gospel Book*, shows the Evangelist, beneath his symbolic image as the winged ox, looking toward the viewer and pointing toward the text of his Gospel, which is also turned to face the viewer, inviting us to read the Word of God. The depiction of St. Mark in the *Gospel Book of Archbishop Ebbo of Reims*, dating from around the second decade of the century, seems strikingly modern, reminiscent in its dynamic sense of movement of the work of El Greco. The cover binding of the *Lindau Gospels*, which dates from the latter half of the century, shows the crucified Christ, rendered in gold, surrounded by numerous embedded semiprecious stones. The manuscript itself was written and illuminated at the famous monastery at St. Gall in Switzerland.

We will conclude this summary of the beautiful art produced in this age of great kings and Vikings with a look at two diminutive gems, very different from the ostentatious splendor of the great illuminated Gospel books. The first is the Stowe Missal, which dates from late eighth- or early ninth-century Ireland. Technically speaking it is not actually a missal but a sacramentary, a book used by a priest for Mass and other liturgical services, which only contains the words spoken or sung by him, unlike a missal, which includes additional texts. Clearly designed as something that the priest could carry with him on his travels, it is only six inches by five inches in size, yet the illumination is still truly masterful, perhaps more so as it is worked in miniature. The initial page of St. John's Gospel has the traditional historiated initial, adorned with swirls, knotwork, and animal figures, and the whole page is framed with an interlaced design. The manuscript itself, which is mostly in Latin with some Old Irish, is important as the oldest surviving example of the Divine Liturgy for the Celtic rites. Although it dates from the late eighth or early ninth century, the text of the liturgy itself probably dates from the sixth century.

The other "diminutive gem", which is known as the Alfred Jewel, is literally a diminutive gem of gold and crystal, so named for its inscription, which reads "Alfred ordered me to be made." The "Alfred" is usually said to be Alfred the Great himself, though, as with so many of the other legends surrounding the great English king, the truth behind this beguilingly small but beautiful work of art is shrouded in mystery.

Tenth Century

Monasteries and Monstrosities

The Good

Insofar as we can truly speak of a Dark Ages, it would be true to say that the tenth century was perhaps as dark as any century before or since. Christendom was being besieged by infidels on all fronts. The pagan Vikings continued their reign of terror in the North, and the Magyars, a pagan tribe, based in what is now Hungary, penetrated to the very heart of Europe, pillaging as they went; to the South and East, Islam continued to flex its military muscle. Even worse than the violence of the pagans and the Muslims was the viciousness of corruption within the Church, even and especially in the highest echelons of the hierarchy, the decadence of Judas proving a greater threat than the barbarian hordes or the Islamic host. And yet, in the very midst of such darkness, a light of renewed holiness would be kindled in Burgundy that would spread the fires of faith across the length and breadth of Christendom. This was the founding of the Cluny Abbey in 910.[1]

What was refreshingly unusual about the founding of this particular abbey was the manner in which the charitable gift of the land by William the Pious, Duke of

---

[1] The date of the founding is sometimes given as 909.

Aquitaine, was made with no strings attached. His charter, issued on September 11, 910, is worth quoting at length:

> Desiring to employ, in a manner useful for my soul, the goods God has given me, I thought I could not do better than to win for myself the friendship of the poor. In order that this work might be perpetual, I wished to maintain at my expense a community of monks. I therefore give, for the love of God and of Our Lord Jesus Christ, to the holy Apostles Peter and Paul, from my own domain, the land of Cluny.... I give it for the soul of my Lord, King Eudes, and for the souls of my parents and servants....
>
> These monks and all these goods will be under the authority of the abbot Berno as long as he shall live; but after his death, the religious will have the power to elect as abbot, according to the rule of St. Benedict, whomever they please, without the prevention of regular election by any authority....
>
> From this day, they will be neither subject to us, nor to our relatives, nor to the king, nor to any power on earth. No secular prince, no count, no bishop, not even the pope himself—I beg them all in the name of God and of the saints and of the Day of Judgment, not to take over the goods of these servants of God, nor to sell, exchange, or diminish them, or to give them in fief to anyone, and not to impose on them a superior against their will.[2]

Considering the appalling levels of corruption in the world and the Church at the time, it was clearly an act of prudence on Duke William's part to seek to extricate the governance of Cluny Abbey from the avaricious grasp of secular and ecclesial power. It was also a great act of

---

[2] Quoted in Diane Moczar, *Ten Dates Every Catholic Should Know* (Manchester, N.H.: Sophia Institute Press, 2005), 69–70.

temperance on the duke's part to relinquish any claim of authority or influence over the gift he was freely giving. As for the charter itself, it serves as an exemplary expression of Christian political philosophy in terms of the sacrosanct place allotted to the principles of subsidiarity and solidarity.

Irrespective of Duke William's self-sacrificial donation of his land to such a worthy cause, his prudence and temperance would have borne little fruit if it had not been for the sanctity of the monks with whom he had entrusted the land, especially that of the first abbot, St. Berno. In the event, God rewarded the duke's piety with a succession of holy abbots, each of whom was also granted great longevity. There would be only seven abbots in the first 250 years of Cluny's existence, all of whom were canonized or beatified. During this same period, there were no fewer than forty-eight popes, most of whom were not saintly examples to their flock. Three of the greatest popes of this period—Gregory VII, Urban II, and Paschal II—were all monks of the Cluniac Order.

The monks at Cluny followed the Benedictine rule with a renewed sense of vigor and rigor. Some were devoted to full-time prayer, and all were subject to holy silence, except for the chanting of the Divine Office. Such was the reverence in which Cluny was held that bishops and secular rulers began to invite Cluny to establish daughter houses in its likeness in many parts of Christendom. Cluniac priories were founded in the Netherlands, Italy, Spain, England, and Germany. By 1100, there were no fewer than fifteen hundred priories, each of which was under the jurisdiction of the Abbot of Cluny who was now the most powerful person in the Church, with the exception of the pope himself.

Parallel with the miraculous expansion of the Cluniac Order throughout Christendom was a Benedictine revival, set in motion by St. Gerard of Brogne, which spread throughout Flanders. Germany had its own monastic revival, inspired by Cluny, centered at Hirschau, and similar revivals met with great success in Italy, in Piedmont in the north and also in the south of the country where the ancient abbey at Cava was the hub for four hundred other religious houses under its authority.

England was blessed in the tenth century by the authoritative presence of the holy monk St. Dunstan, who became Abbot of Glastonbury in 939 and Archbishop of Canterbury in 960, serving as the Primate of All England for twenty-eight years, until his death in 988. His reformation of both monastic and diocesan life was so extensive and so successful that later generations, following the Norman Conquest, looked upon it as a "golden age". Belloc considered the reform of the Church by Pope St. Gregory VII a century later as having its inspirational roots in St. Dunstan's reforms in England: "We must always remember that the revival of the Catholic Church ... was thus launched in England, and by an Englishman."[3] In addition to Dunstan's influence on the universal Church, he was also a pivotal figure in English history. "It has been well said," wrote the historian David Hugh Farmer, "that the 10th Century gave shape to English history, and Dunstan gave shape to the 10th Century."[4]

If, however, the flames of faith had been rekindled by great monastic reformers, such as SS. Berno, Gerard, and Dunstan, the "golden age" that they initiated was taking place within a decidedly dark age of barbarism and decadence. It is into this darkness that we now descend.

[3] Hilaire Belloc, *A Shorter History of England* (London: George G. Harrap, 1934), 95.

[4] David Hugh Farmer, *The Oxford Dictionary of Saints* (Oxford: Oxford University Press, 1987), 139.

The Bad

In the first decades of the tenth century, the menace of Islamic militarism was threatening Rome itself. The Muslims had established a presence in central Italy that was ended only when Pope John X raised an army of Italians that, assisted by Byzantine naval support, drove the Moors out. Unfortunately, this pope's noble example was very much an exception to the ignobility that marked those occupying the See of Peter in the tenth century.

John X would be murdered for endeavoring to free the papacy from Roman aristocratic dominance and decadence. He was imprisoned and then suffocated in the Castel Sant'Angelo at the behest of the notorious matriarch Marozia. This femme formidable and femme fatale then appointed the next two popes, Leo VI and Stephen VII, before appointing her own son as Pope John XI. Another of Marozia's sons, Alberic II, became the secular ruler of Rome in 932 by deposing his mother and stepfather. Imprisoned by her own son, Marozia languished in prison until her death five years later.

During his twenty-two-year reign, Alberic would appoint five popes to do his bidding. It is little surprise that this period in the history of the papacy has become known as the *saeculum obscurum* (the dark century, or the dark age), a time when, according to papal historian Eamon Duffy, "the papacy became the possession of the great Roman families".[5] Yet even in the midst of such anarchic decadence, there were glimmers of goodness. Two of Alberic's appointments, Leo VII and Agapitus II, were great promoters of the monastic revival, the former being a friend and supporter of the saintly Abbot Odo of Cluny.

[5] Eamon Duffy, *Saints and Sinners: A History of the Popes* (New Haven: Yale University Press, 2014), 103–4.

The decadent aristocratic control of the papacy reached a new low point in 955, when Alberic had his eighteen-year-old son and heir appointed as Pope John XII. Mercifully for the Church, the young pope would die at the age of twenty-seven, allegedly while in bed with a married woman. Seeing the hand of Providence in the sordid and sudden death of John XII, the historian Alan Schreck wrote that John "was so corrupt that God delivered the Catholic Church from him through a secular ruler, Otto I (the Great), the first Holy Roman Emperor of the German nation".[6] Although the coronation of Otto I in 962 would free the papacy from being the personal property of Roman aristocrats, there would be a price to pay. The Holy Roman Empire, like the Carolingian Empire before it, would attempt to control the Church and the papacy for its own purposes. Such imperial overreach was better, however, than the power-drunken debauchery of the *saeculum obscurum*, even if only the better of two evils.

The Beautiful

The coronation of Otto I established what has become known as the Ottonian dynasty, so named because of the reign of three successive rulers named Otto: Otto I, who ruled from 936 to 973 (from 962 as Holy Roman Emperor); Otto II, who ruled from 973 to 983; and Otto III, who ruled from 983 to 1002.

Perhaps the finest example of architecture from the Ottonian period is the Church of Cyriakus at Gernrode in Germany. A nobleman, named Gero, founded the convent of St. Cyriakus in 961 and began work on the church

---

[6] Alan Schreck, *The Compact History of the Catholic Church* (Ann Arbor, Mich.: Servant Books, 1987), 39.

in the same year. It took twelve years to build, being consecrated in 973. Inspired by earlier Carolingian structures,
such as the Abbey of Saint-Riquier at the monastery of
Centula in northern France (dedicated in 799), the Church
of Cyriakus would itself inspire architects for the next three
hundred years, proving instrumental to the flourishing of
the Romanesque style.

In around 970, a life-size sculpture of Christ was commissioned by Gero, Archbishop of Cologne, a relative of
the nobleman of the same name who had founded the
convent of St. Cyriakus. The *Gero Crucifix*, as it is known,
can still be seen in Cologne Cathedral. The figure of
Christ is six feet, two inches in height and is sculpted
in painted and gilded oak. Its most remarkable feature
is its graphic realism, so different from the spiritualized
approach of iconography. The corpse of Christ leans forward from the Cross, bereft of life, the head drooped, the
arms stretching and seeming to strain under the weight.
An interesting feature is the small cavity in the back of the
head, designed to hold a fragment of the eucharistic host,
making the crucifix a tabernacle to host the very Lord that
the sculpture represents.

Symbolic representations of the power of the Ottonian
dynasty are represented in a tenth-century painted depiction of the Holy Roman Emperor, robed in Byzantine
imperial purple and surrounded by female figures representing the four provinces that he rules. In his right hand,
he holds the royal scepter, and in his left, an orb, signifying
the cosmos, the latter of which is marked with a cross,
a reminder that the emperor holds his authority "under
God". The same symbolism is evident in an example of
the imperial crown, which has survived and is in a museum
in Vienna. It is surmounted with a gem-embedded cross,
signifying that it is Christ who crowns the emperor.

A framed carving in ivory from this period shows the glorified Christ, flanked by angels and by the Blessed Virgin and St. Maurice. At Christ's feet are three figures paying homage, one of whom, a child, is presumably the young Otto III, beneath whom are the words *Otto Imperator*. A similar symbolic representation is to be found on the charter, decreed by King Edgar of England in 966, transferring Winchester Cathedral from the secular canons to the Benedictine monks, as requested by the great monk and reformer St. Ethelwold. The painting shows Christ glorified surrounded by angels. King Edgar is shown looking up in praise and adoration, flanked by the Blessed Virgin and St. Peter.

The illustration and illumination of manuscripts continued apace. The dedication page of the *Liuthar Gospels*, dating from the end of the century, shows the emperor Otto III enthroned in glory in the same position in which the glorified Christ might be expected to be found. Any suggestion of blasphemy or imperial self-idolization is removed, however, or at least alleviated, by the hand of God that places the crown on the emperor's head and by the orb, surmounted by a cross, that the emperor holds in his right hand. The enthroned emperor is flanked by symbolic representations of the four Evangelists. The dedication on the facing page illustrates the humble subordination of the emperor to the truth of the Gospel: "With this book, Otto Augustus, may God invest thy heart."

An illustration in the so-called *Paris Psalter*, dating from the beginning of the tenth century, entitled *David Composing the Psalms*, shows the young David, harp in hand, in the company of a female figure, presumably his Muse, and surrounded by animals and allegorical figures. Its arcadian setting is reminiscent of the classical heritage of Greece, exemplifying the union of Jerusalem and Athens in the humanistic imagination of Christendom. As for the psalms themselves, the great monastic revival of the tenth century produced some of the finest Gregorian chant, the singing of which still graces monastic life and the liturgy to this day.

Apart from the works of beauty produced in the tenth century itself, two literary works inspired by that century, but written a thousand years later, warrant our attention. The first is Hilaire Belloc's depiction of the pious legends surrounding the life of St. Dunstan.

As was often the case with the more popular saints, folk tales and legends began to proliferate about the life of St. Dunstan. One of the most entertaining, if not one of the most believable, is shown in artistic depictions of the saint holding the devil by the nose with a pair of blacksmith's tongs. Hagiographical tradition had made Dunstan a metalworker, a reference to the metalwork he was known to have done while living as a hermit, prior to his becoming Abbot of Glastonbury. It was believed or claimed that some tenth-century blacksmith's tools, still kept as relics at a convent in Mayfield in Sussex, had belonged to Dunstan. These legends are retold and embellished with rambunctious humor by Hilaire Belloc in *The Four Men: A Farrago* (1911), in which St. Dunstan is credited with saving the county of Sussex from being destroyed by the devil.

The other work, which is inspired by the mists of mystery surrounding the period in which the fearsome Viking races were converting to Christianity, is the 1992 novel *Vinland* by the Catholic convert poet and novelist George Mackay Brown. Its backdrop is the era that saw the twilight of the Norse gods and the dawning of Christianity. In 960, King Harald Bluetooth of Denmark became the first of the Scandinavian Vikings to convert to Christianity. By this time, there were Viking settlements in the remotest parts of the known world. Farmers from Norway had settled the Orkney, Shetland, and Faroe Islands, north of Scotland, in the ninth century. By the end of that century, Norwegian settlers had inhabited Iceland, and by 930, its population had grown to twenty thousand. In 985, Icelanders led by Erik the Red settled in Greenland. Erik the Red's son, Leif Erikson, established a settlement called Vinland on the North American coast, probably in what is now Newfoundland, at the end of the tenth century or the beginning of the eleventh. George Mackay Brown's novel, a modern epic akin to the Norse epics that inspired it, is one of the great works of Catholic fiction of the past century. In its pages, the age that saw the conquest of the Vikings, not by the sword but by the cross, is brought to vibrant and vivid life.

We will conclude with a description of a manuscript page dating from the end of the tenth century that serves to epitomize what was best and worst in this darkest and most monastic and monstrous of centuries. It is the painting in the *Gospels of Otto III* showing Christ washing the feet of His disciples. This great act of humility on the part of Christ serves to illustrate that the greatest must be the servant of the least. This was the spirit of holy poverty that animated the monastic reform and revival heralded by the founding of Cluny Abbey. The absence of such a spirit was seen in the corrupt and decadent aristocrats and the corrupt and decadent popes that they appointed. It is indeed significant that the same chapter of St. John's Gospel in which Christ washes the feet of His disciples is the chapter in which Christ exposes Judas as the one who will betray Him.[7] In the tenth century, as in the first, Christ knows His sheep as He knows the wolves in sheep's and even shepherd's clothing who betray him. The wicked, like the poor, are always with us, but so are the saints.

[7] Jn 13:1–30.

Eleventh Century

Ends and Beginnings

The Good

The end of the Church's first millennium did not lead to the end of the world, as some had prophesied, but to the dawn of a new world in which Christendom blossomed into the majesty of the High Middle Ages. In her book *Ten Dates Every Catholic Should Know*, Diane Moczar singles out A.D. 1000 as the gateway to the Church's most glorious age:

> That millennial year ... may be taken as the gateway to a glorious period in history. The three centuries that followed it included the rise of the papacy to the highest point of its power and prestige, the development of the European nations, the greatest burst of cultural and institutional creativity in Western history, more saints than one can keep track of, and more material prosperity.[1]

The rise of the papacy in terms of prestige, power, and prominence was the consequence of a succession of good popes who stood in stark and refreshing contrast to the miserable menagerie of monstrous men who had occupied the See of Peter in much of the ninth, tenth, and early eleventh centuries. The first of these was Gregory VI,

---

[1] Diane Moczar, *Ten Dates Every Catholic Should Know* (Manchester, N.H.: Sophia Institute Press, 2005), 97.

who, according to papal historian Eamon Duffy, was "a man with a reputation for holiness and a genuine interest in religious reform".[2] Peter Damian, abbot of the monastery of Fonte Avellana and one of the most vocal advocates for reform, declared his hope that Pope Gregory's election in 1045 might herald the return of "the golden age of the Apostles".[3] Other reforming popes followed, including Leo IX, who reigned from 1049 to 1054 and was canonized in 1082 by St. Gregory VII, the greatest of the century's popes. A pope whose courage and tenacity matched his sanctity, Gregory continued the reforms undertaken by Leo, especially with respect to his insistence that priests be faithful to their vows of celibacy and that they reject the corrupt practice of simony, the "selling" of spiritual services for financial gain. Those refusing to obey these much-needed reforms were excommunicated, irrespective of how powerful they were. Even the Holy Roman Emperor himself, Henry IV, was excommunicated by this fearless pope for his obstinacy in corruption. "Since the day when the Church placed me on its apostolic throne," wrote Pope Gregory shortly before his death in 1085, "my whole desire and the end of all my striving has been that the Holy Church ... should recover her honor and remain free and chaste and Catholic."[4]

The historian Sir James Stephen wrote that Gregory VII "kindled the torch of reform and bore it aloft with clear and steady brilliancy to the gaze of the Christian world".[5]

[2] Eamon Duffy, *Saints and Sinners: A History of the Popes* (New Haven: Yale University Press, 2014), 111.

[3] Ibid.

[4] Quoted in Christopher Dawson, *The Historic Reality of Christian Culture* (New York: Harper and Bros., 1960), 54.

[5] Quoted in G. Elliott Anstruther, K.S.G., "Hildebrand, Pope and Reformer", in *Great Catholics*, ed. Claude Williamson, O.S.C. (London: Nicholson and Watson, 1938), 98.

Yet the finest and most effusive tribute came from Gregory's contemporary Paul of Bernried, who wrote a life of Gregory VII in 1128:

> He endured perfidy and temptation, perils, insults, captivity and exile, for the love of God. By the grace of that same God, and by the aid of the apostles—kings, tyrants, dukes, princes, all the jailors of human souls, all the ravenous wolves, all the ministers of Antichrist ... were vanquished by this invincible athlete.[6]

There were three more popes in the eleventh century following Gregory VII's death, all of whom were Benedictine monks. Blessed Victor III sat on the throne of Peter only for a little over a year, but his brief reign was marked by the same spirit of reform that had marked the pontificate of his predecessor. He called the Synod of Benevento in 1087, which condemned the practice of lay investiture. Blessed Urban II is best known for his calling of the First Crusade in 1095, of which more presently. Paschal II, who was elected pope in 1099, continued the reforms of his predecessors, as well as ordering the rebuilding of the ancient fourth-century church of Santi Quattro Coronati after it had been burned to the ground during the sacking of Rome by the Normans in 1084.

Such was the beginning of "the rise of the papacy to the highest point of its power and prestige" as described above by Diane Moczar in her summary of the importance of the eleventh century, but what of "the development of the European nations", which was another aspect of the century that she considers so important? According to Christopher Dawson, the rise of independent nations was a consequence of the emperor Otto III's decentralization

[6] Ibid.

of power to local areas, a policy that would now be called subsidiarist or localist in principle:

> The radical transformation or policy which altered the whole history of Central and Eastern Europe ... was primarily due to the passing of the leadership in the conversion of the new peoples from the Empire ... to the rulers of those peoples themselves.... It was rendered possible by Otto III's wider conception of the Empire as a society of Christian peoples, which made him welcome the formation of new Christian kingdoms and the creation of new Churches in direct dependence on Rome rather than on the German hierarchy.[7]

Otto II, in league with Pope Sylvester II, created the new Christian kingdom and hierarchy of Hungary in A.D. 1000. The new nation's first king, St. Stephen, received the Holy Crown, the sacred symbol of Hungarian royalty, establishing an "Apostolic Kingdom" that, in the words of Christopher Dawson, "was to be the eastern bulwark of Christendom":

> The conversion of Hungary even more than that of Poland opened the way to Christian culture in Eastern Europe, since the Middle Danube has always been the chief gateway between East and West.[8]

St. Bruno of Querfurt led a mission from Hungary to evangelize the pagan nomads of the Russian steppe and the pagan cousins of the recently converted Magyars on the Volga. This mission also enabled him to forge friendly relations with the new Christian state of St. Vladimir in

[7] Christopher Dawson, *Religion and the Rise of Western Culture* (New York: Image Books, 1958), 115.

[8] Ibid., 116–17.

Kiev, a city that according to the eleventh-century chronicler Adam of Bremen was "the rival of Constantinople and
most renowned glory of Greece".[9] Whereas the founding
of the Christian kingdom of Hungary had served as a gateway for the evangelization of the East, the conversion of
Russia made it possible for Christian missionaries to pene-
trate into the farthest reaches of the pagan North.

The unifying and Christianizing of Norway during the
reign of King Olaf from 1016 to 1030 continued the conversion of the various Viking tribes that had begun in ear-
nest in the previous century. Adam of Bremen, writing
only a generation or so after the time of St. Olaf, described
the remarkable transition of the people of Scandinavia
from the days of their piratical past:

> After their acceptance of Christianity, they have become
> imbued with better principles and have now learned to
> love peace and truth.... Of all men they are the most
> temperate both in food and in their habits, loving above
> all things thrift and modesty. Yet so great is their venera-
> tion for priests and churches, that there is scarcely a Chris-
> tian to be found who does not make an offering on every
> occasion that he hears Mass.[10]

He speaks in a similar way of the recently converted
people of Iceland, expressing sympathy for the hardness of
their lives caused by the harshness of the climate:

> Blessed is the people, say I, of whose poverty no one is
> envious, and most blessed in this—that they have now
> all put on Christianity. There is much that is remarkable
> in their manners, above all Charity.... They treat their

[9] Quoted in ibid., 113.
[10] Ibid., 98.

bishop as it were a king, for the whole people pay regard to his will, and whatever he ordains from God, from the scriptures and from the customs of other nations, they hold as law.[11]

The eleventh century also saw a Scandinavian, King Canute, on the throne of England. Reigning from 1016 until 1035, he is best known to posterity for the legendary account of his ordering the tide to obey him. Although this is often cited as evidence of the foolishness of egocentric rulers who "try to stop the tide", the true source of the account, which dates from the twelfth century, demonstrates Canute's piety and humility, not his folly and pride. According to the twelfth-century account by Henry of Huntingdon, Canute ordered his throne to be placed on the beach and then, sitting on it, he ordered the incoming tide to stop. When the tide lapped against his feet, in defiance of the royal command, he used the incident to teach a priceless lesson to his flattering courtiers. "Let all men know how empty and worthless is the power of kings," he declaimed, "for there is none worthy of the name, but He whom heaven, earth, and sea obey by eternal laws." He then hung his crown on a crucifix and, according to the account, never wore it again "to the honour of God the almighty King".[12] The episode shows King Canute to be a kindred spirit to the chastened and converted King Lear, who refers to flattering courtiers as "gilded butterflies" and "poor rogues [who] talk of court news".[13] Such men are not to be trusted, either in history or on the stage.

[11] Ibid., 99.

[12] Henry of Huntingdon, *The Chronicle of Henry of Huntingdon*, trans. and ed. Thomas Forester (London: Andesite Press, 2017), 199.

[13] William Shakespeare, *King Lear*, ed. Joseph Pearce, Ignatius Critical Editions (San Francisco: Ignatius Press, 2008), act 5, scene 3, lines 13–14.

Although most historians question the veracity of this anecdotal episode, seeing it as "apocryphal", the fact that the source for the story dates from only a century after Canute's own time suggests that Canute was known for his wisdom and Christian piety, irrespective of the factual veracity of Henry of Huntingdon's account.

King Canute's reign, as noble as it was, would be eclipsed in terms of its virtue by the reign of his stepson, St. Edward the Confessor, who ruled England from 1042 until the fateful year of the Norman Conquest in 1066.

Edward's reputation for holiness was acknowledged during his reign. He was an accessible ruler, being receptive to the needs and requests of his subjects and demonstrating great generosity to the poor. He was said to have received mystical visions and to have cured people of scrofula with the laying on of his hands. He strengthened links with the papacy, sending bishops to Leo IX's councils in 1049 and 1050 and receiving papal legates in 1061. The most ambitious project he undertook was the founding of Westminster Abbey, which would become and has remained the place for the coronation of the kings and queens of England. It was completed and consecrated shortly before his death and became his place of burial, his tomb and relics being undisturbed to this day, having survived the ravages of the Reformation with its iconoclastic destruction of England's shrines to her saints.

St. Edward's death in 1066 would sound the death knell for Anglo-Saxon England, precipitating rival claims to the English throne and leading a few months later to the Norman Conquest. Both sides claimed Edward's blessing on their respective claims, and both sides, the victorious Normans and defeated Anglo-Saxons alike, would venerate him as a saint. In 1102, his body was found to be incorrupt, adding considerably to the reverence in which he was already held. He would be the accepted patron saint of England until the crusaders brought back their devotion to St. George, the warrior saint who would eventually displace Edward as the country's patron. Shakespeare's devotion to the saint was expressed in *Macbeth* when Edward's sanctity and his miraculous powers of healing are contrasted with the Machiavellian evil of the Scottish king.

Although it might seem apt to bring down the curtain on Anglo-Saxon England with the death of St. Edward the Confessor in 1066, only a few short months before the Battle of Hastings would bring Anglo-Saxondom to a definitive end, the final and climactic moment in the 650-year history of the Anglo-Saxons, and its greatest blessing, was a Marian apparition during St. Edward's reign.

In 1061, a widow and Lady of the Manor, Richeldis de Faverches, received a vision of Our Lady at Walsingham in the East Anglian county of Norfolk. This quickly became one of the most popular pilgrimage sites, not only in England but in the whole of Christendom. For over four centuries, until its destruction by Henry VIII, pilgrims would flock to the shrine from all over Europe. And so it was that Anglo-Saxon England died in a blaze of celestial glory, like a supernova, burning brightest as it passed away.

The Bad

In a letter written in 1075 to the abbot at Cluny, Pope Gregory VII lamented the widespread corruption both inside and outside the Church:

> The Eastern Church has fallen away from the Faith and is now assailed on every side by infidels. Wherever I turn my eyes—to the west, to the north, or to the south—I find everywhere bishops who have obtained their office in an irregular way, whose lives and conversation are strangely

at variance with their sacred calling; who go through their duties not for the love of Christ but from motives of worldly gain. There are no longer princes who set God's honour before their own selfish ends, or who allow justice to stand in the way of their ambition.[14]

We have seen how this saintly pope, showing the courage of his convictions, had set about tackling the corruption with great and growing success, initiating reforms that were reinforced by his successors. Echoing the distinction that St. Augustine had made between the City of God and the City of Man, he insisted that all government must be under God and, therefore, that all secular power must be subject to the magisterial authority of the Church in matters of faith and morals. "Shall not an authority founded by laymen," he asked, "even by those who do not know God, be subject to that authority which the providence of God Almighty for his own honour has established and in his mercy given to the world?" In contrast, the worldly power had no such divinely ordained authority:

Who does not know that kings and rulers are sprung from men who were ignorant of God, who by pride, robbery, perfidy, murders, in a word, by almost every crime at the prompting of the devil, who is the prince of this world, have striven with blind cupidity and intolerable presumption, to dominate over their equals, that is, over mankind?[15]

Although the uncompromising stridency of these words conveys Pope Gregory's formidable personality, there was

---

[14] Quoted in H. W. Crocker III, *Triumph: The Power and the Glory of the Catholic Church* (New York: Three Rivers Press, 2001), 128.

[15] Gregory VII, Letter to the Bishop of Metz, dated 1081, in *Documents of the Christian Church*, ed. Henry Bettenson (Oxford: Oxford University Press, 1954), 145–53.

little he was able to do to heal the Eastern Church's falling away from the faith, which he had lamented. In 1054, the Great Schism between the Eastern and Western churches, deeply rooted in centuries of tension between Rome and Constantinople, had torn the very flesh of the Body of Christ. This tragic division was described by the historian Alan Schreck as "one of the saddest moments of the history of the Church [which] certainly violates the will of God who sent Jesus to form one people, one church".[16]

Apart from lamenting the schism, the pope had also expressed concern that the Eastern Church was "now assailed on every side by infidels". The Byzantine army had suffered a heavy defeat at the hands of Islamic forces at the Battle of Manzikert, in what is now Turkey, in 1071, and, in the words of H. W. Crocker, "the Byzantine empire felt the hot breath of the Muslim invader on its neck".[17] A few years earlier, the short-lived Byzantine protectorate to guard the Christian holy sites in Jerusalem had collapsed, leaving the Holy City once again under Islamic control. It was this state of affairs that prompted Pope Urban II to preach the First Crusade in 1095, the commencement of two centuries of struggle to wrest the Holy Land from Islamic rule.

The Beautiful

The Norman Conquest of England in 1066 saw the eclipse of Anglo-Saxondom and, in consequence, the demise of the Anglo-Saxon language, or what is now called Old

---

[16] Alan Schreck, *The Compact History of the Catholic Church* (Ann Arbor, Mich.: Servant Books, 1987), 42.

[17] Crocker, *Triumph*, 131.

English. The life of St. Wulstan, written by a monk named Coleman shortly after the saint's death in 1095, is the last prose work written in Old English, the language of *Beowulf*, "The Dream of the Rood", and other wonderful literary works. Yet the end of Old English would also signal the beginning of a new hybrid language, in which French and Latin combined with Old English to form what would emerge in the works and words of Chaucer as the Middle English infancy of the modern English language, one thing of beauty passing away to make way for another.

Two works of beauty associated with the conquest of England in 1066 are the famous *Bayeux Tapestry*, which depicts in embroidered cloth the historical narrative of the events leading up to the conquest, as well as the conquest itself, from the Norman perspective, and *King Harald's Saga*, a Norse epic that tells the story of the attempted conquest of England in the same year by Norwegian Vikings led by King Harald Hardradi.[18] The first was probably made in the late eleventh century, only a decade or two after the events it chronicles, whereas the latter was written by the famous Icelandic bard Snorri Sturluson in the early thirteenth century.

Another literary epic inspired by military events in the late eleventh century is the *Poema de Mio Cid*, which recounts the heroic exploits of the legendary El Cid in around 1090 as the Christians were beginning the reconquest of the Iberian Peninsula, the "western front" of the Crusades. In real life, El Cid was Rodrigo Díaz de Vivar, a medieval outlaw who might be seen as the Spanish equivalent of Robin Hood. Even before his death in 1099, he was

---

[18] King Harald Hardradi should not to be confused with his nemesis, King Harold of England, the latter of whom defeated Harald Hardradi at the Battle of Stamford Bridge before meeting his own death three weeks later at the Battle of Hastings.

the subject of a panegyrical Latin poem known as the *Carmen Campidoctoris*, dating from around 1094, and around ten years after his death, he was the subject of a brief Latin chronicle, the *Historia Roderici*, but it is the *Poema de Mio Cid*, written at the beginning of the thirteenth century, that is best known and most celebrated.

Manuscript paintings remained one of the most prominent forms of artistic piety in the eleventh century as they had in earlier centuries. The illustration on the presentation page of the Gospel book made for Hitda, the abbess of a convent near Cologne, shows the abbess presenting the book to St. Walburga, the convent's patron saint, who blesses it. The saint takes center stage, standing on a pedestal to depict the holy ground from whence she bestows her blessing. Her golden halo is itself encircled by a bronze-colored arch creating an aura or sacred space from whence her sanctity radiates outwards.

If Christian art, such as the illustration and illumination of manuscripts, was already well established in the West, it was just beginning to flourish in the newly converted East. Kiev had become a city of churches and monasteries, seemingly overnight, soaking up Byzantine culture and expressing it magnificently. The *Vladimir Madonna*, one of the most sacred and celebrated of all icons, dates from the eleventh century and was in Kiev until the late fourteenth century, when it was moved to Moscow. The Virgin holds her Son, who rests His head on her cheek. Her eyes have a penetrative power that seems to hold the viewer in a solemn and prayerful embrace.

Apart from the evident Byzantine iconographical influence on the newly baptized Russian culture, there is also the presence of its architectural influence. The St. Sophia Cathedral in Kiev, resplendent with Byzantine mosaics and frescoes, dates from the mid-eleventh century and rivals, in

the estimation of Christopher Dawson, St. Mark's Basilica
in Venice as "a witness of the high achievement of Eastern
Christendom at the prime of its medieval development".[19]

Throughout Christendom, this was a time in which
Romanesque architecture flourished. As one eleventh-
century monk noted, "Each people of Christendom rivaled
with the other, to see which should worship in the finest
buildings. The world shook herself, clothed everywhere
in a white garment of churches."[20] Speyer Cathedral dates
from this time, as does the cathedral complex at Pisa.
Other magnificent edifices erected at this time include the
Durham Cathedral in northern England, Sant'Ambrogio
Basilica in Milan, Basilica of Saint-Sernin at Toulouse, and
Abbey of Saint-Étienne at Caen. The breathtaking scale of
these buildings dovetails with the beauty of the divine to
be found in the detail. The bronze doors of Hildesheim
Cathedral, for instance, completed in 1015, show three figures in relief: Christ on the left, with the fallen Adam in the
middle, and Eve on the right with the serpent at her feet.
Their respective gestures speak volumes, painting the proverbial thousand words. Christ points to Adam, who points
to Eve, who points to the serpent. Each blames the other,
but only one is blameless. It is He, the blameless one, who
will take the blame and shoulder the burden of sin.

The eleventh century also saw an explosive growth in
the popularity of pilgrimages to the holy sites of Christendom, such as Jerusalem, Rome, and the shrine of St. James
the Great at Santiago de Compostela Cathedral in Galicia
in northwest Spain. Monasteries, churches, and inns were
built along the main pilgrimage routes to accommodate

---

[19] Dawson, *Religion and the Rise of Western Culture*, 113.
[20] Quoted in Marilyn Stokstad, *Art History* (New York: Harry N. Abrams, 1995), 511.

the spiritual and physical needs of the countless pilgrims, which were likened to the stars of the Milky Way because of the enormity of their numbers. The pilgrim culture was itself a consequence of the rise in the veneration of the saints, which led in turn to the making of beautiful and elaborately decorated reliquaries to contain their holy relics. One of the most famous of these is the statue of St. Foy in Majesty, a gold figure of the child saint, martyred in the early fourth century, which is decorated with gemstones. Dating from the eleventh century and almost three feet high, this masterpiece of Western art was made to contain the relics of the child martyr.

This culture of pilgrimage would contribute to the pope's calling of the First Crusade to liberate the holy places of Jerusalem from the infidel. Pilgrims needed to be protected and guaranteed safe passage to the Church of the Holy Sepulchre and other sacred sites. It is tragically ironic, however, that the desire to worship the Way, the Truth, and the Life, and to venerate the goodness, truth, and beauty of his saints, should lead to the wickedness and ugliness of war. Do such noble ends really justify such violent means? Do such ends justify the beginning of two centuries of bloodshed?

Twelfth Century

Charity and Chivalry

The Good

The twelfth century saw the birth of the great universities that would forge more solidly than ever the indissoluble bond of faith and reason. The first of these was at Bologna in Italy, the origins of which go back to 1088, even though the university was not formally established until 1158. Paris had a university by 1150 and Oxford by 1167. Each of these developed from cathedral schools at which students would gather at the feet of a teacher.

The rise of the universities reflected the revival of interest in philosophy, which had itself been prompted by the first translations into Latin of the works of Aristotle. Considering the violent backdrop made manifest by the Crusades, it was ironic that these translations were a consequence of a healthy intellectual engagement between Christian and Muslim philosophers, the latter of whom had been studying Aristotle's works and those of the Neoplatonists for several centuries. It was natural, therefore, that the Christian clerics who had translated Aristotle's *Logic* and *Physics* should also translate commentaries on these works by Arabic scholars, such as Avicenna and Averroës.

At the helm of this new Scholasticism was St. Anselm of Canterbury, who would be declared a Doctor of the

Church in 1720 in acknowledgment of his place in history as the most important theologian to emerge since Augustine seven hundred years earlier. Another important Scholastic of the twelfth century was Peter Lombard, whose *Four Books of Sentences* became the standard theological textbook of the following century. This period also saw the publication of the *Decretum* by Gratian, a professor at the monasteries in Bologna, which is the most famous and foundational of all canon law texts.

The most exciting development at this time was the founding of a new religious order that would sweep across Christendom as dramatically as had the Cluniac Order two hundred years earlier. These were the Cistercians, who had their origin in the founding of a monastery at Citeaux in France by Robert of Molesme in 1098. The order was formally founded, however, by St. Stephen Harding, an Englishman who was the third abbot of Citeaux, whose *Carta Caritatis* gave the new order its formal structure. The Cistercians followed a reformed version of the Rule of St. Benedict but with an emphasis on strict ascetic practice as penance in expiation of sin. Cistercian abbeys were built in wild, out of the way places, and relied on the manual labor of the monks for their sustenance.

It was the founding of a Cistercian abbey at Clairvaux in 1116 by a charismatic young monk named Bernard that really put the new reforming religious order on the map. Under St. Bernard's spiritual leadership, the Cistercians became the most influential and fastest-growing religious order in the Church. In 1122, there had been nineteen abbeys; by the end of the century, there were 530.

An invaluable insight into the life of a Cistercian monk is given by St. Aelred, who, in 1134, had joined the abbey of Rievaulx in Yorkshire, which had been established by St. Bernard with monks sent from Clairvaux. Being somewhat delicate in terms of health, he found the harshness of the monastic life an ordeal:

> My food is less, my clothes are less soft, my drink is only from the spring. At the day's end I lay my wearied limbs on an uncomfortable mat, my rest is broken, I fall asleep over my books. Only to three men, and that seldom, have I leave to talk. But I see all about me charity, patience, fervor, zeal, affection, such as no Gospel precept nor apostolic epistle nor patristic homily nor ancient monastic practice could better.... Our order is the cross of Christ.[1]

In 1147, thirteen years after entering the Cistercians, Aelred became Abbot of Rievaulx. Under his rule, the abbey became the largest in England. There were 150 choir monks (those ordained to the priesthood) and 500 lay brothers and lay servants. Aelred's leadership was characterized by a gentleness born of charity, inspired by the writings of St. John and St. Augustine. He wrote a treatise on friendship, the *Speculum Caritatis*, and a much-celebrated collection of sermons on Isaiah. At the time of his death in 1167, he was working on a treatise on the human soul.

Aelred's unfailing focus on charity in his life, spiritual leadership and writings was evident in his great love for the Eucharist:

> In this manger under the appearances of bread and wine is the true body and blood of Christ. There in swaddling clothes is our Christ, in the swathed bands of bread and wine, invisible but real. We have no memorial so great of Christ's nativity as the daily reception of His body and blood.[2]

---

[1] Quoted in Maisie Ward, ed., *The English Way: Studies in English Sanctity from Bede to Newman* (Tacoma, Wash.: Cluny Media, 2016), 84.

[2] Ibid., 98.

Commenting on St. Aelred's *Speculum Caritatis*, the Dominican theologian Bede Jarrett distilled the essence of his teaching:

> The center of the argument is that charity is not merely the chief purpose of life, but the remedy and cure for all evils, the protection against threatened dangers; and charity consists in the love of God, out of which must come the love of self and the love of the brotherhood.
>
> The love of God is the foundation of all spirituality; it is the basis also of happiness and peace.[3]

There is no doubt that these charitable principles were being put into laudable practice by the new Cistercian monasteries, which were at the heart of medieval society. The religious congregations, in partnership with brotherhoods of laity, established hospitals, orphanages, homes for the elderly, leper houses, refuges for penitents, and inns for pilgrims. The religious revival also had ramifications in terms of public morality, especially with respect to a renewed reverence for the sanctity and indissolubility of marriage.

The most difficult challenge to charity in the twelfth century as in all centuries was the presence of war. In those instances in which war was deemed to be just, as in the case of the Crusades, how can it be fought without the abandonment of the love of neighbor that is at the heart of the Gospel? It is this challenge that led to the rise of chivalry. In the chivalrous consecration of knighthood as a religious service, soldiers pledged to be subject to certain constraints in time of war. These included a promise to refrain from molesting women, traders, and peasants, and to refrain from damaging crops or destroying orchards. It

[3] Ibid., 94.

was little enough to ask, to be sure, but was at least an effort to remind warriors that they remain subject to the laws of love. At its best, such as in St. Bernard's ideal of Christian knighthood or in the initially austere discipline of the new military orders, it did introduce an element of virtue and noblesse oblige to the practice of warfare. As we shall see, however, it was difficult to retain even the pretense of virtue in the midst of the viciousness of war.

The Bad

Where does one place the Crusades in a history of Christendom? Should they be ranked among that which is good, as a manifestation of a just war against hostile infidels intent on destroying Christendom? This was certainly the view of the Church at the time. Even great saints, such as Bernard of Clairvaux, preached that the Crusades were a good and holy endeavor. The Church's position and that of St. Bernard was that the Crusades were a "just war" in accordance with St. Augustine's teaching on the subject. The liberation of the Holy Land from Muslim control was justified; the defense of Christendom from the military threat of Islam was justified; the protection of pilgrims en route to the holy shrines was justified, as was the protection of the holy shrines themselves. Yet even ardent defenders of the Church, such as the Catholic historian Alan Schreck are forced to question whether the theoretical justice of a cause should be allowed to diminish the wickedness done in its name. "In theory, the crusades might have been justified," he writes, "but due to man's fallen nature, the results of these wars were often tragic."[4] Although the First Crusade had been

---

[4] Alan Schreck, *The Compact History of the Catholic Church* (Ann Arbor, Mich.: Servant Books, 1987), 45.

a military success, Schreck reminds us that the expulsion of the Greek patriarch from Antioch had deepened the division between the Eastern and Western churches. He also condemns, as all Christians must, the indiscriminate killing of hundreds of innocent people by the crusaders after they had captured Jerusalem. The Second Crusade in 1146 was a military failure, and the Third Crusade in 1189 could claim only partial success in terms of the signing of a treaty guaranteeing the safety of Christian pilgrims in the Holy Land. As for the Crusades of the following century, they were increasingly conducted for the very prideful and mercenary motives that Pope Urban II had specifically forbidden in his preaching of the First Crusade.

Another Catholic historian, Christopher Dawson, puts a braver face on things, at least with respect to the success of the First Crusade:

> In any age it would have been an achievement of the first magnitude to march an army overland from France through Asia Minor to Antioch and Jerusalem, to defeat the Turkish and Egyptian forces and to establish a chain of Christian states along the Syrian coast, and inland as far as Edessa on the Euphrates. It marks a turning point in the history of the West: ending the long centuries of weakness and isolation and cultural inferiority and bringing the new peoples of Western Christendom back to the old centres of Eastern Mediterranean culture.[5]

Dawson continues by affirming that the success of the First Crusade "was rendered possible by the overmastering unifying power of religious passion".[6] As for the Crusades taken as a whole, Dawson's final verdict appears to be in

[5] Christopher Dawson, *Religion and the Rise of Western Culture* (New York: Image Books, 1958), 150.
[6] Ibid.

their favor: "So long as the Crusades continued, the unity of Christendom found expression in a dynamic militant activity which satisfied the aggressive instincts of Western man, while at the same time sublimating them in terms of religious idealism."[7] Begging to differ, at least a little, dare we ask why the satisfaction of the "aggressive instincts of Western man" is worth celebrating, irrespective of their being sublimated by "religious idealism"? In the final analysis, however, Dawson appears to agree with Alan Schreck in his confession of an element of ambivalence: "The Crusades expressed all that was highest and lowest in medieval society—the aggressive acquisitiveness of a Bohemond or a Charles of Anjou and the heroic self-abnegation of a Godfrey of Bouillon and a St. Louis."[8]

Far away from the Crusades, the ongoing and perennial tension between church and state came to the fore in a particularly dramatic way in England. In 1166, the Archbishop of Canterbury, Thomas Becket, found himself in conflict with King Henry II, who, like his predecessors, was seeking to impose his royal will on the affairs of the Church. Becket wrote to the king, reminding him that "you have not the power to give rules to bishops, nor to absolve or excommunicate anyone, to draw clerks before secular tribunals, to judge concerning churches and tithes, to forbid bishops to adjudge causes concerning breach of faith or oath, and many other things of this sort."[9] It was this letter that placed the king and archbishop at loggerheads, with neither willing to compromise. In his frustration at the impasse, King Henry allegedly exclaimed, "Will no one rid me of this turbulent priest?" In obedience to

[7] Ibid., 151.
[8] Ibid.
[9] Quoted in James Bruce Ross and Mary Martin McLaughlin, eds., *The Portable Medieval Reader* (New York: Viking Press, 1949), 246–50.

what they perceived to be the king's will, four knights burst into Canterbury Cathedral on December 29, 1170, and butchered Thomas Becket as he knelt in prayer. His last words, before the fatal blows were struck, were the prayers of a saint: "To God and Blessed Mary, to the patron Saints of this Church and St. Denis I commend myself and the cause of the Faith."[10]

The horror felt throughout Christendom by the martyrdom of Thomas Becket forced Henry II to relinquish the powers he had claimed over the Church. Furthermore, on May 21, 1172, he performed a ceremony of public penances for his role in Becket's martyrdom, solemnly swearing to restore to the Church all property that he had confiscated or otherwise acquired unjustly, promising not to obstruct any appeals to Rome by the clergy, and promising to provide money for two hundred knights for the Crusades.

Hilaire Belloc was in no doubt of the historical importance of St. Thomas' martyrdom, which was the consequence of what he called the saint's "heroic resistance".[11] The principle for which St. Thomas suffered martyrdom was as clear as it was noble:

That the Church of God is a visible single universal society, with powers superior to those of this world, and therefore of right, *autonomous*. That principle is the negation of the opposite ... the principle that the divine and permanent is subject to the human and passing power. St. Thomas died for the doctrine, the truth, that the link with eternal things must never be broken under the pressure of ephemeral desires, that the control of eternal things cannot, in morals, be subjected to the ephemeral arrangements of men.[12]

[10] Quoted in Ward, *English Way*, 125.
[11] Ibid., 105.
[12] Ibid., 103.

Having stated the principle for which St. Thomas of Canterbury laid down his life, Belloc proceeds to an appraisal of the historical significance and importance of the saint's "heroic resistance", which struck a blow for religious liberty against the encroachments of secular tyranny, the impact of which would reverberate down the centuries:

> Those few moments of tragedy in the North Transept of Canterbury had done what so many years of effort had so far failed to do. The whole movement against the autonomy of the Church was stopped dead. The tide ran rapidly backward—within an hour St. Thomas was a martyr, within a month the champion not only of religion but of the common people, who obscurely but firmly knew that the independence of the Church was their safeguard. A tale of miracles began, and within a year the name of St. Thomas of Canterbury was standing permanently above and throughout Christendom. Everywhere there were chapels and churches raised to his name, and then came the great uninterrupted pilgrimages to his shrine year after year, until it rivalled St. James of Compostela, becoming the second great center in the West and loaded with gems and gold and endowment.[13]

The Beautiful

Following the relative success of the Crusades on its "western front" in Spain, pilgrimages to the shrine of St. James the Great in Galicia were becoming more popular than ever. The importance of Santiago de Compostela is evident in the beauty of its twelfth-century cathedral, not least in the Glory Portico, the door by which pilgrims entered

[13] Ibid., 125–26.

the cathedral. It is so named because it depicts the heavenly Jerusalem following the Last Judgment, with Christ as Judge. The symbolism connects the pilgrimage that the pilgrim has just completed on foot with the pilgrimage of life he is called to complete thereafter, life itself being a pilgrimage with its sole purpose being to pass through the ultimate "Glory Portico" to heaven itself.

The Romanesque portal at Santiago is typical of other such portals built at this time. The south portal of the Cluniac priory of Saint-Pierre at Moissac in France follows the theological typology of that at Santiago. Christ is shown in majesty at the Last Judgment, surrounded by the four Evangelists and by angels. Beyond them are Old Testament kings and prophets who worship the triumphant King who is the fulfilment of the Law. A similar but more solemn scene is depicted in the west portal of the Cathedral of Saint-Lazare in Burgundy in which Christ sits in judgment surrounded by the souls being judged, weighed on scales held by angels and demons. These apocalyptic sculptures framing the entrance to churches serve as a reminder to those entering that the church represents the City of God, the heavenly Jerusalem. The scenes of judgment remind the living of their imminent death and of the Four Last Things to be kept in mind always: death, judgment, heaven, and hell.

Apart from these wonderful examples of sculpture, the Romanesque churches of the twelfth century were also resplendent with marvelous wall paintings. Nowhere is this more evident than in the Benedictine Abbey Church of Saint-Savin-sur-Gartempe in western France and in the Church of San Clemente in Lérida in Spain, the latter of which has an apse painting of Christ in Majesty that has retained an intensity of color due to the glazing technique used by the artist.

Space precludes saying much about the many surviving examples of manuscript illustration, but a page from the *Winchester Psalter*, dating from the mid-twelfth century, is really remarkable. It is known, understandably enough, as *Hellmouth* because it shows the souls of the damned being devoured by a monstrous mouth, which is opened by an angel placing a key in the lock. It is so luridly imaginative and grotesque that it seems to prefigure the works of Dante and Hieronymus Bosch, and even the surrealistic nightmares of Salvador Dali.

The twelfth century was also a time of innovation in terms of poetry and music, both sacred and profane. With respect to the latter, this was the time of the troubadours, wandering minstrels who sang of courtly love who might be considered the first Romantic poets. One of the most famous troubadours was Bernart de Ventadorn, a lowly born son of lowly born parents whose dashingly good looks and poetic and musical talent made him very popular with the wives of noblemen. If his biographer can be believed, he was dismissed from the service of the Count of Ventadorn after his relationship with the countess was discovered. He then moved to Normandy, where he won the heart of Eleanor of Aquitaine, wife of the future king of England, Henry II. His amorous adventures at an end, he spent his final years as a penitent at the Cistercian Abbey of Dalon. Typical of Bernart's art is his song entitled *Can vei la lauzeta mover* (When I see the lark moving), which exhibits the troubadours' obsessive lament or lamentable obsession with unrequited love:

> Alas! I thought I knew so much about
> Love, but know in truth so little,
> For I cannot help myself loving
> One who gives me nothing in return

My whole heart, myself,
Herself, and the whole world
She has taken from me, and left me nothing
But desire and a yearning heart.[14]

If for no other reason, the troubadours are noteworthy for their influence on Dante, the greatest of poets. In
his treatise on vernacular poetry *De vulgari eloquentia* (On
eloquence in the vernacular), he quotes from the works
of three troubadours: Bertan de Born, Arnaut Daniel, and
Folquet of Marseilles. Interestingly, each of these would
find himself placed in different parts of Dante's *Divine
Comedy*. Bertran de Born is placed in the *Inferno*, Arnaut
Daniel in *Purgatory*, and Folquet of Marseilles in *Paradise*.
The placing of Folquet in heaven might be due to the fact
that, like his predecessor Bernart de Ventadorn, he ended
his life as a penitent in the Cistercian Order after fifteen
years as a worldly wandering poet. It is intriguing, however, that Bertran de Born, who is condemned to Dante's
hell, also spent the last twenty years of his life in a Cistercian monastery. Whatever else we might like to say about
Dante's *Commedia*, we can certainly proclaim that Dante's
judgment of the dead is decidedly quixotic on occasion.

There was another literary movement in the late eleventh and twelfth centuries that did not so much parallel
the spirit of the troubadours as contradict it. These were the
chansons de geste, the tales of heroic deeds, the most famous
of which is *The Song of Roland*. Whereas the troubadours
waxed lyrical with conscious affectation, singing of cour-
tesy, courtly manners, emotions, and romantic love, suggestive of moral decadence and self-absorption, the *chansons*

[14] Quoted in Susan Treacy, *The Music of Christendom: A History* (San Francisco: Ignatius Press, 2021), 31.

de geste were masculine tales of duty, courage, and self-forgetfulness for the sake of a greater or common good. They had much more in common with the epic narratives of Homer and Virgil, or the Anglo-Saxon heroic poem *Beowulf*, than with the romantic musings of the wandering minstrels. This radical difference was highlighted by Christopher Dawson:

> The gradual leavening of the heroic ethos by the influence of the Church finds its literary expression in the *chansons de geste*, which represent the authentic spirit of feudal society, in contrast to the romantic poetry of the troubadours and the courtly epic which seem to belong to an entirely different world.[15]

If the troubadours represented the spirit of innovation in secular music, the twelfth-century Benedictine abbess St. Hildegard of Bingen was the great innovator in the field of sacred music. In 1141, she received a vision of "a fiery light, flashing intensely",[16] a scene that is illustrated in the *Liber Scivias*, the book she wrote in around 1151 or 1152, describing the visions she had been having since she was a child. This book contains fourteen of her songs, or chants, that would presumably have been used in the liturgies at the monastery of which she was abbess. The total number of extant notated musical works that she wrote is seventy-seven, including antiphons, responses, sequences, hymns, a Kyrie, and an Alleluia. She wrote chants in honor of the Trinity, the Blessed Virgin, the apostles, angels, saints, martyrs, patriarchs, prophets, and virgins. Although her music is monophonic, like Gregorian chant, it also has distinctive qualities. "Her melodies will remind the listener

---

[15] Dawson, *Religion and the Rise of Western Culture*, 152.
[16] Marilyn Stokstad, *Art History* (New York: Harry N. Abrams, 1995), 538.

somewhat of Gregorian chant," writes musicologist Susan Treacy, "and yet because of their unique style, many of the melodies sound soaring and ecstatic. Very often the range of Hildegard's melodies span an octave and a fourth of fifth, exceeding that of typical Gregorian chant."[17]

A woman of astonishing genius, she is also credited with writing the first morality play, the *Ordo virtutum*, which tells of the rescue of the soul from the devil by sixteen personified virtues. Containing eighty-two distinct melodies, each of the characters sings, except for the devil, who simply shouts his lines, lacking the harmony necessary for song. As for her own understanding of the harmony necessary for song, she wrote that "the words symbolize the body, and the jubilant music indicates the spirit; and the celestial harmony shows the Divinity, and the words the Humanity of the Son of God."[18]

Such is the place and importance of St. Hildegard of Bingen that Pope Benedict XVI, in 2012, proclaimed her a Doctor of the Church.

One final musical note needs to be sounded before we conclude our time in the twelfth century. It was at this time that some of the most beautiful prayers make their first appearance, such as the *Ave Maria* and the *Salve Regina*, beautiful lyrical anthems to the Mother of God that will inspire sublime musical settings throughout each of the following centuries.

[17] Treacy, *Music of Christendom*, 26.
[18] Ibid.

Thirteenth Century

The Best and Worst of Times

The Good

According to Church historian Alan Schreck, the thirteenth century was "the greatest century of spiritual, cultural, and intellectual advancement in the history of Western civilization":

> The thirteenth century was the flower of the Middle Ages and the height of Christendom. In almost every area of life we see the influence of the Church and the advancement of culture and learning. Certainly there were dark moments, such as the crusades and the Inquisition launched against heresies. But the light of the achievements of this century far outshines the darkness and illumines the Catholic Church even today.[1]

The century began in the reign of Innocent III, a faithful and formidable pope. In 1215, he called the Fourth Lateran Council, which would prove to be the most important and influential Church council of the Middle Ages. In the same year, in England, King John signed the Magna Carta at the behest of the Church and the barons, albeit reluctantly. This groundbreaking and foundational document, limiting the power of the monarchy and laying

[1] Alan Schreck, *The Compact History of the Catholic Church* (Ann Arbor, Mich.: Servant Books, 1987), 48.

the foundations for the English legal system, was partially drafted by the Archbishop of Canterbury, Stephen Langton, who was the first witness to sign it. Such was Archbishop Langton's role in this historic event that the political philosopher Ernest Barker has called Langton the "father of English liberty".[2]

Perhaps the most important work of Pope Innocent III, superseding his calling of the Lateran Council and his success in securing the independence of the Church from secular power, was his support for the new mendicant orders. He had given his blessing to St. Francis from the very beginning of the great saint's apostolate, when only a handful of pioneering disciples accompanied the beggar of Assisi. He was also very supportive of St. Dominic, the founder of the Dominican Order.

Innocent's support for the embryonic Franciscan and Dominican orders was continued by his successors. Honorius III formally established the Dominicans in 1216, and his successor, Gregory IX, canonized Francis in 1228, only two years after the saint's death. Such was the meteoric rises of both these mendicant orders that their presence became part of the very fabric of life over the following decades. Franciscan and Dominican friars were everywhere, begging on the streets, helping the poor, teaching in the newly founded universities, and rising to the highest echelons of the Church's hierarchy. In 1271, Blessed Gregory X, a third order Franciscan, was elected to the papacy, and his successor, Blessed Innocent V, was the first Dominican to become pope.

It would be somewhat remiss of the author and something akin to a sin of omission to mention the miraculous

---

[2] Robert R. Reilly, *America on Trial: A Defense of the Founding* (San Francisco: Ignatius Press, 2020), 75.

growth and spread of the Franciscan and Dominican orders without saying something about their charismatic founders.

"Two men, at the beginning of the thirteenth century, were raised up by God to season his Church, that seemed in danger of perishing through its own corruption."[3] Thus wrote Ronald Knox whose words seem to evoke the famous dream of Innocent III in which the pope had a vision of St. Francis bearing the weight of the entire Lateran Basilica on his shoulders, "an impoverished monk, yet an Atlas of the Church".[4] This dream is found in the legends of St. Dominic, as well as St. Francis, and is depicted in an engraving by Claude Boizot,[5] which shows both saints, arm in arm, shouldering the weight of the crumbling basilica that towers above them. Apart from its allusion to the pope's dream, the engraving also commemorates the meeting of St. Francis and St. Dominic in Rome in 1218.

Totally devoted to Mother Church, St. Francis also rejoiced in Brother Sun and Sister Moon, seeing the Creator's presence in his creatures. Wedded utterly and ascetically to Lady Poverty, he became the richest of men when he was sealed with the holy stigmata, the mystical wounds of Christ, which he received shortly before his death. This miraculous blessing ensured his almost immediate canonization by popular acclaim as well as by papal decree, and worked wonders in helping the Franciscan Order to take the world by storm, or rather by the peace of Christ.

"Saint Francis ... expressed in loftier and bolder language than any earthly thinker the conception that laughter

[3] Ronald Knox, *Captive Flames: On Selected Saints and Christian Heroes* (San Francisco: Ignatius Press, 2001), 51.

[4] H. W. Crocker III, *Triumph: The Power and the Glory of the Catholic Church* (New York: Three Rivers Press, 2001), 164.

[5] *Francis and Dominic Hold Up the Lateran Basilica*, an engraving by Claude Boizot (Rome, Franciscan Museum).

is as divine as tears," wrote G. K. Chesterton. "He called his monks the mountebanks of God. He never forgot to take pleasure in a bird as it flashed past him, or a drop of water as it fell from his finger: he was, perhaps, the happiest of the sons of men."[6]

If St. Francis and the order he founded could be said to represent the mystical marriage of love and beauty, the order that St. Dominic founded could be said to represent the marriage of love and reason. It was to the Dominicans, in a special sense, through the teaching and preaching of St. Albert the Great and St. Thomas Aquinas, that we owe the rise of Scholasticism and its rooting of the Church ever more strongly in the indissoluble union of faith and reason (*fides et ratio*).

At the heart of Scholasticism was the rediscovery of Aristotle, the great Greek philosopher whose work had been neglected but which would now be wielded as a sword. "The old weapon, soiled and rusty, useless, you would have thought—but there were men ready to scour and polish it, and make use of it, an instrument as keen as ever, for the confuting of false doctrine and the systematization of knowledge."[7] There were two men, beyond all others, who scoured and polished the old sword of truth, which Aristotle had wielded. These were St. Albert the Great and St. Thomas Aquinas.

Born in 1200, at the very birth of the century itself, and living to the ripe old age of eighty, St. Albert the Great, or Albertus Magnus, straddled the greatest of centuries as the greatest of its philosophers, with the exception of his own student, Thomas Aquinas. There was almost no area of the sciences in which he was not a pioneer. He

[6] G. K. Chesterton, "St. Francis of Assisi", *The Speaker*, December 1, 1900.
[7] Knox, *Captive Flames*, 70.

studied chemistry, astronomy, and most especially philosophy. He was eclipsed, however, by the sheer brilliance of St. Thomas Aquinas, whose magisterial and monumental magnum opus, the *Summa Theologica*, spanning twenty-one weighty volumes, and still unfinished at the time of his death, represents the greatest single achievement in the history of philosophy, unsurpassed and seemingly unsurpassable. Given the title of the Angelic Doctor, he holds the preeminent position among all the thirty-seven Doctors of the Church and was described by the twentieth-century philosopher Ralph McInerny as "the lodestar of intellectual sanity".[8]

Although the Dominicans have the places of precedence among the thirteenth-century Scholastics, the Franciscans were also represented prominently by St. Bonaventure, Blessed John Duns Scotus, and Roger Bacon.

This briefest overview of what was good in the "greatest century" would be incomplete without a brief litany of the century's greatest saints. In addition to those already mentioned, it would be a gross and grotesque sin of omission to fail to bow with due deference and reverence to Anthony of Padua, Elizabeth of Hungary, Clare of Assisi, Louis IX, and Celestine V, all of whom demand more than the merest passing mention that they are afforded here.

The Bad

"It was the best of times, it was the worst of times."—The opening words of Charles Dickens' classic novel *A Tale of Two Cities* seem especially appropriate as we consider

---

[8] Crocker, *Triumph*, 168.

the dark underbelly of the "greatest century". Indeed, we should remind ourselves that all of history, in both the best of times and the worst of times, is a tale of two cities. All that is good and beautiful belongs to the City of God; all that is bad and ugly belongs to the City of Man. This is true in the greatest as in the least of centuries.

Alan Schreck reminds us, even as he calls the thirteenth century the "greatest", that "there were dark moments, such as the crusades and the Inquisition launched against heresies." It is to these dark moments that we now turn.

"It was the age of wisdom, it was the age of foolishness." The additional opening words of *A Tale of Two Cities* continue to be appropriate. Even as the universities were opening, the mendicant orders flourishing, and the life of the mind flowering, there were times when foolishness prevailed and in which pride was allowed to take pride of place, with the usual tragic consequences.

Pope Innocent III called the Fourth Crusade to liberate Jerusalem from the infidel, but when it was launched in 1202, it unleashed the rabid dogs of war, and worse than war. Long before the crusaders reached the Holy Land, they were attacking fellow Christians. The siege and subsequent sacking of Zadar, a city in Croatia, was the first time that a Catholic crusading army had attacked a Catholic city. Although Pope Innocent had sent letters explicitly forbidding the siege and threatening excommunication of those who disobeyed, the crusaders (with a few notable and noble exceptions) ignored him. After the city was sacked, the "crusaders" fought among themselves in a dispute over the distribution of the plundered property they had stolen. It beggars belief that anyone could really claim that the grace of God was with such people or that their military endeavor was a crusade in any meaningful sense of the word.

As if this unpromising start were not bad and portentous enough, worse was to follow. Long before the crusaders reached the Holy Land, they were lured into the sordid political intrigues of Constantinople. They sacked the ancient city with diabolical abandon:

> For three days they murdered, raped, looted and destroyed on a scale which even the ancient Vandals and Goths would have found unbelievable. Constantinople had become a veritable museum of ancient and Byzantine art, an emporium of such incredible wealth that the Latins were astounded at the riches they found. Though the Venetians had an appreciation for the art which they discovered ... and saved much of it, the French and others destroyed indiscriminately, halting to refresh themselves with wine, violation of nuns, and murder of Orthodox clerics. The Crusaders vented their hatred for the Greeks most spectacularly in the desecration of the greatest Church in Christendom. They smashed the silver iconostasis, the icons and the holy books of Hagia Sophia, and seated upon the patriarchal throne a whore who sang coarse songs as they drank wine from the Church's holy vessels. The estrangement of East and West, which had proceeded over the centuries, culminated in the horrible massacre that accompanied the conquest of Constantinople. The Greeks were convinced that even the Turks, had they taken the city, would not have been as cruel as the Latin Christians. The defeat of Byzantium, already in a state of decline, accelerated political degeneration so that the Byzantines eventually became easy prey to the Turks. The Fourth Crusade and the crusading movement generally thus resulted, ultimately, in the victory of Islam, a result which was of course the exact opposite of its original intention.[9]

[9] Speros Vryonis, *Byzantium and Europe* (New York: Harcourt, Brace & World, 1967), 152.

Further Crusades followed throughout the century, culminating in the final defeat of the Christian army at Acre in 1291. According to Alan Schreck, painful lessons were learned from the ultimately futile efforts to liberate the Holy Land by force of arms: "The lesson of these crusades to capture the Holy Land has remained with the Church until the present day. Never again has the Catholic Church attempted to wage a war to capture territory, even the Holy Land, for the sake of Christ; nor has it condoned warfare among nations for this reason."[10]

It should be added, however, that the Christians were successful in the "crusade" on its western front. In 1212, an army led by the kings of Aragon and Castille defeated a Muslim army at Las Navas de Tolosa in Spain. This would prove to be the turning point in the struggle to wrest the Iberian Peninsula from Islamic control, and by 1248, most of Spain was in Christian hands.

We will conclude our survey of the dark underbelly of the "greatest century" with a brief consideration of the role of the Inquisition.

It is the Church's responsibility to refute error and to counter its harmful effects. This is best done, however, through the use of reason employed with charity. The great philosophical and theological weapons provided by the great Scholastics of the thirteenth century, such as St. Thomas Aquinas, provide all that is necessary for the refutation of error, together with sanctity and the edifying power of beauty. The use of barbaric methods of "persuasion", such as torture, should always be anathema. Christ did not crucify His enemies; He was crucified by them. He took up His own Cross and called upon His followers to take up theirs; He never called on them to nail sinners to the cross.

---

[10] Schreck, *Compact History of the Church*, 50.

The Beautiful

It is interesting and telling that the chapter on the thirteenth century in E. H. Gombrich's 1950 bestselling book, *The Story of Art*, is entitled "The Church Triumphant". Whether this is a mark of the author's theological ignorance (the Church Triumphant being the technical term for the Church in heaven, i.e., the saints and angels in the beatific presence of God), or whether he was using the term rhetorically to suggest the Church's temporal political triumph, or its triumphalism in the light of such political success, is unclear. His view is, in any event, at odds with that of G. K. Chesterton, who saw the spirit of the thirteenth century, as exemplified in Gothic architecture, as the fighting presence of the Church Militant:

> The truth about Gothic is, first, that it is alive, and second, that it is on the march. It is the Church Militant; it is the only fighting architecture. All its spires are spears at rest; and all its stones are stones asleep in a catapult.[11]

Chesterton is right. The great Gothic edifices that were built across Europe in the thirteenth century signify the presence of a fighting Church in the midst of a miserable world. These cathedrals and churches are the true crusaders. They enshrine the tabernacles that house the Real Presence of Christ in the Eucharist. They are themselves tabernacles that enshrine the Real Presence. They are the temples in which the priest in the sacred liturgy re-presents the sacrifice of Christ, day in, day out, week in, week out, even unto the consummation of the world. They are hymns of praise and

---

[11] G. K. Chesterton, *In Defense of Sanity: The Best Essays of G. K. Chesterton* (San Francisco: Ignatius Press, 2011), 71.

a battle cry. They are alive. They cry out. They are charged with the grandeur of God.

Apart from the great and glorious march of the Gothic across the landscape of Christendom, the century also saw the embryonic beginnings of the great Western tradition in painting. Florence became a great center of artistic creativity, exemplified by the work of Cimabue, whose celebrated *Madonna* was borne in triumph from his studio to the Church of Santa Maria Novella. Cimabue's great Florentine contemporary Gaddo Gaddi, remembered for his *Coronation of the Virgin*, would be eclipsed, as would Cimabue himself, by the great Giotto, a friend of Dante, both of whom were active in the late thirteenth century but whose greatest work was produced in the early decades of the following century, which is where we will encounter them more fully. Other centers of artistic excellence flourishing at this time included the cities of Pisa, Lucca, and Siena, where artists, such as Guido, Ugolino, Segna, Duccio, and Berlinghieri, were producing masterpieces of devotional art.

As for poetry, two of the greatest saints of the century also wrote some of its finest poetry. St. Francis of Assisi's "Canticle of Brother Sun" and St. Thomas Aquinas' wonderful eucharistic hymns have both stood the test of time, retaining that timelessness that is the mark of all great art, remaining as fresh as they are profound. St. Thomas composed the Latin hymn *Pange Lingua*, for Vespers of Corpus Christi, the last two verses of which form a separate hymn, *Tantum Ergo*, which is sung at Benediction of the Blessed Sacrament. *O Salutaris Hostia*, another hymn sung at Benediction of the Blessed Sacrament, comprises the last two verses of *Verbum Supernum Prodiens*, Aquinas' hymn for Lauds of Corpus Christi. In addition, St. Thomas composed the Propers for the Mass of Corpus Christi, including the sequence *Lauda Sion Salvatorem*. It is truly astonishing that this great saint, who is rightly lauded as the Angelic Doctor, could be the greatest philosopher and theologian in the history of the Church and also one of her greatest poets.

We began our look at this century with the claim by historian Alan Schreck that it was the "greatest century ... in the history of Western Civilization". We will end with another historian who agrees with him. James J. Walsh wrote a book entitled *The Thirteenth, Greatest of Centuries*, in which he justifies the enormity of the claim with the enormity of the achievement that makes the claim justifiable:

> Is it any wonder ... that we should call the generations that gave us the cathedrals, the universities, the great technical schools that were organized by the trades guilds ... and of art carried to such heights that artistic principles were revealed for all time, and, finally, the great men and women of this century—for more than any other it glories in names that were born not to die—is it at all surprising that we should claim for the period which, in addition to all this, saw the foundation of modern law and liberty, the right to be hailed—the greatest of human history?[12]

[12] James J. Walsh, *The Thirteenth, Greatest of Centuries* (New York: Catholic Summer School Press, 1924), 17.

Fourteenth Century

Holy Women and Divine Poets

The Good

There is no better way of beginning a discussion of the fourteenth century than the summary and overview offered by the great Catholic historian Christopher Dawson:

> The fourteenth century was an age of profound social and spiritual change: an age of ruin and rebirth, of apocalyptic fears and mystical hopes. It was the age of the Great Schism and the Black Death and the Hundred Years' War, but it was also the age of Dante and Petrarch, of St. Catherine and St. Bridget ... an age of poets and mystics and saints. It saw the breakdown of the theocratic order of medieval Christendom and the rise of political nationalism and religious division.[1]

We will come presently to all that was bad about this most confused and confusing of times: the Great Schism, the Black Death, the wars, the ruin, the breakdown of order, the religious division. We will also look at the beauty of the art and literature that shone forth the light of divinity in the midst of the darkness. We will begin, however, with the mystics and the saints.

[1] Quoted in Maisie Ward, ed., *The English Way: Studies in English Sanctity from Bede to Newman* (Tacoma, Wash.: Cluny Media, 2016), 162.

It is no mere coincidence that the only saints whom Dawson mentions by name are women. The fourteenth century had a feminine touch that was present in most of what was best and good in an otherwise dark and uninspiring age. It was these holy women who represented a civilized presence in uncivilized times.

The most prominent and important female presence, aside from the perennial presence of the Virgin, was that provided by the two towering prophetesses whom Dawson names specifically, St. Bridget of Sweden and St. Catherine of Siena, who sought to heal the divisions in the Church through their prayers, holy example, and wisdom.

St. Bridget of Sweden was a wife and the mother of eight children, one of whom would also become a saint. In 1344, following the death of her husband, Bridget founded a monastery on Lake Vättern in her native Sweden for sixty nuns and twenty-five monks who lived in separate enclosures but shared the same church. The rule of the Bridgettine Order, as it became known, was austere. All superfluous income was given to the poor, and all trappings of luxury were forbidden. On the other hand, there was no limit to the number of books that members of the order could request for purposes of study.

In 1349, Bridget went to Rome on pilgrimage, never returning to Sweden. She spent the rest of her life in Italy or on pilgrimage to various shrines, including to the Holy Land. Her reputation as a woman of great virtue was based on her austere life, her devoted service to pilgrims at the many shrines she visited, and for her ministering to the poor and the sick. She was also gifted with mystical visions, some of the Passion of the Christ and others connected to the political and religious issues of her day. She endeavored to dissuade King Magnus IV of Sweden from launching an ill-advised "crusade" against the pagans of

Estonia and Latvia, and she warned Pope Clement VI that he needed to return to Rome from Avignon and that he needed to work to end the Hundred Years' War between England and France. She was, therefore, a tireless advocate of both peace and tradition.

St. Catherine of Siena was a lay Dominican whose influence on her own century has been more than matched by her enduring influence in the centuries since. Like St. Bridget, she urged the return of the pope from Avignon to Rome, and she worked tirelessly and heroically to broker peace between Florence and the papacy. Following the Great Schism caused by the establishment of a rival pope in Avignon in defiance of Urban VI's election in Rome, she was a vociferous defender of Pope Urban, calling for the restoration of Church unity.

St. Catherine's influence on the Church since her death in 1380 is due largely to the theological importance of her spiritual teaching, published as *The Dialogue of Divine Providence*. She was canonized in 1461, declared a patron saint of Rome by Pope Pius IX in 1866 and of Italy (along with St. Francis of Assisi) by Pope Pius XII in 1939. She would be only the second woman to be declared a Doctor of the Church, being elevated to the ranks of the *illustrissimi* and *eminenti* of the Church's theologians by Pope Paul VI in 1970, only days after he had bestowed the same honor on St. Teresa of Ávila. It says something of the significance of both St. Catherine of Siena and St. Bridget of Sweden that they were both named as co-patron saints of Europe in 1999 by John Paul II, alongside three others, SS. Cyril and Methodius and St. Teresa Benedicta of the Cross (Edith Stein).

St. Catherine of Sweden, one of St. Bridget's eight children, followed in her mother's footsteps. She married an invalid whom she nursed devotedly until his death and then became a member of her mother's new religious order at the mother house on Lake Vättern, becoming abbess. Travelling to Rome to promote the cause for her mother's canonization, she befriended Catherine of Siena.

Another peacemaking holy woman of the fourteenth century was St. Elizabeth of Portugal. A princess, the daughter of the king of Aragon, she married King Denis of Portugal, with whom she had two children. Pursuing a life of prayer and devotion, she founded hospitals, orphanages, and homes for fallen women, and she was known for her hospitality to pilgrims and help to the poor. Working for peace and reconciliation in an age of war and division, she reconciled her son with her husband after the former had taken up arms against his father in the Civil War between 1322 and 1324. Toward the end of her life, she also prevented the outbreak of war between Portugal and Castile. Following her husband's death, Elizabeth went on pilgrimage to Compostela and expressed a desire to end her days as a Poor Clare nun. She was dissuaded from doing so but spent her last days as a lay Franciscan at one of the Poor Clare monasteries she had founded, living in great simplicity, like her namesake and distant relative, St. Elizabeth of Hungary.

Probably the greatest cross that St. Elizabeth of Portugal had to bear was the way she was treated by her abusive and adulterous husband. This connects her with a lesser-known fourteenth-century holy woman, St. Margaret the Barefooted, who was abused by her husband because of her devout life of prayer and her love and help for the poor. She is now the patron saint of brides, difficult marriages, and victims of abuse.

Our survey of fourteenth-century holy women continues with two English mystics, Margery Kempe and Julian of Norwich, who were contemporaries living in the English county of Norfolk.

Margery Kempe is the author of what has become known as *The Book of Margery Kempe*, possibly the first autobiography written in the English language. It documents the trials and tribulations of marriage and motherhood but also her many pilgrimages to shrines across Christendom, including the Holy Land, and her mystical visions and conversations with Christ, which have not been formally approved by the Church. Her book offers a priceless view of late fourteenth- and early fifteenth-century England, such as the veneration accorded to the Blessed Sacrament as a priest bore it through the streets of Kings Lynn, the town in which she lived, on his way to minister to the dying, the townsfolk falling to their knees as he passed.[2]

Julian of Norwich, a mystic and anchoress, received a number of mystical visions in 1373, centered on the Holy Trinity and the Passion of Christ. Living a solitary life walled up in a cell, attached to the wall of St. Julian's Church in Norwich, from which she presumably took her name, she spent a solitary life of prayer meditating upon the visions she had received. These meditations and reflections were written down and were subsequently published as *Revelations of Divine Love*. From her cell, Julian could see into the church through a small window, enabling her to see Mass being celebrated and to receive Communion. The cell, which had evidently become a place of pilgrimage in the century or so following her death, was destroyed during the iconoclasm of the English Reformation.

We will conclude our veneration of the holy women of the fourteenth century with the devotion shown to the holiest woman of all. Throughout the century, Walsingham, the site of a Marian apparition in England in 1061,

---

[2] Eamon Duffy, *The Stripping of the Altars* (London: Yale University Press, 1992), 101.

continued to wax as a place of pilgrimage. In 1361, King Edward III granted funds toward the expenses of his enemy, the Duke of Brittany, a prisoner of war, so that the latter might make a pilgrimage to Walsingham. Three years later, he gave safe conduct to King David II of Scotland to make a pilgrimage to Our Lady's shrine, accompanied by twenty knights, one of several pilgrimages to Walsingham that the Scottish king undertook. King David's father, Robert the Bruce, who commanded the Scottish army in its great victory over the English at the Battle of Bannockburn in 1314, was also said to have been given safe conduct to Walsingham, shortly before his death in 1329.[3] Such were the numbers arriving at Walsingham from continental Europe that there was a fixed scale of charges for pilgrims visiting from Flanders.

In 1381, the fourteen-year-old king Richard II knelt and prayed before an image of the Virgin before riding out to meet the rebels during the Peasants' Revolt in 1381. As the fourteenth-century chronicler Jean Froissart wrote:

> The king went to Westminster and heard Mass in the church there, and all his lords with him.... And beside this church there was a little chapel with an image of Our Lady.... There the king made his devotions before this image; and having made his offerings to it, he then mounted and rode off to meet the rebels.[4]

According to legend, it was at this time that the king dedicated England as "Our Lady's Dowry", offering the nation to her as England's "protectress", a momentous event that was probably the inspiration for the painting of the Wilton diptych, which is discussed at the conclusion

[3] H. M. Gillett, *Shrines of Our Lady in England and Wales* (London: Samuel Walker, 1957), 302.
[4] Quoted in ibid., 344.

of this chapter. According to Eamon Duffy, "Englishmen were encouraged to think of their country as being in a special way 'Mary's Dowry', a notion propagated ... by the custodians of the shrine at Walsingham."[5] In around 1350, a mendicant preacher stated in a sermon that "it is commonly said that the land of England is the Virgin's dowry."[6] By the end of the century, the Archbishop of Canterbury, Thomas Arundel, wrote that "we English, being ... her own Dowry, as we are commonly called, ought to surpass others in the fervour of our praises and devotions."[7] By the reign of Henry V, the title *dos Mariae* (dowry of Mary) was being applied to England in Latin texts. On the eve of the Battle of Agincourt in 1415, according to the contemporary chronicler Thomas Elmham, English priests prayed to "the Virgin, protectress of her dower".[8]

England was by no means unique, of course, in her devotion to the Mother of God, as can be seen by the aforementioned pilgrimages to Walsingham by the Duke of Brittany and the king of Scotland, both of whom were from countries with which England was at war in the fourteenth century. Even in the midst of the maelstrom of incessant conflicts that plagued the age, the Queen of Peace had the power to touch the hearts of the most war-like of men.

The Bad

Even as holy women were applying the feminine touch to the fourteenth century, fostering peace and praying for

[5] Duffy, *Stripping of the Altars*, 256.

[6] Nigel Saul, *For Honour and Fame: Chivalry in England, 1066–1500* (London: Random House, 2011), 208.

[7] Quoted in Sarah Jane Boss, *Mary* (London: Continuum, 2004), 118.

[8] Saul, *For Honour and Fame*, 209.

unity, the macho machinations of many of the secular and ecclesial rulers were a cause of much scandal.

During the Siege of Metz, one of the internecine feudal conflicts that were the time's plague, a new weapon was unleashed on the citizens of the besieged town. This was the cannon, the first weapon of mass destruction made possible by the invention of gunpowder. Invented in China and making its way to Europe via the Mongols, the introduction of gunfire to the sphere of human conflict was the beginning of the industrialization of warfare. This new technology was employed by both the French and English armies during the Hundred Years' War, which began in 1337 and would continue intermittently until 1453, although the superiority of the "primitive" English longbow over the innovative mechanical French crossbow would also play an important factor in the English victories.

The divisive conflicts between the emergent nations of Europe left Christendom weakened and vulnerable to the power of Islam. In 1389, the Ottoman Turks defeated the Serbs at the Battle of Kosovo, the beginning of the rise of the Ottoman Empire. Within a century, most of the Balkans south of the River Danube were under Muslim control, heralding a renewal of the conflict between Islam and Christendom on the soil of Europe.

The biggest killer of the century was not warfare but plague, the Black Death spreading across Europe, having originated, like gunpowder, in China. Within four years, it had wiped out between a third and a half of Europe's population. It was no wonder that a pestilence of such biblical proportions should have been blamed on the wickedness of the world, not merely in terms of the interminable warfare between nations but also with respect to the insufferable divisions within the Church, both man-made "plagues" that St. Bridget of Sweden and St. Catherine of Aragon had sought to heal through prayer and protestation.

Divisions in the Church were brought to a head by the removal of the papacy from its divinely ordained seat of authority in Rome to its politically expedient new home in France. "For most of the fourteenth century, the bishops of Rome lived far away from Rome, in the fortified city of Avignon," wrote Eamon Duffy. "The seventy-year exile of the popes at Avignon was a disaster for the Church, and came to be known as the Babylonian Captivity of the papacy."[9] One inevitable consequence of the transplanting of the popes to Avignon was the suspicion that the popes were now effectively in the pocket of the king of France, a suspicion that was borne out by the fact that the seven French popes between 1305 and 1378 created 134 cardinals, of whom no fewer than 113 were French.[10]

At the urging of St. Catherine of Siena, Pope Gregory VI returned the papacy to Rome in 1377. In 1378, following Gregory's death and the election of Urban VI, the French cardinals elected a rival pope, technically an antipope, who continued to reside in Avignon. Thus began the Great Schism, which would last until 1417, in which true pope and antipope vied for supremacy within the Church. Although this tragic scenario did much to harm the Church, it was not as damaging, in the view of Christopher Dawson, as the period in which the true popes had resided in Avignon:

It was not ... the great schism so much as the translation of the Papacy to Avignon that marked the turning-point,

[9] Eamon Duffy, *Saints and Sinners: A History of the Popes* (New Haven: Yale University Press, 2014), 163.

[10] Philip Hughes, *A Popular History of the Catholic Church* (New York: Macmillan, 1962), 154.

by destroying the super-national prestige of the Holy See. It is true that the Popes of Avignon did not deserve the indiscriminate condemnation that was passed upon them by contemporary writers like Villard and Petrarch. They included men of high character and ability, such as Benedict XII and Urban V, who were not unmindful of their universal responsibilities. Nevertheless, the divorce of the Holy See from the sacred associations of the Holy City had a disastrous effect on public opinion.[11]

The Beautiful

If the fourteenth century was a time of plague, both natural and sinful, it was also a time of renewal and rebirth, a time of "renaissance". Although historians usually date the Renaissance as beginning in the following century, it is in this century that Giotto, the first of the "modern" painters, emerges as a pioneer of a new naturalism in art. His contemporary Giovanni Villani wrote that Giotto was "the most sovereign master of painting in his time, who drew all his figures and their postures according to nature".[12] Giorgio Vasari, the sixteenth-century artist, architect, and art historian, concurred with Villani's judgment, declaring that Giotto had initiated "the great art of painting as we know it today, introducing the technique of drawing accurately from life".[13]

Giotto's avant-garde approach becomes evident if we compare his *Ognissanti Madonna* with the *Madonna and Child* of his famous predecessor Cimabue. Whereas Cimabue's

---

[11] Quoted in Ward, *English Way*, 193.

[12] Kenneth R. Bartlett, *The Civilization of the Italian Renaissance* (Toronto: D.C. Heath and Company, 1992), 37.

[13] Giorgio Vasari, *Lives of the Most Excellent Painters, Sculptors, and Architects* (London: Penguin Classics, 1965), 15.

depiction of the Virgin and Child, surrounded by angels, is executed with the stylized reverence of Byzantine iconography, Giotto shows the Mother and Child in a relatively relaxed and natural posture. Whereas Cimabue's angels meet the eye of the viewer, as do his Virgin and Child, Giotto's angels have their eyes on the seated Virgin, Child on lap, joining the viewer in adoration.

Dante, Giotto's contemporary, references the celebrated status that Giotto had acquired in his own day, in the famous speech by the artist Oderisi in the *Purgatorio* on "the empty glory of man's frail ambition":

> Once, Cimabue thought to hold the field
> In painting; Giotto's all the rage today;
> The other's fame lies in the dust concealed.[14]

As for Dante himself, it could be argued that he is the greatest writer of all time, and few would argue that, at the least, he stands shoulder to shoulder with his own mentor, Virgil, and with Virgil's mentor, Homer. Inspired by the Scholasticism of the previous century and especially by the philosophy and theology of St. Thomas Aquinas, *The Divine Comedy* is the definitive masterpiece of Christian literature, a literary edifice that edifies the reader with the beauty of its musing on the Four Last Things: death, judgment, heaven and hell. As supremely sublime art, it towers over the literary landscape as the Gothic cathedrals tower over the natural landscape. If Thomas Aquinas is the Angelic Doctor, well might it be said that Dante, his disciple, is the Angelic Poet. Ultimately, we are left bereft of adequate words to convey the enormity of his achievement and are forced to agree with T. S. Eliot, the greatest

[14] Dante, *Purgatorio*, Canto XI, 94–96, trans. Dorothy L. Sayers (Penguin Classics (New York: Penguin Books, 1955).

poet of the twentieth century, in his awe-struck praise of the greatest poet of all time. "I feel so completely inferior in his presence," Eliot wrote. "There seems really nothing to do but to point to him and be silent."[15]

Although Dante's work is timeless in the truest sense of the word, it can also be seen to be the final and finest fruit of the Middle Ages. There is something distinctly medieval about Dante, even as he speaks to all ages. The same cannot be said of Petrarch, the other great fourteenth-century Italian writer, whose sonnets are the final and finest fruit of the courtly love tradition of the troubadours, and also the first flowering of the humanism of the Renaissance. He marks the transition from the medieval to the modern and is somehow stuck there, very much belonging to the spirit of the age that inspired him and which he in turn inspired.

The fourteenth century also witnessed the rebirth of great literature in the English language, almost seven hundred years after the first golden age of English literature during the age of Bede and *Beowulf*. Although the language had changed greatly in the intervening centuries, metamorphosing from the Old English of the Anglo-Saxons to the Middle English of the Anglo-Norman ascendency, writers such as William Langland and the anonymous author of *Sir Gawain and the Green Knight* still employed the alliterative accentual meter that their Anglo-Saxon ancestors had used. As for Langland, he was, in the judgment of Christopher Dawson, "the Catholic Englishman par excellence, at once the most English of Catholic poets and the most Catholic of English poets ... a man in whom Catholic faith and national feeling are fused in a single flame.": "He saw Christ walking in English fields in the

---

[15] *The Letters of T. S. Eliot: Volume I, 1898–1922*, ed. Valerie Eliot (London: Harcourt Brace Jovanovich, 1988), 374–75.

dress of an English labourer, and to understand his work is to know English religion in its most autochthonous and yet most Catholic form."[16]

And yet, Dawson continues, irrespective of his Christian idealism, Langland was "also a realist who does not shrink from describing in pitiless detail the corruptions of the Church, the wrongs of the poor and the vices of the rich".[17] The same could be said of the unflinching candor of Dante and Chaucer. These great writers served as the conscience of Christendom, holding up a mirror to the times in which they found themselves, penetrating the miasma and malaise with the incisive moral presence of Christ.

We will end with a wonderful work of art that serves as a metaphor for this most messy of centuries and provides the moral to be learned from it. The Wilton Diptych, one of the finest examples of late medieval art, shows King Richard II of England kneeling before the Virgin and Child, who are surrounded by angels, one of whom holds aloft a St. George's Cross flag. The king is presented to the Madonna and Child by three saints: St. John the Baptist (King Richard's personal patron) and the two patron saints of England, St. Edward the Confessor and St. Edmund the Martyr.[18] It illustrates the moment when the king had knelt before the image of the Virgin seeking deliverance for himself and his kingdom from the Peasants' Revolt and consecrating England as Our Lady's Dowry. This illustration of a secular ruler's humility in the presence of Christ and His mother illustrates what was sorely lacking in a century in which the secular powers, aided and abetted by corrupt or weak popes and cardinals, rode

[16] Quoted in Ward, *English Way*, 161.
[17] Ibid.
[18] It was not until the Reformation that St. George emerged definitively as England's patron.

roughshod over the rights of the Church. If only the secular and ecclesial rulers of the fourteenth century had spent
less time seeking to bring the Church to her knees and
more time on their own knees in prayer, if only they had
listened to the holy women and heeded the voice of the
poets, peace might have reigned instead of incessant war.

Fifteenth Century

Rebirth and Rebellion

The Good

Following the ending of the Great Schism in 1417, a period of slow spiritual healing began. This found expression in a revival of popular piety, especially a growing devotion to the Suffering Christ, no doubt prompted by the gross and grotesque sins of those who had nailed Christ's Mystical Body to the Cross during the previous century. The Passion of Christ and the sufferings of His mother became the central focus of the spiritual life of Christians. In art, this is manifested in paintings and statues of Christ crowned with thorns, or with images of His carrying the Cross as well as hanging from it. Conjoined with this mystical union of the sinner with the Passion of the Lord was meditation upon the Sorrows of Mary. The most enduring legacy of this period of religious renewal was the publication of *The Imitation of Christ* by Thomas à Kempis, which has proved to be one of the bestselling and perennially popular books of all time. Its success was immediate, capturing the spirit of the time. Over the next two hundred years, it would be published in more than seven hundred editions and would be translated into more languages than any other book except for the Bible itself.

The revitalization of the Church was evident during the Jubilee Year of 1450, the astonishing success of which exceeded all expectations. So many pilgrims flooded into Rome that there were not enough beds in the city to accommodate them. Thousands camped in fields and vineyards on the edge of the city, there being no room at the proverbial inn. Pope Nicholas V ordered that the relics of the saints be put on public display so that pilgrims arriving at the Eternal City could venerate those noble souls who had served Christ so faithfully across the centuries. Endless queues of pilgrims made their way through the major basilicas, from dawn till late into the night. Such were the numbers that the pope was forced, in prudence, to shorten the required time that pilgrims needed to stay in Rome from eight days to only three. According to papal historian Eamon Duffy, "The Jubilee was a formative event for the Renaissance papacy": "After the long traumas of the schism ... it confirmed beyond argument the centrality of Rome and the Pope in popular Catholicism."[1]

In the Netherlands, the Augustinian Canons Regular flourished in a new congregation at Windesheim. Under the enigmatic leadership of the second prior, Johann Voss, new foundations were made across the Netherlands and Germany. In 1407, there were twelve monasteries; by the end of the century, there were 102: eighty-six houses of canons and sixteen of nuns. Meanwhile, in Italy, Benedictine monastic life was being reformed by the new congregation of St. Justina. It was, however, the Franciscan Order that produced two of the greatest saints of the century, Bernardine of Siena and John of Capistrano.

Having become a Franciscan in 1402, St. Bernardine earned a reputation as a highly gifted preacher, traveling across Italy, always on foot, where the crowds who came

---

[1] Eamon Duffy, *Saints and Sinners: A History of the Popes* (New Haven: Yale University Press, 2014), 182.

to see him were so large that he was forced to preach in the open air. With a powerfully resonant voice, he preached the need for penance and voluntary poverty, denouncing gambling, usury, superstition, and the wickedness of the politics of Italy's city-states. A gifted orator, he moved his audience to both laughter and tears, employing mimicry and anecdotal humor to lighten and relieve the intensity of his denunciation of sin and his call for repentance. As he tramped across Italy, he left a trail of conversions in his wake.

In 1437, Bernardine became vicar-general of the Observant branch of the Franciscan Order. Such was his charismatic presence and leadership that the number of Observant Friars increased at this time by more than tenfold. Aware that ignorance of Church doctrine was as much of a threat to the Franciscan life as worldly riches, he established schools of theology for the friars at Perugia and Monteripido. By 1444, his body broken by age and toil, he became unable to journey from place to place on foot, traveling instead on the back of a donkey. He died in May of that year, on his way to Naples in the midst of a long and arduous speaking tour. Following his death, there were many reports of miracles due to his intercession, and he was canonized only six years later, on the Feast of Pentecost, the ceremony in Rome proving to be the highlight of the city's Jubilee Year. Hugely popular, he was depicted by artists as small and emaciated, with the burning eyes of a fiery preacher. Sometimes he is shown with three mitres placed at his feet in recognition of the three bishoprics he had refused, those of Siena, Ferrara, and Urbino.

St. John of Capistrano had enjoyed a successful life in the secular world before joining the Franciscans in 1416. He had studied law and had become the governor of Perugia before embracing a life of poverty. Ordained to the priesthood in 1420, he studied theology under St. Bernardine and then followed in Bernardine's footsteps by becoming a wandering preacher. As gifted as his mentor in the art of Spirit-guided rhetoric, he also attracted huge crowds wherever he went. He enjoyed particular success in central Europe, where his preaching brought many followers of the heretic John Huss back to the Catholic fold.

Although he was truly an instrument of peace as a true follower of St. Francis, he is also known as the soldier saint for his involvement in the defense of Christendom from the threat of the Turks who, following the fall of Constantinople in 1453, were now threatening to invade Christian Hungary. Although he was seventy years old, he joined forces with the Hungarian general John Hunyadi, becoming the spiritual leader of the Hungarian army that defeated the Turks at the Battle of Belgrade in 1456. Both he and Hunyadi died shortly after the victory, probably due to disease caused by neglect of the unburied corpses at the scene of battle. Having fought the good fight in a life of service to Christ and His Church, preaching the Gospel, he died defending Christian Europe from the military threat of its ancient Islamic foe.

One other fifteenth-century Franciscan saint should also be lauded before we turn to the century's dark underbelly. St. Colette was, in some ways, the female equivalent of SS. Bernardine of Siena and John of Capistrano. Between 1410 and her death in 1447, she founded seventeen new convents and reformed several old ones, mostly in her native France and in Flanders and Savoy.

The Bad

The first seventeen years of the century were overshadowed by the scandal of the Great Schism. At one point, there were not merely two rival "popes", the true pope in Rome and the antipope in Avignon, but three "popes". This bizarre scenario arose in 1409 when a self-styled "General Council" at Pisa elected its own "pope", who went by the name of Alexander V. This absurd situation was finally brought to an end at the Council of Constance in 1417, which deposed two "popes", persuaded the third to retire, and elected a new pope, Martin V, who was recognized by the whole Church. Mercifully, the Great Schism had finally ended.

The newly reunited Church had many challenges to face, two of which had their ignominious roots in fourteenth-century England. The first was the rise to increasing prominence of the fourteenth-century philosopher and theologian William of Ockham, whose nominalist ideas were growing in popularity and popular acceptance, sowing the seeds for the Protestant Reformation and for the later philosophical relativism that would follow in Protestantism's wake. The other was the influence of John Wycliffe, whose translation and misinterpretation of Scripture laid the foundations for the de facto theological relativism of sola scriptura and sola fide, two of the pillars of Protestantism. Although these seeds of error had been sown in the previous century and would not come to full destructive fruition until the following century, the fifteenth century became a battleground on which these ideas were tried, tested, and contested.

In England, the followers of Wycliffe, known as Lollards, had limited success, largely due to the unpopularity of their attacks on the Eucharist, but his followers in distant Bohemia, under the leadership of John Huss, had much popular support. Huss, a Catholic priest, was excommunicated in 1412 for his rejection of Catholic sacramental theology and his denial of papal authority. Huss' popularity had as much to do with his being the leader of Czech

national resistance to the Germans as with his theological
ideas, a popularity that grew after his execution in 1415.
Seeing him as a "martyr" for the emergent Czech nation,
his followers, known as Hussites, fought a series of wars
in the 1420s and 1430s, seeking to "liberate" the Czech
nation from German and papal control.

One of the sad and grim ironies of history is that a Catholic saint, Joan of Arc, faced the same fate as the anti-
Catholic rebel John Huss, both of whom were burned at
the stake as heretics. The conviction of St. Joan for heresy
in 1431 by a corrupt French court would be overturned
after Callistus III, the first Spanish pope, ordered a retrial.
In 1456, the original trial and its verdict were judged to
be illicit due to improper procedures, deceit, and fraud.
"The Maid of Orleans was a devout, visionary, and sword-
wielding heroine of France," wrote H. W. Crocker. "She
essentially won the Hundred Years War for her country.
By rescinding her conviction, Pope Callistus undid one
of the worst miscarriages of justice since the dissolution of
the Templars."[2]

In a sermon preached on the feast day of St. Joan of
Arc, Ronald Knox imagines the saint's unshaken resolu-
tion that the promises of France's deliverance, which she
had received mystically from God, would be kept, even
though she was doomed to die a horrific and unjust death
before seeing them come to pass:

She was to deliver France—the voices had told her so—
and France was not yet delivered. And so she went to the

---

[2] H. W. Crocker III, *Triumph: The Power and the Glory of the Catholic Church*
(New York: Three Rivers Press, 2001), 214. The Knights Templar, a Catholic
military order founded in 1119, was dissolved in 1312 by Pope Clement V
at the behest of King Philip IV of France. It is now generally acknowledged
that the accusations against the order were unfounded and that the suppression
of the order was unjust.

stake, her hopes still unfulfilled, but never doubting for an instant that the voices were true. Five years later the King entered Paris; twenty-two years later, England had no possessions left on French soil. She believed he was faithful who had promised.... She could not foresee that her unjust condemnation would be reversed, point by point, twenty-five years after her death: she could not foresee that, nearly five hundred years after her death, France ... would receive the tidings of her canonization by the tribunal to which, in life, she never ceased to appeal, the tribunal of the Holy See. But she believed that he was faithful who had promised.[3]

Such faith in the midst of such tribulation. Such faith in the promises of Christ even in the absence of any tangible evidence that the promises will be kept. It was such faith that had earned St. Joan of Arc her heavenly reward. Inspired by such faith, Ronald Knox ended his sermon in honor of the saint with heartfelt hope: "Whither may God of his great mercy bring us, that we may see with open vision, among the choir of Virgins that are our Lady's handmaids, the Saint whose glorious merits the Church commemorates today."[4] Knox's words remind us that the saints always triumph over evil, even in the most tragic circumstances, christening their "wild-worst Best"[5] by uniting themselves to Christ.

Perhaps the "wild-worst" moment of the whole century was the fall of Constantinople to the forces of Islam in 1453. The tragedy was, however, a long time in the making, in the sense that the city had become enfeebled by decadence and was, in consequence, unable and

[3] Ronald Knox, *Captive Flames: On Selected Saints and Christian Heroes* (San Francisco: Ignatius Press, 2001), 84–85.

[4] Ibid., 86.

[5] A phrase plucked from Gerard Manley Hopkins' poem "The Wreck of 'The Deutschland' ".

unwilling to defend itself. Only five thousand Byzantines, just 5 percent of the city's population, were willing to take up arms in its defense. Instead, continuing an ignoble tradition that went back centuries, the city relied on foreign mercenaries to do its fighting. These warriors from the Catholic West formed the backbone and military leadership of the defense of their estranged Eastern brethren. Hopelessly outnumbered, they would fight a courageous last stand against the 150,000 Ottoman Turks besieging the city. The commander in chief of the small Byzantine army was an Italian, Giovanni Giustiniani. It was a German, Johan Grant, who foiled the Turkish attempts to mine the city; and it was a Spanish knight, Don Francis of Toledo, who died, side by side with the Byzantine emperor, in one final heroic but hopeless charge against the Turks. Thus, the glory of Constantinople passed away. "The Turk had finally crushed enfeebled Byzantium," wrote H. W. Crocker. "The Catholic West would prove hardier stock."[6]

The difference between the decadence of Byzantium and the "hardier" character and culture of the Catholic West was evident in 1480, when the southern Italian city of Otranto was attacked by the Turks. The city fell after a fifteen-day siege. Upon reaching the cathedral, the Turks found the archbishop fully vested and with a crucifix in hand. He was beheaded; the priests that were with him were also slain, and the cathedral desecrated. Then all the women and older children were rounded up to be sold into slavery. Older men, younger children, and all infants were killed. It is thought that around twelve thousand people were killed, and around five thousand women and older children sold as slaves.

[6] Crocker, *Triumph*, 213.

Eight hundred able-bodied men were rounded up and told that they would be spared if they converted to Islam. In response, a tailor by the name of Antonio Primaldi stepped forward and proclaimed that since Christ had died for Christians, it was fitting that Christians should die for Christ. At these words of defiant faith, the other captives cheered. Witnessing the subsequent execution of these Christian martyrs, which began with the beheading of Antonio Primaldi, it is said that one of the Muslims converted on the spot and was killed instantly by his companions.

The Otranto Martyrs were beatified by Pope Clement XIV in 1771 but were not canonized until 2013. Pope Benedict XVI issued a decree in 2007 recognizing that Primaldi and his companions had been killed "out of hatred for their faith".[7] In 2012, he authorized the Congregation for the Causes of Saints to promulgate a decree regarding the miraculous healing of a religious sister, Francesca Levote, which was attributed to the intercession of Blessed Antonio Primaldi and his companions. Then, on February 11, 2013, the day on which he announced his resignation, Pope Benedict also announced the date for the canonization of the Otranto Martyrs. They were canonized by the newly elected Pope Francis three months later.

Further evidence of the "hardier" character of the Christian West was revealed twelve years after the Otranto massacre when a Spanish army took the city of Grenada, the last bastion of Islam in Western Europe. The liberation of the Iberian Peninsula from the grip of Islam secured the victory of Christendom on the "western front" of its centuries-old conflict with its old enemy. In the same year, 1492, Christopher Columbus landed in the "New World"

---

[7] Iván de Vargas, "The 800 Martyrs of Otranto", *Zenit*, May 13, 2013.

of the Americas, opening up a whole new "western frontier" and beginning a whole new chapter in the history of Christendom.

The Beautiful

If the thirteenth century had been the age of Gothic architecture and the great cathedrals, the fourteenth century the age of the divine poets, the fifteenth century would be the age of the great artists of the Renaissance. They are so many in number that we can offer only a tantalizing glimpse of their multifarious works.

Masaccio's *Madonna and Child* is almost earthy in its depiction of a somewhat plain Virgin, more homely than comely, and a thumb-sucking Christ worshipped by very human-looking angels. Paradoxically, the painting's beauty is in the artist's masterful grasp and execution of the new science of perspective, the throne on which the Virgin is seated gaining three-dimensional solidity, accentuated by the shadows that fall upon it. In *Expulsion from Paradise*, Masaccio's presentation of the grief-stricken Adam and Eve is so graphically successful that we can feel their anguish with the intensity that we can see the terror in Edvard Munch's *The Scream*, the former prefiguring and prophesying the expressionism of modern art.

Fra Angelico's *Annunciation* and *Deposition* display a reverence and deference to religion that seems lacking in Masaccio's work, an indication of the former's deep faith and holy life as a Dominican friar, which was recognized by the Church when he was beatified by Pope John Paul II in 1982. The creative juxtaposition of the religious life with the life of art, exemplified by Fra Angelico, is also present in the life and work of Fra Filippo Lippi, a Carmelite monk. His *Adoration in a Wood* combines doctrinal symbolism with naturalism and a vibrant use of color. The symbolic presentation of the Trinity and the Incarnation reveals the power of art as apologetics, as well as shining forth the work itself as an act of worship on the part of the artist. In addition, the realistic realization of the fabric of the Virgin's robe is so successful that its enshadowed folds are almost tactile. Such realism encapsulates the purity of vision that the Pre-Raphaelites would seek to emulate four hundred years later.

In contrast, Antonio Pollaiuolo's *Martyrdom of St. Sebastian* is almost bereft of any reverence for the saint in its focus on the physical anatomy of those who are putting him to death. It seems, in fact, that the artist has spent more time and creative energy on highlighting the flexed muscles of the man in the foreground than in the saint whose form, by comparison, is rather flaccidly understated and nondescript. The work appears to be animated by a humanism that elevates the life of man over those who die for Christ.

It could be said that the Renaissance loses its virginity, its divine innocence and purity, when it loses the Virgin in its pursuit of Venus. This aesthetic and erotic fall does not divorce art from beauty, however, as can be seen by the magnificence of Botticelli's *Primavera* and his *Birth of Venus*. In both works, the goddess takes the place of the Mother of God as the center of focus, pregnant and bounteously fruitful in the former painting and nakedly and erotically alluring in the latter. And yet Botticelli's *Pietà* is one of the most sorrowfully glorious of all religious art, the muscular dead body of the clean-shaven Christ draped dramatically across the lap of His mother, who appears to be almost fainting with grief, while being supported and surrounded by saints and holy women.

No survey, however brief, of the great art and artists of the Quattrocento could omit the great Leonardo da Vinci. The real problem is knowing where to start or finish. A good place to start would be one of his earliest works, *Madonna of the Carnation*, which shows the Virgin, her face bathed in light, her eyes looking down at the flower or possibly closed in prayer, while her Son reaches out toward the flower while his eyes meet those of the viewer. His gaze invites us into the painting while His hand leads us to join the Virgin in contemplating the flower, the red carnation signifying the Incarnation and the Crucifixion. According to legend, red carnations sprang forth miraculously wherever Mary's tears touched the earth as she wept for her Son. This legend, which was well known in medieval culture and would surely have been known by Leonardo, is the probable etymological explanation for the carnation being named after the Incarnation. The flower serves, therefore, as the artist's invitation to the viewer to contemplate the theological connection between the birth of Christ and His Crucifixion.

A later painting by Leonardo, *Virgin of the Rocks*, is reminiscent of Fra Filippo Lippi's *Adoration in a Wood*. In both paintings, the Madonna and Child are al fresco, in the midst of a wild landscape. In Leonardo's painting, the rocky background falls into shadow in the presence of the glorious light that falls on the faces of all four figures. The Virgin holds her hand out in maternal blessing over her Infant Son, who, seated on the ground, raises His own hand in blessing, while the slightly older child, St. John the Baptist, kneels in adoration. The final figure, the Archangel Uriel, is seated beside the Christ Child. None of the faces meet the eye of the viewer, as if each is caught up in the meditative moment.

At the end of the century, in 1498, Leonardo executed one of his most famous paintings and, indeed, one of the most famous of all works of art. This is his *Last Supper*, a mural painted for a convent in Milan. Christ is seated in the center with the twelve apostles, six on each side of Him. He remains calm while the apostles gesticulate wildly following His revelation that one of them will betray Him. He is the calm at the center of the storm, even as He knows of the impending storm that the betrayal of Him will unleash.

Although the masterpieces of the Renaissance demand center stage in any discussion of beauty in the fifteenth century, we would be remiss were we not to mention that this was also the century in which the architect Filippo Brunelleschi designed the dome of Florence Cathedral, which was completed in 1436 and remains one of the wonders of human achievement in the arts. A triumph of innovative engineering, it remains the largest brick dome in the world.

Only a passing deferential nod can be made in the direction of the music of the fifteenth century in which the French composer Guillaume Du Fay was preeminent. In 1467, Piero de' Medici described Du Fay as "the greatest ornament of our age",[8] which is a truly remarkable tribute considering that Piero de' Medici was the de facto ruler of Florence, which was at the very center of the Renaissance. It says something of the status and brilliance of this French composer that he should be considered superior to Italian artists, such as Botticelli, Fr. Angelico, and their illustrious ilk.

We will end with a fitting tribute to a Catholic saint who was also an artist and is the patron saint of artists. This is St. Catherine of Bologna, a Poor Clare nun who was a writer, teacher, and mystic, as well as being an artist and a saint. As a Franciscan, it is little surprise that she

[8] David Fallows, *Dufay* (New York: Vintage Books, 1988), 1.

painted many portraits of St. Francis and St. Clare and many images of the swaddled Christ Child, reflective of St. Francis' own special devotion to the Infant Jesus. Other saints she painted were Paul, Jerome, Thomas Becket, Anthony of Padua, Mary Magdalene, and Catherine of Alexandria. Perhaps the most famous work attributed to her is a Madonna and Child, in which a fresh-faced and rosy-cheeked Virgin holds what appears to be a peach in her left hand while holding the Christ Child with the other. The Infant Jesus holds his right hand in blessing while His other hand grabs the Virgin's veil.

Apart from her art, St. Catherine wrote a significant mystical work, *Seven Spiritual Weapons Necessary for Spiritual Warfare*, which was very popular in the sixteenth and seventeenth centuries and was translated from the original Italian into Latin, French, Portuguese, English, Spanish, and German. She also wrote a five-thousand-line Latin poem called the *Rosarium Metricum*, on the life of Christ. In an age in which Franciscans were at the forefront of the life of the Church, especially in the holy example of St. Bernardine of Siena and St. John of Capistrano, it is apt that we should end with another Franciscan saint who incarnated the goodness and truth of the Gospel with the beauty of art.

Sixteenth Century

Rupture and Reformation

The Good

One of the most egregious errors of secular history is its account of the Reformation. The general view that the Reformation was Protestant and that the Catholic reaction to it was the Counter-Reformation is simply at variance with the reality of the situation in sixteenth-century Europe. From a purely secular perspective, there were three separate reformations, all very different from each other. There was the Protestant Reformation, heralded by Luther; the English Reformation, imposed mercilessly by Henry VIII; and the Catholic Reformation, which was the bona fide reform movement within the Church. From a Catholic perspective, only one of these movements was an authentic reformation; the other two were ruptures from the Body of Christ.

We will begin with all that was good about the one authentic reformation in the sixteenth century, which secular historians have labeled the Counter-Reformation.

Since there is no doubt that the Church was in need of reform at the beginning of the century, it is plausible, providentially speaking, to see the Protestant "Reformation" as God's way of prompting such a reform. The Church's response to the Protestant rupture was made manifest at the Council of Trent, which was held between 1545 and

1563. Decrees were made on purgatory, the invocation of the saints, the veneration of relics and images, on fast and feast days, on the catechism, and on the revision of the breviary and the missal. In addition, and particularly important to the reform of the Church, was the reading and passing of the General Reform Decree, with its insistence on simplicity of life among cardinals and bishops. These decrees of the Council laid the foundations of the Tridentine Reformation, which revitalized the Body of Christ, paving the way for a new spirit of evangelization and inspiring a golden age of saints.

In 1540, five years before the beginning of the Council of Trent, Pope Paul III had formally approved the Society of Jesus, a new religious order soon to be known worldwide as the Jesuits, which had been founded in Paris in 1534 by St. Ignatius Loyola and six associates, one of whom was Francis Xavier. It was also in 1540 that King John III of Portugal requested that Jesuit missionaries be sent to evangelize the new Portuguese colonies on the Indian subcontinent. Answering the call, Francis Xavier set sail for Goa in the following year. Described by an early biographer as "the Glory of his Age and the Society of which he was a member",[1] Francis Xavier was a pioneer of the new missionary evangelization that carried the truth of the Gospel to new frontiers and new worlds. He devoted almost three years among the people of southern India and Sri Lanka, converting many to the faith and building nearly forty churches along the coast, in spite of being hampered in his labors by the vicious habits and scandalous example of many of the Portuguese soldiers. In Travancore, in southwestern India, he made more converts, tramping on foot from village to village, than

[1] Anonymous, *The Lives of the Saints* (London: Thomas Meighan, 1729), 4:282.

the Portuguese clergy, traveling in the relative luxury of horse and carriage, had made in thirty years. Although his preaching to the lower-caste people met with great success, his efforts to evangelize the high-caste Brahmins were to no avail. The poor were eager to hear the Word of God. The rich turned away.

Francis Xavier reached Japan in 1549 and an island off the coast of China, truly virgin territory for the Church, in 1552. It was here, a little over three months after his arrival, that he died. A few short years afterward, in 1556, Ignatius Loyola died in Rome. At the time of his death, the Society of Jesus had more than a thousand members in Europe and in missions around the world. Four hundred years later, in 1956, the Society of Jesus had more than thirty thousand members, its influence bearing fruit in ways too manifold and multifarious to fathom.

Two great reformers who helped to revitalize the Church in Italy at this time were St. Philip Neri and St. Charles Borromeo.

St. Philip Neri, known as the Apostle of Rome for his work of evangelization among the people of the Eternal City, had a "delightful sense of humour, always charitable but calculated to knock the conceit out of self-satisfied Pharisees or to blow away scruples like a healing wind".[2] St. Charles Borromeo supervised work on the new catechism of the Church, summarizing the whole of Catholic teaching in accordance with the decrees of the Council of Trent. Part I was devoted to the Creed; Part II to the sacraments; Part III to the Ten Commandments; and Part IV to the Lord's Prayer. As with the *Catechism of the Catholic Church* published more than four hundred years later during

[2] Margaret Yeo, *Reformer: St. Charles Borromeo* (Milwaukee: Bruce Publishing, 1938), 69–70.

the pontificate of John Paul II, the publication of the Tridentine Catechism gave the Church a powerful tool to fight the errors being propagated by Protestantism as well as providing the means to dispel the widespread ignorance of the faith among the public at large. In addition, Charles Borromeo was a key member of the commission on the reform of church music, including the judgment of three new Masses by Palestrina, thereby ensuring that the Catholic Reformation was infused with the goodness of sanctity, the truth of catechesis, and the beauty of the liturgy. On these three pillars would reformers such as Charles Borromeo rebuild the tattered and battered Church of Christ, even as missionaries, such as Francis Xavier, were spreading the Gospel to the four corners of a largely newly discovered world.

The sixteenth century was also blessed with one of the holiest and greatest popes in the Church's history. Leading by his own ascetic example, St. Pius V ate only two meager meals a day, vegetable soup and a couple of eggs at lunchtime, and a small serving of fish, salad, and fruit in the evening. He rose at dawn to say Mass and then spent long hours in work and prayer. "It was as if St. Francis had become pope," wrote Harry Crocker. "He shocked Rome with his personal care for the sick and the poor, his unstinting prayer and penance [and] the demanding moral standards he enforced on the clergy."[3]

Elected pope in January 1566, he began as he meant to continue by distributing in alms to the poor the money usually spent by a newly elected pope on lavish entertainment or in extravagant shows of largesse toward the rich and powerful. He sought to tackle the widespread vice, so prevalent in Rome, by ministering to the poor in general and to

[3] H. W. Crocker III, *Triumph: The Power and the Glory of the Catholic Church* (New York: Three Rivers Press, 2001), 277.

the city's prostitutes in particular. "His charitable endeavours for reclaiming those unhappy persons met with no small success, and to prevent the increase of their number, he gave fortunes to a great many poor girls, whose circumstances might otherwise have exposed them to temptation."[4]

Having sought to restore virtue and order close to home, Pius set about combating the spread of Protestantism throughout Europe. He supported the Catholics in Germany who were being persecuted by Protestant princes, and he sought to strengthen Catholic resistance to the ideas of Luther and Calvin in Austria, Poland, Prussia, France, and Holland. As for England, Pius locked horns with Elizabeth I, "the cold queen of England", as Chesterton dubbed her in his poem "Lepanto",[5] whom Pius called "the pretended queen of England and the servant of crime",[6] excommunicating her for her relentless war of attrition against the Catholics of her realm.

The crowning achievement of Pius V's papacy was, however, his role in the defeat of the Muslim armada at the Battle of Lepanto in 1571, which would not have been possible without his tireless efforts to form a Holy League to counter the Islamic threat. The Christian victory was a devastating blow for the Ottoman Empire, which lost all but thirty of its ships.

In gratitude for this triumph and the devastating blow that it had dealt to the power of Islam, he instituted the Feast of Our Lady of Victory[7] to celebrate the anniversary of the Battle of Lepanto. He also added to the Litany of

[4] Anonymous, *Lives of the Saints*, 2:240.

[5] G.K. Chesterton, "Lepanto," Poetry Foundation, https://www.poetry foundation.org/poems/47917/lepanto#:~:text=The%20cold%20queen%20 of%20England,is%20laughing%20in%20the%20sun.

[6] St. Pius V, Regnans in Excelsis (February 25, 1570).

[7] Now usually known as the Feast of Our Lady of the Rosary, the Church still celebrates the victory of Lepanto every year on October 7.

Loreto the supplication "Help of Christians" ("Auxilium Christianorum"), in honor of the role that he believed the intercession of the Blessed Virgin had played in bringing victory to the Christian forces.

On May 1, 1572, a few short months after the victory at Lepanto, Pius V died. He would be canonized in 1713, the official recognition that the holy pope who had founded the Holy League had gone to bask in a glory beyond all the victories that this world has to offer.

The crowning glory of the sixteenth century was not, however, the appearance of so many great saints but the appearance of the greatest of all saints. It was the apparition of Our Lady of Guadalupe in Mexico in 1531, only a decade after the conquest of the Aztec Empire by the Spanish conquistador Hernán Cortés, which opened the hearts of the indigenous people of Mexico to the new religion being preached by the Spanish missionaries. It was, therefore, with the miraculous blessing of the Mother of God that these missionaries began to conquer the New World with the light of the Gospel. They could not be in better or safer hands.

The Bad

There were two spirits at work during the European conquest of the Americas. On the one hand, Christian missionaries sought to bring Christ to cultures that practiced the systematic sacrifice of children to pagan gods, liberating the indigenous peoples from their possession by demonic "deities"; on the other hand, the European conquerors, drunk with power and the avaricious quest for gold, were often as barbaric as the people whom they conquered. Most horrific of all the crimes of those who owed their allegiance to the City of Man was the African slave trade. Beginning in around 1500 and continuing for almost four hundred years, it is estimated that more than ten million Africans were transported as slaves to the Americas before the trade in human flesh was finally abolished.

Meanwhile, in Europe, the Protestant rupture was ripping flesh from the Body of Christ. It did so with viciousness and violence in a series of religious wars that was Christendom's civil war. The ideas of Luther led to the German Peasants' War in 1524 and to a war between German Protestant princes and the Holy Roman Empire in 1546. From 1562 until the end of the century, France was torn asunder in its own series of civil wars as Protestants and Catholics struggled for supremacy in the land known as the Oldest Daughter of the Church.

Irrespective of its bitter and bloody fruits, the Protestant Reformation in Europe was at least rooted in theological differences, Luther and Calvin breaking with the Church's traditional teaching. In England, however, the so-called "Reformation" had nothing to do with theological differences and everything to do with the king's determination to have his wicked will obeyed by his unfortunate subjects. Having no grounds to divorce his loyal and pious wife, Henry VIII declared himself head of the Church in England, effectively founding a state religion and using its "authority" to sanction his divorce. Demanding the servile obedience of all the English bishops to the new state religion, all but one kowtowed in recreant submission. The one courageous bishop who refused, the elderly Bishop of Rochester, St. John Fisher, was imprisoned and subsequently executed. Demanding the same servile submission of his political ministers, Henry VIII imprisoned and executed the one minister, St. Thomas More, who had the courage to defy his will.

Having ridden roughshod over the holy sacrament of matrimony, Henry would divorce and remarry at will. Of his six wives, two were beheaded on his orders.

If the Catholic hierarchy in England had shown itself pathetically weak in the face of Henry's threats, the monks and nuns were more resistant to his will. Henry responded by forcibly closing all of England's numerous monasteries, abbeys, and convents, handing over the land and property of the Church to those members of the aristocracy who put avarice ahead of their immortal souls. Henry was as merciless as ever to all those who had the courage of their convictions. To take but one example, Blessed Richard Whiting, the last abbot of Glastonbury Abbey, was seventy-eight years old when he and two other monks were dragged on a hurdle to a hill overlooking the abbey, where they were hanged, disemboweled, beheaded, and quartered. The abbot's head was stuck on a pike above the entrance to the abbey for all to see. His quarters were boiled in pitch and then displayed in the nearby towns.

The people of England rose in anger at the dissolution of the monasteries in an uprising known as the Pilgrimage of Grace. Throughout the sixteenth century, they rose repeatedly in defense of the faith, which was being ripped away from them by Henry VIII and by his successors, Edward VI and Elizabeth I. There were uprisings across the length and breadth of the country when Edward VI banned the Mass, and there was a major uprising, known as the Northern Rebellion, during the reign of Elizabeth.

The fate suffered by Blessed Richard Whiting—hanging, disemboweling, and quartering—would be shared by many other English Martyrs during the Tudor Terror, which reigned in England throughout the century. Especially noteworthy were the courageous Jesuits, such as St. Edmund Campion and St. Robert Southwell, who returned to their native land knowing that such a tortuously slow death awaited them upon their being captured.

Sadly, persecution of the saints was not restricted to the northern parts of Europe. In the Catholic heartland of Spain, the holy reformers St. Teresa of Ávila and St. John of the Cross were being hounded by their lukewarm confreres. In 1577, St. John of the Cross was arrested on the orders of the prior general of the unreformed Carmelites, who was seeking to suppress the reformed Discalced Carmelites, which Teresa of Ávila had founded. Although John and a companion priest did not resist the arrest, they were nonetheless bound and gagged. Later that night, the two friars were severely scourged for being rebellious children of the order they had sought to reform. On the following day, upon hearing of the news of their arrest, Teresa wrote a letter to Philip II, in which she told the king of "the exceedingly great good" that John had done, adding that "people take him for a saint", adding her own judgment that in her opinion he was one.[8]

The enclosed space in which the saint was imprisoned could not really be called a cell but rather a small closet, not quite six feet wide and under ten feet in length. There was no window and no lighting except for that which crept in through a loophole not three inches wide, situated in the wall near the roof. It was light enough to read for only a short time each day when the sun shone in the corridor outside the room. At this time, he read his breviary by standing on a bench and holding the book up under the scanty sunlight peeping through.

Only the friar appointed to be his jailer was allowed to speak to him or see him. Every evening he was led down

---

[8] Fr. Paschasius Heriz, *Saint John of the Cross* (Washington, D.C.: College of Our Lady of Mount Carmel, 1919), 71.

to the refectory, and there, on the floor, he ate his daily portion of bread and water. After he had eaten, the prior berated him in the presence of the other brothers and then had him scourged for his recusancy. Such was the viciousness of these daily beatings that the saint carried the scars of them for the rest of his days. After a while, the prior got tired of this daily routine of brutality, or perhaps (one might dare to hope) he had pangs of conscience about it and lost his cruel appetite. Thereafter, the saint was simply left alone in his cell for days on end, seemingly forgotten and left to rot. He was in this squalid little room for more than eight months, never once being permitted to even change his clothes, which must have been saturated with dried blood and horribly soiled. As if to add spiritual insult to physical injury, he was also deprived of his priestly calling to say Mass and, as we have seen, was able to say his daily Office only with great difficulty. And yet the state of his own soul during this time of trial transcended the physical misery in its flights toward God, a fact all too clearly seen in the wonderful poetry he wrote during these months of dreary and solitary confinement. It was here, in the dark, alone and seemingly forgotten, that he wrote his most famous poem "On a Dark Night" (*En uno noche oscura*) and a thirty-one stanza version of his celebrated "Spiritual Canticle". In the absence of any writing materials, these masterpieces of Christian literature were composed in his head and memorized. Almost four centuries later, the Russian dissident Aleksandr Solzhenitsyn would memorize hundreds of lines of poetry in this way during his years in the Soviet prison system. It is a sobering thought that lukewarm Catholic monks could treat one of their own dissident brethren in the manner that atheistic communists would later treat dissident "comrades". It has always been this way. The enemy within the Church is always as deadly as the enemy without, and perhaps more so.

The Beautiful

If the assault on the Church by the rise of Protestantism had led to the Tridentine Reformation and a golden age of reforming and missionary saints, it would have no real impact on the golden age of religious art that had begun in the previous century.

At the beginning of the century, prior to Luther's launching of the Protestant assault, Pope Julius II commissioned Raphael to paint some of the greatest masterpieces of all time, including *The School of Athens*, the *Disputation of the Holy Sacrament*, and *The Miracle of Bolsena*. The first of these three frescos celebrates the Church's embrace of classical philosophy and the union of faith and reason that it represents; the other two celebrate the Church's teaching on the Eucharist, which would soon be under attack from the Protestants.

Having commissioned work by Raphael, Pope Julius II then commissioned Michelangelo to paint the ceiling of the recently constructed Sistine Chapel. Perhaps there is little or nothing that can be said about the sheer brilliance of Michelangelo's multifaceted fresco, or perhaps there is so much to say that it is difficult to know where to start. In any event, we will do what most people do when visiting the chapel. We will point, gaze in wonder, remain in awe-struck silence for a few moments, and then move on.

In 1512, at around the time that Michelangelo was finishing his work on the Sistine Chapel, the German artist Matthias Grünewald began painting the Crucifixion for the Isenheim altarpiece. It would be finished in 1516, only a year before the Lutheran rupture. Its gruesome depiction of the dying Christ, whose fingers curl convulsively in excruciating agony, serves as a prophesy of the impending ripping of the Body of Christ by the spread of heresy.

Perhaps the greatest artist of the late sixteenth century, and certainly the most innovative, was El Greco. In paintings such as the *Assumption of the Virgin* and the *Burial of Count Orgaz*, he abandoned the solidity of Raphaelesque perspective, which drew the viewer into the physical depths of the work, in favor of a spiritual perspective that drew the viewer vertically toward the spiritually ecstatic and contemplative, emphasizing the ethereal over the material. In the *Assumption of the Virgin*, the astonished apostles at the bottom of the painting gaze upward to the ascending Virgin, the vertical orientation of the composition seeming to take the viewer with the Virgin to the heavens, to which she is bound. In the *Burial of Count Orgaz*, the figures in the bottom half are seemingly less substantial than the vision of the Church Triumphant that fills the top half of the canvas. It is as though the mourners at the count's funeral are living in a shadow reality, whereas the count is about to be lifted into the very Presence of Reality Himself, the whole composition pointing toward Christ Triumphant at its apex.

In architecture, the building of St. Basil's Cathedral in Moscow signified the rise of Russia as a new center of Eastern Christianity in the wake of the fall of Constantinople a century earlier. In music, the sixteenth century marked the golden age of polyphony. Giovanni Pierluigi da Palestrina and Tomás Luis de Victoria were the leading composers of liturgical music in Rome. St. John Paul II said of Palestrina: "It would seem that, after a troubled period, the Church regained [in Palestrina] a voice made peaceful through contemplation of the Eucharistic mystery, like the calm breathing of a soul that knows it is loved by God."[9] As for Victoria, his music has been likened in its mystical fervor to the paintings of El Greco, his contemporary.[10]

Ironically, two of the greatest composers of the sixteenth century were Thomas Tallis and William Byrd, both of whom were Catholics living in the very anti-Catholic political climate of Elizabethan England. Even as Elizabeth was putting Catholics to death, she was happy to turn a tolerant blind eye toward the faith of Tallis and Byrd, even showing them considerable favor. In 1588, William Byrd set to music a poem by Henry Walpole that eulogized the Jesuit martyr St. Edmund Campion, who had been exe-cuted seven years earlier. In 1592, he began composing three settings of the Mass, even though the celebration of the Catholic liturgy was illegal in England.

In literature, the century was blessed with two great poets who also became saints. The first was St. John of the Cross, whose poetry we have already mentioned; the second was St. Robert Southwell, an English Jesuit mar-tyred in 1595 whose holy example and fine poetry would prove to be influential on his contemporary William Shakespeare, whom he almost certainly knew. His work would also influence other poets. According to literary scholar Gary Bouchard, "Southwell's works ... provoked Edmund Spenser, prompted George Herbert, haunted John Donne, inspired Richard Crashaw and—two and a half centuries later—consoled Gerard Manley Hopkins."[11] As for Shakespeare himself, he was clearly a believing

[9] Address to the Plenary Assembly of the Pontifical Council for Culture, March 18, 1994, quoted in Susan Treacy, *The Music of Christendom: A History* (San Francisco: Ignatius Press, 2021), 64.

[10] Treacy, *Music of Christendom*, 67.

[11] Gary Bouchard, *Southwell's Sphere: The Influence of England's Secret Poet* (South Bend, Ind.: St. Augustine's Press, 2018), backcover copy.

Catholic whose faith was a formative and pervasive influence on his work.[12] Since, however, most of his greatest plays were written in the first decade of the seventeenth century, we will defer further discussion of his place in the history of Christendom until the next chapter.

[12] There are numerous works showing the evidence for Shakespeare's Catholicism, the discussion of which is beyond the scope of this book. See especially two books by Joseph Pearce: *The Quest for Shakespeare: The Bard of Avon and the Church of Rome* (San Francisco: Ignatius Press, 2008) and *Through Shakespeare's Eyes: Seeing the Catholic Presence in the Plays* (San Francisco: Ignatius Press, 2010). The former book offers a five-page bibliography of other books on the topic.

Seventeenth Century

Old and New

The Good

Many of the greatest saints of the seventeenth century came from France, the oldest if not always the most virtuous daughter of the Church.

St. Francis de Sales became Bishop of Geneva in 1602, having gained a reputation in the previous decade for his fearlessness in preaching orthodoxy in the Calvinist heartland of the Chablais country, winning many converts from heresy. He was celebrated for the lucidity and eloquence of his teaching and preaching, and for spiritual direction. His greatest achievement, however, at least in terms of his enduring influence, is the fruit of his pen. It is as the author of ever-popular spiritual classics such as the *Introduction to the Devout Life* and his *Treatise on the Love of God* for which he is most remembered. He died in 1622, was canonized in 1665, declared a Doctor of the Church in 1877, and was named patron saint of writers in 1923.

St. Jeanne de Chantal had St. Francis de Sales as her spiritual director, and it was with him that she founded the Order of the Visitation in 1610. She was described by St. Vincent de Paul as "one of the holiest souls I ever met".[1]

---

[1] David Hugh Farmer, *The Oxford Dictionary of Saints* (Oxford: Oxford University Press, 1987), 96.

As for St. Vincent de Paul himself, he was assuredly one of the holiest souls of the seventeenth century, working tirelessly and ceaselessly for the poor. Along with St. Louise de Marillac, he founded the Sisters of Charity, the first uncloistered female religious order, which enabled the sisters of the order to live and work among the poor and the sick to whom they were ministering.

Another religious order founded at this time were the Order of Reformed Cistercians of Our Lady of La Trappe, now popularly known as the Trappists. As with the reform of the Carmelite Order in the previous century by St. Teresa of Ávila and St. John of the Cross, the Trappist reform of the Cistercians involved a more rigorously demanding life of prayer and penance, which is why they later became known as Cistercians of the Strict Observance.

These new religious orders, taken together with the charism of saints, such as Francis de Sales and Vincent de Paul, were a reflection of popular Catholic piety. The Church historian Alfred Lapple wrote of "an upsurge in religious life, with the practice of eucharistic adoration, devotions to the Child Jesus, the Sacred Heart, and Mary [and] the nuptial mysticism practiced in many convents".[2] Popular devotion to the Sacred Heart of Jesus and to the Holy Heart of Mary was spearheaded by St. John Eudes, who wrote the devotions for the Mass and the Office for the Feast of the Holy Heart of Mary, which was first celebrated in 1648, and for the Feast of the Sacred Heart of Jesus, which was first celebrated in 1672. He was also a great evangelizer, preaching more than a hundred missions all over his native France, as well as working for the poor and sick and founding a refuge for fallen women.

[2] Alfred Lapple, *The Catholic Church: A Brief History* (New York: Paulist Press, 1982), 70.

Devotion to the Sacred Heart was also nourished by the mystical visions received by St. Margaret Mary Alocoque, a nun of the Visitation Order. In these visions, Our Lord revealed to her that the great love of His Heart for humanity was unrequited and was met with a cold indifference. Inspired by these visions, she promoted the Feast of the Sacred Heart and the First Friday devotion, which is still widely practiced today.

The seventeenth century was graced by one really great pope, Blessed Innocent XI, who made it his first business to "clean house" within the Vatican itself. Inheriting a debt of fifty million scudi upon his election in 1676, he greatly reduced papal expenditure, streamlined the Curia by abolishing unnecessary honorary posts, and introduced an array of economic measures aimed at keeping the Vatican on a firm financial footing. In so doing, he not only balanced the books but began to build a financial reserve. In addition, he helped to unite the Holy Roman Emperor and the king of Poland in a military alliance against the invading Turks, which would prove successful in lifting the Turkish Siege of Vienna in 1683. Following this defeat, the Turks were forced into wholesale retreat from most of Europe. In this sense, like St. Pius V in the previous century, Innocent XI could be said to have saved Europe from Islam.

It is also noteworthy that Pope Innocent expressed strong disapproval of religious persecution, condemning Louis XIV's treatment of the Huguenots, and strongly promoted Catholic missionary activity around the world. It is to these Catholic missions, especially those in the Americas, that we now turn our attention.

Pope Gregory XV had established the Sacred Congregation of the Propagation of the Faith in 1622 to promote and oversee Catholic missionary activity in the Americas and elsewhere. These missions often helped to allay the suffering of the indigenous peoples and the transported slaves at the hands of merciless and avaricious Europeans. One noble example of such selfless missionary activity is provided by St. Peter Claver, a Spanish Jesuit who devoted his life to helping African slaves. Arriving at Cartagena in what is now Colombia in 1610, he was horrified at the conditions in which he found the slaves who had been transported from Angola and other parts of western Africa. At this time, thousands of slaves were arriving at the port city of Cartagena every year. Following his own arrival, Peter Claver began helping an elderly priest, Fr. Alfonso de Sandoval, who had already spent forty years ministering to arriving slaves. Emulating his tireless predecessor, Fr. Claver would himself minister to the slaves for the next forty years until an illness in 1650 left him paralyzed. He died four years later. Throughout his life, he had served the African slaves, ministering to their material as well as their spiritual needs and emphasizing their inherent human dignity as children of God who were made in God's image. Seeking to put himself at the service of the poorest of the poor, he called himself "the slave of the Negroes for ever".[3]

Further south, in Lima, St. Martin de Porres worked among the poor of the city, establishing an orphanage and a children's hospital. He was no stranger to poverty himself, having been raised by his mixed-race mother, a freed slave of African and indigenous descent. His father, a Spanish nobleman, abandoned his mother when Martin was only two years old. Becoming a lay brother of the Dominican Order, his life of sanctity was widely acknowledged at the time of his death in 1639 and would be recognized by

---

[3] Farmer, *Oxford Dictionary of Saints*, 102.

the Church with his canonization in 1962. Much earlier, in 1671, another native of Peru would be the first person born in the Americas to be canonized. This was St. Rose of Lima, who lived a life of penance serving the poor until her early death, at the age of thirty-one, in 1617.

Even as Jesuits, such as St. Peter Claver, were ministering to the indigenous people and the slaves in the Spanish and Portuguese colonies in the southern parts of the New World, other Jesuits were spreading the Gospel in the French colonies in the northernmost parts of the continent. These Jesuits helped to bring the Huron, Algonquin, and Iroquois peoples to Christ, with eight of their number being tortured and brutally martyred by the Iroquois between 1642 and 1649. Martyrdom on a much larger scale was inflicted upon the Catholics of Japan during the years of intense persecution between 1617 and 1632 with more than two hundred being glorified with the laying down of their lives for Christ.

We will leave our survey of all that was best in the seventeenth century with a few words about St. Kateri Tekakwitha. Born in 1656, she was the daughter of a pagan Mohawk chief and an Algonquian Christian mother, both of whom died in a smallpox epidemic when she was young. Raised by her uncle in the village of Ossernenon in what is now upstate New York, she was drawn to the piety and teaching of the Jesuit missionaries and was baptized in 1676. Seeking to avoid an arranged marriage, she fled her home village and settled in a Jesuit mission near Montreal. Her subsequent life of penitential suffering might seem excessive to many comfort-seeking modern readers, but historian Christopher Shannon has no doubt that such asceticism served as a powerful witness to others and was exemplified by the willingness of the Jesuit missionaries to suffer and die for Christ: "The Jesuits' ability to endure pain spoke more eloquently to a warrior culture than any sermons they could possibly have preached."[4] St. Kateri died in the Holy Week of 1680 at the tender age of twenty-four. Yet, in spite of her very short life, the impact she had on her contemporaries was immense. Her eighteenth-century Jesuit biographer wrote that her heroic sanctity was evident in "the unalterable gentleness, patience, [and] joy" with which she endured her final illness and that the "example of her most holy life ... produced a very great fervor among the Iroquois of Sault St. Louis," who soon "had recourse to her intercession".[5] Her tomb became a shrine, a place of pilgrimage, with reports of miracles being granted after prayers for her intercession. By the middle of the following century, she was popularly perceived as "the protectress of Canada", though it would not be until 2012 that she would be canonized.

The Bad

Even as courageous missionaries and zealous converts were bringing the faith to the New World, the Old World was ripping itself asunder with war and heresy. The Thirty Years' War, which raged from 1618 to 1648 and involved many of the nations of Europe, would cause utter devastation, altering the political map of Europe forever. If there could be said to be a victor, it was France, with the biggest losers being the Germanies and the Holy Roman Empire. It might be said, therefore, that the seventeenth century was one in which the French dominated, both in terms of the City of God and the City of Man, the former in the

[4] Christopher Shannon, *American Pilgrimage: A Historical Journey through Catholic Life in a New World* (San Francisco: Ignatius Press, 2022), 126.

[5] Quoted in ibid., 126.

many French saints who brought the peace of Christ to the world, and the latter in the Machiavellian realpolitik that the French had employed in the Thirty Years' War, ironically under the cynical political leadership of a prince of the Church, Cardinal Richelieu.

France was also the center of some of the worst heresies being spread at the time, especially Jansenism and Gallicanism.

Jansenism was named after Cornelius Jansen, the Bishop of Ypres in Flanders who emphasized the complete corruption of human nature by Original Sin in terms that sounded more like the heresy of Calvin than the orthodoxy of a Catholic bishop. Indeed, the Church historian Philip Hughes described Jansenism's "heretical theory about grace" as "a kind of 'calvinized' Catholicism".[6]

Although Bishop Jansen died in 1638, his ideas continued to grow in influence, especially in France, so that Pope Innocent X felt constrained in 1653 to condemn several of the theological propositions of his writings. Jansen's supporters in France defied the pope and denied that their ideas were wrong. The stand-off escalated in 1664, when Innocent's successor, Pope Alexander VII, reiterated the papal condemnation of Jansenism. Four French bishops strongly resisted papal teaching, affirming their recalcitrant commitment to Jansenist theology. Matters got worse when the next pope, Clement IX, endeavored to bring the four Jansenist bishops in line with Church teaching. This time, no fewer than nineteen French bishops protested against the pope's interference and made a public declaration, no doubt under the watchful and perhaps threatening eye of the pro-Jansenist king, that any action against their four heretical colleagues would be "harmful to the interests of

---

[6] Philip Hughes, *A Popular History of the Catholic Church* (New York: Macmillan, 1962), 210.

the State".[7] This subservience of the French hierarchy to "the interests of the State", even to the point of defying or denying the authentic doctrinal teaching of the Church, was an example of the other heresy afflicting France at the time. This was Gallicanism, which called for the creation of a French national "Catholic" church in which the pope would be stripped of all meaningful authority. Needless to say, the real motive force behind Gallicanism was King Louis XIV, who was seeking absolute authority over his realm without the interference or tempering influence of the Church. It was only the courage of Blessed Innocent XI, the century's greatest pope, as we have seen, that caused King Louis to compromise his Gallicanism in order to seek an acceptable rapprochement with the Church.

A much more subtle heresy came in the form of the philosophy of another Frenchman, René Descartes, whose philosophical works, published between 1637 and 1649, rejected the Aristotelian-Thomistic foundations of philosophical realism, replacing them with the fallacious foundations of essentially egocentric relativism. His influence would be so great that the German philosopher Georg Wilhelm Friedrich Hegel would describe him as "the father of modern philosophy".[8]

Having spent much time discussing the importance of France during the seventeenth century, let us cross the Channel to England, where the anti-Catholic tyranny instituted by the Tudors in the previous century continued unabated under the Stuarts.

Elizabeth I, the last of the Tudors, died in 1603, bringing to an end the lamentable dynasty. Upon the queen's

[7] Ibid., 215.

[8] G. Vesey and P. Foulkes, eds., *Collins Dictionary of Philosophy* (London: HarperCollins, 1990), 84.

death, James VI of Scotland became James I of England, promising to bring an end to the persecution of England's Catholics. Facing opposition from the increasingly puritan Parliament, James reneged on his promise and reinstated all the anti-Catholic laws. Ironically, his failure to stand up to Parliament would lead to the violent death of his own son at Parliament's hands, Charles I being beheaded in 1649 after the Parliamentary forces had defeated their Royalist adversaries in the English Civil War. As in the previous century, when the Catholic Mary Tudor had become queen for a few brief years, the Catholics enjoyed a brief respite from persecution when James II, a Catholic, became king in 1685. Three years later, his enemies paid for an army of foreign mercenaries to invade their own country to depose the rightful ruler. It is grimly and perversely ironic that this act of gross treachery is called the "Glorious Revolution" by Protestant historians.

The treachery of England's rulers ensured that Catholic priests and laity would continue to be martyred throughout the seventeenth century. We will offer just two examples of the many that could be given. At the beginning of the century, on February 26, 1601, St. Anne Line, a convert to the faith, was hanged for the heinous crime of sheltering Catholic priests from the authorities. She had been arrested when priest hunters had raided her apartments in London during the celebration of Mass. The Jesuit who had been celebrating the Mass managed to remove his vestments in time and had escaped by mingling into the congregation. Standing trial for hiding priests, Mrs. Line remained heroically defiant to the last, declaring that "would God that where I had harboured one, I had harboured a thousand".[9]

---

[9] Martin Dodwell, *Anne Line: Shakespeare's Tragic Muse* (Sussex, England: Book Guild Publishing, 2013), 112.

Almost eighty years after the martyrdom of Anne Line in London, an elderly Catholic priest, Blessed Nicholas Postgate, was martyred at the other end of the country in York, having served the Catholics of the Yorkshire moors secretly and faithfully for almost fifty years. He was certainly in his late seventies and perhaps in his early eighties when he suffered the customary gruesome execution by hanging, disemboweling, and quartering.

Truly, St. Anne Line and Blessed Nicholas Postgate have their reward, and so presumably do those who hunted them down and put them to death.

The Beautiful

The seventeenth century began in a blaze of literary glory. In England, William Shakespeare was writing his greatest plays, while in Spain, Miguel de Cervantes was writing one of the greatest novels ever to be written.

Although Shakespeare had graced the London theaters in the 1590s with plays such as *Julius Caesar*, *Romeo and Juliet*, and *The Merchant of Venice*, his greatest works would not be written and performed until the first decade of the seventeenth century. As a Catholic living in very anti-Catholic times, his tragedies reflect the darkness of the age. *Hamlet* is set in a world of spies who are at the service of a malevolent monarch; *Othello* depicts a diabolical Machiavellian villain who uses the weakness of others to bring about their downfall; *Macbeth* depicts a man who becomes a treacherous murderer to fulfill his worldly ambition; *King Lear* shows a monarch who demands absolute loyalty from his subjects but discovers that the sycophants betray him, whereas the recusants, those who refuse to obey his unjust decrees, are those who truly love him. These plays are timeless in their presentation of unchanging morality and philosophical verity, but they were also timely, holding up a mirror to the wickedness of the world in which the playwright lived. Thus, the famous graveyard scene in *Hamlet* connects closely and intertextually with St. Robert Southwell's poem "Upon the Image of Death", and Southwell's poetry is also present allusively in other Shakespeare plays, particularly *The Merchant of Venice* and *King Lear*. It is also, surely, no coincidence that the two plays that Shakespeare wrote immediately after King James had broken his promise to England's Catholics that he would end religious persecution were *Othello* and *Macbeth*, the former presenting a Machiavellian monster named Iago (i.e., James), and the latter telling of a wicked Scottish king.

Apart from Shakespeare, seventeenth-century England produced many other great writers, making this period something of a golden age of English literature. It was the age of the Metaphysical poets, of which John Donne, George Herbert, and Richard Crashaw were preeminent, the last of whom wrote two masterful poems in praise of St. Teresa of Ávila, and died in exile following his conversion to Catholicism. It was also the age of Bunyan, Milton, and Dryden, the last of whom, following his conversion to Catholicism, wrote a brilliant satire of the religious situation in England called "The Hind and the Panther".

In Spain, Cervantes' *Don Quixote* was the progenitor of the novel as a literary genre. It is one of the best novels ever written and also probably the bestselling novel of all time. The two great playwrights of the Spanish Golden Age were Lope de Vega and Pedro Calderón de la Barca, the latter of whom was trained by the Jesuits, who were at the forefront of the dramatic arts in Europe at the time. Molière, the great French playwright of the period, was also Jesuit-trained. Blaise Pascal, the greatest of the French

Jansenists, is also one of the finest prose stylists in French literature, as is evident in his justly celebrated *Pensées*.

In music, Monteverdi was the giant of the century. His *L'Orfeo*, which was premiered in 1607, was praised by music historian Susan Treacy as "the first truly great opera".[10] One of the hallmarks of French music at the time was the court ballet. Louis XIV was such an aficionado of ballet that he danced frequently in court productions of Molière's *comédie-ballets*.

The century brought forth a host of great artists, most especially Caravaggio, Rubens, Velazquez, and Rembrandt. Although Caravaggio and Velazquez were born into the deeply Catholic cultures of Italy and Spain, whereas Rubens and Rembrandt were raised in the religiously ruptured Netherlands, the breathtaking beauty of the work of these maestros transcends the religious differences and political divisions of their age. It shows that beauty is a salve for the soul, irrespective of whether it can save the world.

One final giant needs to be lauded. This is Gian Lorenzo Bernini, a sculptor who has no peer except for Michelangelo and whose *Ecstasy of Saint Teresa* has no equal other than Michelangelo's *Pietà*. His importance and status was encapsulated by art historian Katharine Eustace: "What Shakespeare is to drama, Bernini may be to sculpture: the first pan-European sculptor whose name is instantaneously identifiable with a particular manner and vision, and whose influence was inordinately powerful."[11] Bernini worked as both an architect and a sculptor on the final stages of the building of St. Peter's Basilica in

[10] Susan Treacy, *The Music of Christendom: A History* (San Francisco: Ignatius Press, 2021), 79.

[11] Katharine Eustace, Editorial, *Sculpture Journal* 20, no. 2 (2011): 109.

Rome, adding the finishing touches to one of the wonders of the world.

There would seem to be no better place to end our discussion of the seventeenth century than in the newly finished St. Peter's. In a century in which a new world was opening for the spread of the Gospel and in which the old world was ripping itself asunder with war and heresy, we find ourselves in the presence of the Vicar of Christ in the Eternal City. Beyond all that is merely old and all that is merely new is that which simply is. Christ is. He is the Alpha and the Omega. The Church is His Mystical Body. Like her Founder, she sees the old and perceives the new from the perspective of the ever ancient and ever new.

Eighteenth Century

Religion and Superstition

The Good

In common with every other century in the Church's heroic history, the eighteenth century had its fair share of saints. It says something about this particular century, however, that the saints of the first half of the century died in their beds whereas many of those in the latter half of the century died as martyrs.

St. Louis de Montfort was ordained in 1700, at the dawn of the century itself, and would make a profound impact in the short time allotted to him. At his untimely death in 1716, his missionary zeal had touched numerous people, especially in the Vendée region of France. He is best known to posterity for his spiritual writing, especially *True Devotion to Mary*, *The Secret of Mary*, and *The Secret of the Rosary*, all of which remain enduringly popular, and for his advocacy of total consecration to Jesus through Mary.

St. Paul of the Cross was a mystic who lived a life of penance and prayer, united to the suffering of Christ on the Cross. In 1720, he founded a religious order, the Congregation of the Passion of Jesus Christ, now commonly known as the Passionists. By the time of his death in 1775, there were 180 fathers and brothers of the Passionist Order in twelve monasteries.

Perhaps the greatest evangelist of the time was St. Alphonsus Liguori, who founded the Congregation of the Most Holy Redeemer, more commonly known as the Redemptorists, in 1732. The mission of both the saint and the religious order he founded was the preaching of missions. From 1745, after twenty years as a missionary to the poor peasantry of Italy, St. Alphonsus began to write. Thereafter, his literary output was prodigious. His nine-volume *Moral Theology* has been so influential that he was named a Doctor of the Church and the Prince of Moral Theologians. In addition to works of such scholarly gravitas, he wrote works of popular devotion, most notably his *Way of the Cross*, which is still used by many people and parishes around the world as part of their Lenten devotions. A man of multifarious talents, he was a gifted poet and musician who composed many hymns. Last but not least, he was a tireless and effective Catholic apologist whose wisdom and knowledge helped to defeat the harmful influence of Jansenism within the Church and the wider culture.

A missionary of a different sort was the Franciscan, St. Junipero Serra, who established missions in Mexico between 1750 and 1760 before blazing a pioneer trail in what is now California, founding missions from San Diego to San Francisco. On the other side of what is now the United States, the intolerant bigotry of the Puritan ascendancy resulted in widespread persecution of the Catholic minority. The plight of Catholics in Maryland was encapsulated by Fr. Peter Guilday in his biography of John Carroll, the first Catholic bishop of the United States:

Nothing more noble in American life can be found than the determination of the Catholic parents of Maryland to preserve amongst their children the Faith for which their ancestors had fought, suffered, and died. The transmission of the doctrines and the discipline of the Church was a sacred obligation imposed upon them by their conscience; and at a time when to apostatize from the Catholic Faith was the open road to social and political advancement in the English dominions, there was a strength of purpose in the hearts of these Maryland mothers comparable in every respect to the mothers of the martyrs.[1]

John Carroll's cousin, Charles Carroll of Carrollton, returned to the United States in 1765 after a period of study in Europe, to find himself a second-class citizen in his own country:

> It must be realized that, in spite of his wealth, education and culture, in spite of the social standing of which the anti-Catholic laws of Maryland could not rob him, Charles Carroll of Carrollton ... returned a disenfranchised citizen, with no voice in the political affairs of the province.... He was denied the public exercise of his religion, and was forced by these same laws to pay a double tax for the support of a clergy that could never be his own.[2]

Fighting fearlessly for his civil rights and those of his fellow Catholics, Charles Carroll became embroiled in 1773 in a public debate, known as the Carroll-Dulany controversy, in which he not only won the argument but also the hearts of his fellow Marylanders, Catholic and Protestant alike. Within three years he had risen to such political prominence that he was among those chosen to be signatories of the Declaration of Independence, the only Catholic to be so honored.

[1] Peter Guilday, *The Life and Times of John Carroll, Archbishop of Baltimore (1735–1815)* (New York: Encyclopedia Press, 1922), 1:15.

[2] Peter Guilday, "Charles Carroll of Carrollton", in *Great Catholics*, ed. Claude Williamson, O.S.C. (London: Nicholson and Watson, 1938), 318–19.

The Bad

Leaving the New World in the midst of the birth pangs that would lead to the founding of the United States, we will return to the Old World and to the Holy Roman Empire, which had been at the broken heart of Europe, for better or worse, for almost a thousand years.

Following the death in 1740 of the Holy Roman Emperor and king of Austria, Charles VI, his twenty-three-year-old daughter, Maria Theresa, became empress and queen. She inherited a bankrupt treasury and a poorly equipped army, a perilous combination in the politically turbulent times in which she found herself. France, Prussia, and Bavaria viewed the death of the emperor and the accession of the young and inexperienced empress as an opportune time to curtail the Holy Roman Empire's power. They were thwarted in these designs by an alliance of nations, which came to the empress' aid. These were Britain, the Dutch Republic, and Hanover. Other countries soon became involved, including Spain, Sweden, and Russia. With Britain and France at war, the conflict became global. British and French forces fought each other in what is now New York, New England, and Nova Scotia and also on the Indian subcontinent, whereas British and Spanish forces fought each other in the Caribbean. In this sense, the War of the Austrian Succession has a claim to being the first "world war", almost two centuries before the conflict of 1914–1918 laid claim to the name.

By the war's end, after eight years of military struggle, an estimated 450,000 combatants had been killed. One consequence of the Treaty of Aix-la-Chapelle in 1748 was the confirmation of Maria Theresa in her titles. With her succession finally secured, Empress Maria Theresa ruled as one who was led by her devoutly Christian conscience as a monarch who saw herself as a servant of her subjects.

As historian Carlton Hayes has written of Maria Theresa, "Love of her subjects was not a theory with her—it was a religious duty."[3] As with the reign of that other devoutly Catholic queen, Mary Tudor, two centuries earlier, a good heart did not necessarily lead to good government. During her long reign, Maria Theresa reduced the taxes and established schools for the poor and began the emancipation of the serfs. Yet, as with Mary Tudor before her, she was overzealous and overreaching in her efforts to fight sin and error, enacting policies that were often draconian and tainted with cruelty.

Irrespective of her failings as a secular ruler, Maria Theresa would prove to be a dedicated wife and the mother of no fewer than sixteen children. Of these, it is her fifteenth child, Marie Antoinette, who is best known to posterity. By the time of her mother's death in 1780, Marie Antoinette would be queen of France and would be destined to fall foul of the first great atheist and proto-communist revolution, which would descend on Europe like a storm cloud and portent of doom in 1789.

Before we turn our attention to the French Revolution, we will look at the so-called "Enlightenment", which laid the revolutionary foundations of atheist tyranny. We will begin by offering the Enlightenment's supercilious view of itself as encapsulated by the authors of the *Smithsonian History Year by Year*:

During the 18th century, people began to cast aside their old beliefs based on religion and superstition, and started to reason for themselves. Scientists and philosophers across

---

[3] Carlton Hayes, *A Political and Social History of Modern Europe* (New York: Macmillan, 1916), quoted in Diane Moczar, *The Church under Attack: Five Hundred Years That Split the Church and Scattered the Flock* (Manchester, N.H.: Sophia Institute Press, 2013), 82.

Europe dared to think differently and their new ideas influenced politics, economics, and science. This exciting movement became known as the Enlightenment or the Age of Reason.[4]

The sheer arrogance and chronological snobbery of this "enlightened" view of history speaks for itself. Religion and superstition are juxtaposed as synonyms; people had never reasoned for themselves before the eighteenth century; Socrates, Plato, Aristotle, Augustine, Aquinas, and all other preenlightened philosophers could not reason for themselves because they were shackled by religion and superstition. It is only those scientists and philosophers who dared to break with the living tradition and the great conversation of intellectual history who were "enlightened"; the past was anathema. There was no age of reason until the eighteenth century. The past could be dismissed as irrelevant to the "new ideas" or even as the enemy of these ideas. The Enlightenment had nothing to learn from its elders. It had nothing to learn from the collective experience of humanity over two millennia. Like ignorant and arrogant cads, the children of the Enlightenment had contemptuously kicked down the very ladder by which they had climbed.

The stepping stone from Christian faith to atheistic unbelief was the philosophy of deism, which held that God was unknown and unknowable. John Locke had pioneered deism in the previous century, and it was Immanuel Kant who raised the philosophical flag of deism in the years immediately prior to the French Revolution.

France was by this time ripe for revolution. Deist and atheist intellectuals, such as Denis Diderot, Jean Le Rond

[4] Peter Chrisp, Joe Fullman, and Susan Kennedy, *Smithsonian History Year by Year* (New York: DK Publishing, 2019), 187.

D'Alembert, and Jean-Jacques Rousseau, were at the forefront of the cynical attack on Christian faith, as was Voltaire, one of the most brilliant men of the century. "When
we have destroyed the Jesuits," wrote Voltaire in 1761,
"we shall have easy work with the Infamy."[5] For Voltaire, "the Infamy" was the Church and the destruction of
the Jesuits a necessary prerequisite for the destruction or at
least the taming of the Church.

Voltaire was not by any means alone in his belief that
the power of the Jesuits needed to be defeated as a means
of defeating the power of the Church.

In 1770, the Society of Jesus numbered twenty-three
thousand members who were spread not merely across
Europe but also in 273 mission stations around the world.
Its other-worldly and "unenlightened" power was a threat
to secular rulers everywhere. Three years later, Pope Clement XIV, kowtowing to pressure from the "enlightened"
tyrants ruling in Spain, Portugal, and France, suppressed
the Jesuits. The papal decree was proof, if such were
needed, that the papacy was now dancing marionette-like
to the secular tune. It was ironic indeed that the pope's
greatest defenders should be betrayed by the pope himself.

Apart from the traditional theological and philosophical
stand that the Jesuits were taking against the philosophy of
the Enlightenment, they were also despised by the colo-
nial powers for their political "interference" in the New
World, especially in their establishment of Catholic vil-
lages for the indigenous peoples of South America.

The suppression of the Jesuit Order led to the closing
of six hundred religious houses, hundreds of schools, and
the dispersion of more than twenty thousand Jesuit priests

---

[5] Quoted in Philip Hughes, *A Popular History of the Catholic Church* (New
York: Macmillan, 1962), 224.

and brothers. The most powerful and effective religious order in the world, which had been at the vanguard of the Church Militant's response to the Protestant rupture and was in the forefront of Catholic missionary efforts around the world, had been killed at the insistence of the world's most powerful secular rulers and on the orders of the pope to whom, ironically, the Jesuits had sworn allegiance. Seldom in the long and convoluted history of Christendom had such ignominy been enacted.

Evidently, a church that was too weak to defend the Jesuits was not going to be strong enough to defend itself. Throughout Europe, secular rulers threw off the shackles of "religion and superstition" and began to "reason for themselves" unimpeded by antiquated notions of morality. Joseph II, eldest son of Maria Theresa, became emperor in 1764 and immediately began to make the Church a tool of his government. In one edict after another, he strengthened his position as supreme governor of the Church. Bishops were forbidden to receive or take account of papal decrees without first seeking the permission of the emperor himself. They were forbidden to communicate with Rome and forbidden to issue pastoral letters until the imperial censor had approved them. Religious orders of contemplative monks or nuns were deemed "useless" and were suppressed.

The state was to decide which clerics were to be promoted to higher office, and all priests were to be trained in new state-run seminaries. Those chosen to run the seminaries were the most liberal and "enlightened", many of them Freemasons. The emperor also imposed his imperial will on the practice of the liturgy. He decided how many candles could be lit on the altar for Mass, which prayers were to be used, and which hymns were to be sung. Only one Mass was permitted daily in each church, and this must be said at the High Altar; all side altars were to be removed. The breviary was censored, and certain liturgical feasts were banned. Sermons on Christian doctrine were forbidden, as were Marian devotions, such as the Litany of Loreto and the Rosary. Nor was adoration of the Blessed Sacrament spared. According to imperial decree, the monstrance must not be used for exposition of the Blessed Sacrament.

Joseph II's example was followed by other countries, including Spain and Germany, which also passed laws designed to bring the Church under the governance of the state. Thus was the unity of Christendom being shattered by the rise of secularist nationalism; thus was "enlightened" monarchy as much an enemy of the Church as the "enlightened" republicanism that would inspire and unleash the French Revolution. Indeed, one French historian even quipped that "God now saved the Church by sending the French Revolution to destroy princely absolutism."[6]

The revolution erupted in 1789 and would then simmer and fester until finally boiling over into the Reign of Terror, the culmination of the cult of enlightened "reason" that the revolutionaries idolized. After the king finally resolved to take a stand, vetoing the revolutionary Assembly's passing of laws to persecute the priesthood, he was overthrown. The mob stormed the palace at Versailles, and the king and his family were taken prisoner. In 1792, the king was stripped of all his rights, and, in the following year, he and his queen, Marie Antoinette, would be guillotined in front of the jeering and cheering mob.

The spirit of the French Revolution was encapsulated brilliantly by Church historian H. W. Crocker:

[6] Quoted in ibid., 232.

The state had its own church. It began with priests whose vestments included the tricolor of the Revolution. It moved on to a cult of Reason, and Reason's altar replaced Christ's at the cathedral of Notre Dame. The state also endorsed a cult of Nature ... and of course a cult of the State. Heroes of the Revolution replaced the saints of the Church. In all this, the French Revolution presaged the state religions of Nazism and Communism, and, indeed, in its mass murders, nationalist uniformity, militarism, and lootings in the name of the state and of equality, it embodied the same principles. But the Revolution also hearkened back to the Reformation. The revolutionaries congratulated themselves as if they were Protestant reformers, "wiping out eighteen centuries of error" by abolishing the Catholic Church.... Churches were stripped and religious art desecrated in the Protestant fashion.[7]

And yet, for all its irrational worship of "reason", its enlightened debauchery, and its murderous barbarism, the Reign of Terror also opened the gates of heaven to thousands of heroic martyrs who laid down their lives for their friends in Christ. Thousands of priests who chose death over exile were killed, and the holy Carmelite nuns of Compiègne went singing to the guillotine, assured of the heaven-haven of the reward that awaits all those who are martyred for Christ. As for the laity, the people of the Vendée region in the west of France rose against the atheism of the revolution, fighting for freedom and the faith under the banner of "Dieu le Roi" (God the King). After mounting heroic resistance, seldom surpassed in human history, the Vendée rising was put down with ruthless and merciless cruelty, resulting in the deaths of possibly a quarter of a million men, women, and children.

[7] H. W. Crocker III, *Triumph: The Power and the Glory of the Catholic Church* (New York: Three Rivers Press, 2001), 347.

Ironically, the French Revolution consumed itself in its own blood, the revolutionaries putting each other to death in a diabolical debauch as the Reign of Terror reached its tragicomic climax. In 1799, the imposition of a military dictatorship under Napoleon put an end to the decaying remnant of the revolution and sowed the seeds of a new Europe-wide war. In the same year, Pope Pius VI died as a prisoner of Napoleon, who had brought him to France following the French invasion of Italy. And so it was that a century of philosophical error ended in a reign of terror and the death in prison of a weak and politically powerless pope.

The Beautiful

It will come as little surprise perhaps that the darkness of this darkest of centuries caused a partial eclipse of the beautiful. In an age in which only empirical measurement, philosophical materialism, and a clockwork deity were considered "enlightened", the transcendental spirit of beauty was destined to be largely neglected, ignored, or perverted.

In literature, there was little of lasting merit, save perhaps Jonathan Swift's broadside in *Gulliver's Travels* against the scientism of the Enlightenment and the coldness of its "reason". The world of art was similarly uninspired and consequently uninspiring. There were noble and notable exceptions, but even the finest artists seemed content to cast the pearls of their Muse before the swine of the spiritless age.

"The eighteenth century is perhaps the first period when art freed itself from convictions," wrote art historian Michael Levy. "No longer did painting *need* to state religious beliefs, record the natural world or explore space. Significantly, painting held little interest for most of the century's great intellectuals; and with new emphasis on it as decoration it often passed unperceived."[8] These words are particularly interesting because Levy, an atheist who campaigned against "religion and superstition" as a member of the British Humanist Association, is a child of the Enlightenment and no friend of the Catholic Church. Even so, he is forced to concede that the architects of the Enlightenment had "little interest" in art, seeing it as being merely decorative, ornamental, and therefore ephemeral and ultimately irrelevant, passing "unperceived". He continued with a lament that the eighteenth century seemed to represent the passing of the true golden age of painting. The beauty had not merely passed; it had apparently passed away. "Men felt there would never again be a Raphael, a Poussin, an Annibale Carcacci."

"Indeed," Levy continued, "belief in art as a power had weakened. The eighteenth century could hardly fail to be sceptical and scrutinising of imagination, for it accomplished so much by its rationality and could advance civilization only by destroying myths."[9] Here we see the philosophical abyss that separates faith and reason from those who seek to divorce faith from reason. For the sons of faith and reason, a *myth* is a fictional or creatively artistic story that points to deep truths that transcend the merely measurable "facts". For the sons of the Enlightenment, of which Levy is a disciple, *myth* is a lie, something that is untrue because not empirically measurable; it is something that must, therefore, be "destroyed". The former is the very breath and life of the imaginative arts; the latter is the puritanical spirit that assassinates art and kills the beauty of which art is an expression and manifestation.

---

[8] Michael Levy, *From Giotto to Cézanne: A Concise History of Painting* (London: Thames and Hudson, 1964), 211.
   [9] Ibid.

In spite of the spiritless age, the century still produced some great artists and some wonderful works of art, albeit inspired by the mundane or the profane. François Boucher's *Reclining Girl* exhibits all the creative gifts of the great artist, though its subject is erotically suggestive. By way of contrast, Giovanni Battista Piazzetta's painting of saints Vincent, Hyacinth, and Lawrence Bertrando has all the mannerism and symbolism of his great Renaissance forebears without their technical abilities. Jean-Étienne Liotard's *Girl with Chocolate* is portraiture at its finest, from the light reflected on the glass and the cup that the girl is carrying to the realism of the hands and the play of light and shadow on the creases and folds of her dress. (As an aside, chocolate was a newly discovered New World delicacy in Europe at the time.)

Perhaps the greatest artists of the period, at least arguably, were the Italian landscapists Canaletto and Francesco Guardi, whose sweeping panoramic scenes of Venice are resplendent with both naturalistic color and the precision of definitive detail. Aptly enough, one of the greatest paintings of the century is Joseph Wright's *Experiment with an Air Pump*, which employs chiaroscuro to great effect, in the manner of Caravaggio or Rembrandt. The difference is that the masters of the Renaissance had used it to illumine the truths of Scripture or the beauty of the human form, whereas Wright uses it to highlight the enlightenment of the physical sciences.

It is, however, in music that the goodness and truth of beauty shine forth most magnificently in this most endarkened of times. At the beginning of the century, between 1700 and 1725, Antonio Stradivari created violins and other string instruments of such sublime quality that nobody in the following three centuries has been able to match them. Such priceless works of art were put at the service of some of the greatest composers of the century. Vivaldi was a contemporary of Stradivari, whose greatest work, *The Four Seasons*, displays the composer's "originality ... in a unique and pioneering way".[10] Specifically, he was a pioneer of what would become known as pictorialism in which the composer tries to depict events, scenes, or ideas that are extramusical.

In contrast to the pioneering style of Vivaldi, Johann Sebastian Bach was considered old-fashioned by his contemporaries and would not be fully appreciated until the following century, long after his death. It was then that he would be rediscovered by the emergent Romantic movement with its deep desire for the spirit of the past: "German Romantics, in particular, were seeking for all that was distinctively German and all that was best in their past, and this, combined with religious revival, led to a renewed focus on Bach as an icon of German Christianity."[11] One is reminded of the words of Ben Jonson, who said of Shakespeare that he was "not of an age but for all time". Great artists are not of their age, or of any particular age, but of all ages. Genius is timeless.

Bach's two greatest works, which would be revived in the following century, were his *Saint Matthew Passion* and his *Mass in B Minor*.

Another great composer, born in 1685, the same year as Bach, was George Frideric Handel, whose most famous and celebrated work is his *Messiah*. The *Messiah* is an oratorio that, as its name suggests, has its etymological roots in the Latin word *orare*, "to pray", and its historical roots in the type of prayer set to music that was pioneered by St. Philip Neri and his Congregation of the Oratory almost two hundred years earlier.

[10] Susan Treacy, *The Music of Christendom: A History* (San Francisco: Ignatius Press, 2021), 96.

[11] Ibid., 103.

Handel's *Messiah* is a meditation in three parts on the mystery of salvation. It was suggested to Handel by Charles Jennens, a scholarly and fervent Christian who was what might be called a "stealth" evangelist. As music historian Susan Treacy explains:

> Jennens' genius was that he saw the value of music, especially Handel's exalted and dramatic music, as a way to inculcate the Christian faith into a society that was becoming tepid on account of spreading Enlightenment attacks on orthodox Christianity and supernatural faith.[12]

Another composer whose omission would be worse than an oversight is Joseph Haydn, who is often referred to as the father of the symphony and the father of the string quartet. It is, however, to Wolfgang Amadeus Mozart that we must turn to bring the curtain down on the eighteenth century.

Susan Treacy suggests what might be called a Shakespearean dimension to Mozart's genius in the manner in which he adds a humanistic gravitas to the levitas of comedy:

> One facet of the remarkable genius of Mozart and his librettist Da Ponte is that they infused seriousness into a comedy. Beaumarchais' play [the literary source for *Figaro*] has a lighter, more frivolous tone despite its political overtones, but Mozart's *Figaro*, in its satire on the aristocracy—the count and countess—shows them as both laughable and appealing. Figaro and Susanna, although servants, are depicted as intelligent and enterprising; in fact, Susanna's guiding hand can be discerned over everything. Mozart's music sparkles and wounds as we follow the humanity of the protagonists.[13]

[12] Ibid., 113.
[13] Ibid., 131.

We will lay the century to rest with Mozart's *Requiem*, which was unfinished at the time of his death in 1791. According to his widow, Constanze, Mozart believed that he was writing the *Requiem* for his own funeral. Whether this is so or otherwise, a Requiem is always meant to remind all of us of the Four Last Things: death, judgment, heaven, and hell. It is surely appropriate to end with a memento mori this discussion of the century that, beyond all others, had forgotten the First Things and the Last Things. The century, which had been a living death, had died. It would not, however, rest in peace. On the contrary, its ghostly and ghoulish presence would haunt the century to come and the one after it.

Nineteenth Century

Revolution, Revelation, and Revival

The Good

At the beginning of the nineteenth century, dispassionate skeptics and cynics could have been forgiven for believing that the Catholic Church was finished. Even the faithful must have faltered in their belief that the Church could survive the precarious predicament in which she found herself. After being bruised and abused by the rise of absolutist monarchs, and after the pope had been bullied into suppressing the Jesuits, his greatest allies, the Church had then found herself betrayed by France, its oldest daughter, with the French Revolution's unleashing of hell itself on the Catholic population and priesthood. As the sun set on the eighteenth century, with a weak pope dying as a prisoner of Napoleon in France, it must have seemed that the sun was finally setting on the Church. And yet, as Chesterton reminds us, the Church, as the Mystical Body of Christ, has the ability to conquer death itself: "Christendom has had a series of revolutions, and in each one of them, Christianity has died. Christianity has died many times and has risen again; for it had a God who knew the way out of the grave."[1] It is, therefore, in the spirit of resurrection that the nineteenth century begins.

[1] G. K. Chesterton, *The Everlasting Man* (San Francisco: Ignatius Press, 1993), 250.

The first sign of resurrection was the Concordat signed by Napoleon and the new pope, Pius VII, in 1801. Napoleon realized that he needed to pacify and placate the Catholics of France and Italy in order to consolidate his political power. The rising in the Vendée had shown how large sections of France still held firm to the faith, and the armed resistance of Catholic loyalists in Italy had indicated the need to come to terms with the moral authority of the Church, even if militarily Christendom was defenseless. Napoleon considered the pope "a lever of opinion" whose moral authority was equivalent "to a corps of 200,000 men".[2] It was, therefore, Napoleon's fear of insurrection that led to the Church's resurrection.

Napoleon began his rapprochement to the Church and courtship of the pope in a speech to the clergy of Milan in June 1800. Considering that he had been one of the political and military leaders of the rabidly anti-Christian revolution, his words reflect a startling change of heart, or, in any event, a firm and cynical grasp of realpolitik:

> I am sure that the Catholic religion is the only religion that can make a stable community happy, and establish the foundations of good government. I undertake to defend it always.... I intend that the Roman Catholic religion shall be practiced openly and in all its fullness.... France has had her eyes opened through suffering, and has seen that the Catholic religion is the single anchor amid storm.... Tell the Pope that I want to make him a present of 30,000,000 Frenchmen.[3]

Even though Napoleon was no doubt motivated by a cynical desire to use the Church, he was simultaneously

---

[2] Eamon Duffy, *Saints and Sinners: A History of the Popes* (New Haven: Yale University Press, 2014), 262.

[3] Ibid.

acting as an unwitting agent of divine providence, enabling the Church to rise from the dust and ashes of her own apparent defeat.

Following the signing of the Concordat, Napoleon was as good as his word, at least for a time. He restored religious education for children and returned seminaries to the Church. Then, in 1804, he became emperor and allowed the absolute power to go to his head. In the same manner as the absolutist monarchs of the previous century, he asserted his imperial right to oversee Church appointments and to judge matters of teaching, as well as imprisoning dissident cardinals, bishops, and priests. A stand-off between the pope and the emperor ensued when Napoleon demanded that the pope take his side in his wars with Britain and other nations. The pope refused. Napoleon responded by ordering his army to invade Rome and the papal states, taking the pope prisoner. Pius VII would be a captive of the French for six years, from 1808 to 1814, and would emerge triumphant in terms of the great moral victory he accomplished in his resolute refusal to surrender his authority to the emperor. He became a hero of resistance in the eyes of the wider world, bolstering the status of the papacy internationally.

In England, horror at the barbarism of the French Revolution and the Reign of Terror that followed in its wake led to a spontaneous outpouring of sympathy for the revolution's victims. Britain opened its doors to refugees from France, including no fewer than eight thousand *emigré* priests who were permitted to minister to England's beleaguered Catholics. Such was the unforeseeable blessing that the French Revolution bestowed upon England, albeit contrary to the designs of the revolutionaries. Such are the ways in which the hand of Providence writes straight with crooked lines, bringing ineffable good from unutterable evil.

Something similar to what was happening in England was also happening in the United States:

> The vicious anti-clericalism and persecution of the Church under the French Revolution caused [Bishop John] Carroll and other American clerics to temper their enthusiasm for the new politics; so too, many of those clerics were in fact French priests living in exile from revolutionary France and not inclined to entertain fine distinctions between good and bad republicanism.[4]

By the 1830s, Catholicism was growing so fast in the United States that the French writer Alexis de Tocqueville remarked that "America ... is the country in which the Roman Catholic religion is making the most progress".[5] Such progress was due in large part to the large-scale emigration from Catholic countries in Europe. From being only 3 percent of the population at the time of the nation's founding, Catholicism would become the largest Christian denomination by the middle of the nineteenth century.

One of the chief marks of the resurrected power of the Church was the reestablishment of the Society of Jesus by Pius VII in 1814. In the following year, even as Napoleon was meeting his literal Waterloo, the Society of Foreign Missions was reestablished. With the resurrected Jesuits at the helm, Catholic missions were revitalized around the world.

The fearlessness of Pius VII set the tone for his successors throughout the century. Leo XII was active in supporting the Jesuits; his successor, Pius VIII, condemned Masonic

---

[4] Christopher Shannon, *American Pilgrimage: A Historical Journey through Catholic Life in a New World* (San Francisco: Ignatius Press, 2022), 199.

[5] Alexis de Tocqueville, *Democracy in America* (New York: Doubleday/Anchor, 1969), 450.

secret societies, an acknowledgment of the key role that such societies had played in the French Revolution and would continue to play in revolutionary movements throughout the nineteenth century. Gregory XVI, especially in his encyclical *Mirari Vos*, issued in 1832, was even more resolute in his attacks on the spirit of the Enlightenment and its promotion of secularism and philosophical materialism. It was, however, the giant figure of Blessed Pius IX, known popularly as Pio Nono, who would stamp the papal seal of authority on the century.

Although Pius IX was a firm tradition-oriented Catholic, he was not an enemy of technology. Shortly after his election in 1846, he set up a commission to introduce railways into the papal states and he installed gas street lighting in Rome. The enemy was not technological progress but the "progressive" determinism of Enlightenment philosophy and its political manifestation in the form of secularist revolution. In 1848, this philosophy led to revolutions across the length of Europe. In France, the restored monarchy was once again overthrown and replaced with a new secularist and anti-Catholic republic. A secularist republic was also established in Rome, forcing the pope to flee the city. He responded with characteristic resolve by excommunicating all the participants in the short-lived republic.

For all his resolve in the war on secularism, Pius IX was resolute above all in his practice of the faith. A saintly man, he was so poor at the time of his election that he had to borrow the money to get him to the Conclave that elected him. Following his election, he was hands-on in his pastoral ministry to the people of Rome, visiting hospitals and schools, confirming children, and distributing Communion in obscure churches and chapels. The effects of his papacy can be seen in the deepening and renewal of the spiritual life of the Church. He encouraged frequent reception of the sacraments and devotion to the Sacred

Heart of Jesus and to the Blessed Virgin. In his encyclical *Ubi Primum*, he emphasized Mary's role in salvation, and in 1854, he promulgated the dogma of the Immaculate Conception, confirming with papal authority the age-old Catholic belief that the Mother of God was conceived without the stain of Original Sin.

Pius IX's promulgation of the dogma of the Immaculate Conception was confirmed miraculously by heaven itself in 1858 with several apparitions of the Blessed Virgin to a fourteen-year-old peasant girl, Bernadette Soubirous. At one of these apparitions, the Virgin told St. Bernadette, "I am the Immaculate Conception."

So much could and should be said about these miraculous apparitions and the numerous miracles of healing that followed afterward. The very fact that Our Lady should choose to reveal herself in this way to a virgin of about the age that she was herself when she conceived the Son of God is testament to the poetic symmetry of this revelation of God's love for fallen humanity. The fact that the place chosen for such an apparition was fallen France is itself symbolically charged. The Mother of the Church appears miraculously to the oldest and most rebellious of the Church's daughters. Like her Son, she comes to call not the righteous but sinners to repentance. This aspect of the apparitions was emphasized by Ronald Knox:

> It was during the sixth apparition that our Lady said suddenly, "Pray for Sinners".... When our Lady stood at the grotto, the first command she gave was not, Heal the sick; was not, Convert the unbeliever. Her command was, Pray for sinners. Man's sin, that is our real malady; man's impenitence, that is the crying problem.[6]

---

[6] Ronald Knox, *Captive Flames: On Selected Saints and Christian Heroes* (San Francisco: Ignatius Press, 2001), 167.

Such was the good news of the Church's resurrection and Our Lady's revelation of herself that the many great saints of the century are reduced to being a mere post-script. Here is a litany of some of the most noteworthy in vaguely chronological order: Elizabeth Anne Seton, Peter Chanel, Jean-Marie Vianney, John Neumann, Anthony Mary Claret, John Bosco, John Henry Newman, Thérèse of Lisieux, and, last but not least, the Korean, Chinese, Ugandan, and Vietnamese martyrs.

We will conclude with Ronald Knox once again wax-ing lyrical, this time on the saints in general and St. Thérèse of Lisieux in particular:

> The Saints ... are our Lord's crown; and in that crown one particular jewel catches the light, now and again, so as to shine out more than ever. All the Saints have possessed the virtue of simplicity; but it was not till God saw fit to give us a really glaring example of saintly simplicity in St. Theresa that the Church really noticed what a wonderful thing it is.[7]

The Bad

The nineteenth century could be seen as the age in which the worst sort of nationalism emerged as an even worse sort of imperialism. It might be said, in this context, that there are two types of nationalism. There is the healthy nationalism of small nations that seeks independence from the imperial designs of larger neighbors, and there is the unhealthy nationalism of large nations that exerts imperial power over smaller neighbors.

[7] Ibid., 171–72.

The century began with two large and imperial nations at loggerheads. Napoleon would rise from being the ruler of France to becoming a self-styled emperor of all he surveyed, expanding his dominions through military conquest. His main rival was the emergent imperial power of Britain, which, in 1801, annexed Ireland in an "Act of Union". The new British flag, the Union Flag, or, more popularly, the Union Jack, consisted of the juxtaposed crosses of St. George, St. Andrew, and St. Patrick, signifying the union of England, Scotland, and Ireland through the coming together symbolically of those nations' patron saints. Under this flag, the British would conquer large parts of the world. By the century's end, almost a quarter of the world's population and almost a quarter of the world's land area would be part of the British Empire. It was, therefore, through the monstrous politics of scale that imperialism would replace nationalism as the defining element of global politics.

In the United States, the North and South went to war over the issues of slavery and states' rights. The South, unable to unshackle itself from the abomination of slavery, was defeated by the industrial North, which then imposed a strong central government on the states of the Union, empowering a federal government that has inexorably centralized power to a degree that has rendered the individual states relatively powerless.

Whereas Britannia "ruled the waves", facilitating the expansion of its global empire, Germany sought to rule the landmass of Europe through the flexing of its political muscle. In 1866, Prussia defeated Austria and then, in 1870, it defeated France in the Franco-Prussian War. In the following year, to rub salt into the wounds of the defeated French, Wilhelm I of Prussia chose to have himself crowned emperor of the German Empire in Paris.

The new German Empire would be no friend of the Church. Under the leadership of the ruthless Otto von Bismarck, the first chancellor of the empire, war was declared on the Catholic population of the new unified Germany. Between 1871 and 1875, Bismarck abolished the Church's control of its own schools, imposing state education, and expelled the Jesuits and other religious orders from Germany. The state took over Catholic seminaries and claimed the right to appoint the clergy. Those Catholics who defied the government were severely punished.

The Catholic resistance was truly admirable. Hundreds of priests were imprisoned, as were the archbishops of Poznan and Cologne and the Bishop of Trèves. This war on the Church became known as the *Kulturkampf*, the culture struggle, or, in modern parlance, the culture wars. In spite of Bismarck's determined efforts to crush the Church, the people rallied in defense of their religion. The Catholic Centre Party was gaining ground in elections, and there was a proliferation of pro-Catholic newspapers and journals. Eventually, after seven years of relentless persecution and equally relentless and resilient resistance, Bismarck admitted defeat. Unable to crush the Church, he sought reconciliation. The anti-Catholic laws were repealed, and the Church once again began building her schools, colleges, hospitals, universities, and all the multifarious social organizations, which reestablished and fortified the role of the faith in the very fabric of German society.

In 1870, even as Prussia was invading France, Italian unification was achieved by the conquering of the papal states and the invasion of papal-controlled Rome. Pius IX, as fearless and indomitable as ever, refused to abandon the Eternal City, even though he was now deprived of any temporal political power. As "the prisoner of the Vatican", Pius IX gained both respect and sympathy from around the world, increasing his spiritual power, even as his temporal power had been lost. The same was true of the loss of the papal states, which was seen at the time as a disaster. The liberation of the popes from the burden of being secular rulers enabled them to focus on their spiritual mission to the world at large.

Following France's defeat in the Franco-Prussian War, the government of the "Third Republic" mimicked the policies of its Prussian enemy by initiating a new anti-Catholic pogrom, which was itself a *Kulturkampf* as draconian as Bismarck's. Convents and monasteries were closed, resulting in more than one hundred thousand monks and nuns being made homeless, and no religious congregation could exist without gaining explicit approval from the government.

The last twenty years of the nineteenth century were marked by a manic scramble by the major European powers to claim as much of the defenseless continent of Africa as their military and economic resources could deliver. In 1881, Tunisia became a French protectorate, and Egypt became part of the British Empire a year later. At the Berlin Conference, held in 1884 and 1885, the European nations decided to carve up the African continent peacefully, ostensibly with the laudable goal of stamping out slavery. In practice, however, it was all about grabbing power in an increasingly competitive global economy. France, Britain, Spain, Germany, Italy, Portugal, and Belgium all claimed their piece of the cake. France ended up with most of the northern part of the continent with Britain claiming the lion's share of the rest. By 1900, 30 percent of the African population had been annexed to the British Empire. In addition, Britain now ruled the Indian subcontinent, enabling Queen Victoria to claim the title of the empress of India.

In terms of secular politics, the nineteenth century can be seen as an age of revolutions and an age of imperialism. The revolutions had sought to destroy the City of God in the name of the City of Man, whereas the emerging imperial powers had sought to turn the City of Man into the Empire of Man. Napoleon had claimed the imperial crown in 1804, Wilhelm I in 1871, and Queen Victoria five years later. In each case, the "omnipotent" empire would prove short-lived. In Napoleon's case, the empire would die before he did; as for the German and British empires, they would both begin to crumble in the trenches of World War I, less than two decades after the demise of the century that had given them birth. *Sic transit gloria mundi* (Thus passes the glory of the world).

The Beautiful

It is no surprise and no coincidence that the resurrection of the good in the nineteenth century should be accompanied by the revival of the beautiful. Ever the two go hand in hand.

The revival of beauty was connected to the rise of Romanticism, which was itself a healthy reactionary response to the cold-hearted empiricism and scientism of the Enlightenment of the previous century. In addition, it was also, at least in England, a healthy reactionary response to the wickedness of the French Revolution.

English Romanticism can be said to have been born with the publication in 1798 of *Lyrical Ballads*, a volume of poetry coauthored by William Wordsworth and Samuel Taylor Coleridge. These two poets had been initially disillusioned with Christianity and admirers of the revolution in France; in the event, the grim reality of the Reign of Terror that followed the revolution led both poets to become disillusioned with the revolution and admirers of, and then believers in, Christianity. Their path would be followed by many others, the Romantic movement in England giving birth to various forms of neo-medievalism, especially the Gothic Revival, the Pre-Raphaelites, and the Oxford Movement.

The Gothic Revival was led by Augustus Pugin, a young architect whose love for the aesthetic of the Middle Ages led to his conversion to Catholicism. Pugin's best-known neo-Gothic architectural masterpiece is the Houses of Parliament in London, but he was also responsible for the design of many of the Catholic churches being built across England in the years following Catholic Emancipation in 1829.

The Pre-Raphaelites, as their name suggests, were a group of artists in Victorian England who sought a purer vision of art "pre-Raphael". Seeking inspiration from medieval and early Renaissance art, these artists also chose medieval subjects for their paintings, such as the Arthurian legends and Dante's *Divine Comedy*, as well as the works of Shakespeare.

The Oxford Movement was led by a young Anglican clergyman, John Henry Newman, who sought to unite the modern Anglican church, of which he was a member with the pre-Reformation English church. Through the study of history and theology, he came to the inescapable conclusion that the Anglican church was founded by Henry VIII and could not be seen, therefore, as part of the Catholic apostolic succession. Following his principles to their logical conclusion, Newman was received into the Catholic Church in 1845, his reception proving to be the birth of a Catholic cultural revival that would last for the next century or more. As for Newman himself, he wrote novels and poetry, as well as works of theology, history, and philosophy, and was one of the finest prose stylists of his age. In 1866, he received into the Church a young man, Gerard Manley Hopkins, who was destined to become a Jesuit priest and arguably the finest poet of the Victorian age.

The nineteenth century was also the golden age of the novel. Space precludes any discussion of the great novelists who graced this greatest of literary centuries, but we must at least list the *illustrissimi*: Jane Austen, Charles Dickens, Alessandro Manzoni, Victor Hugo, Leo Tolstoy, and Fyodor Dostoyevsky. Each of these giants of literature represented aspects of the widespread Christian revival that characterized cultural renewal throughout the century, each in his own individual and sometimes idiosyncratic way.

In France, François-René de Chateaubriand was a literary giant who defended the Church with great lucidity and literary eloquence in the first half of the century. Take, for instance, the epigrammatic brilliance of his defense of the Church as a divine institution: "Christianity is perfect; men are imperfect.... Christianity, therefore, is not the work of men."[8]

In Germany, there was a Catholic revival in the early decades of the century, which was led by accomplished writers and scholars, many of whom were converts to the faith. Leaders of this revival included Friedrich Leopold Stolberg, Friedrich Schlegel, Joseph Görres, and Johann Adam Möhler. Accompanying this intellectual aspect of the Catholic revival in Germany was the influence of German Romanticism, which, like its contemporary

---

[8] Quoted in H. W. Crocker III, *Triumph: The Power and the Glory of the Catholic Church* (New York: Three Rivers Press, 2001), 357.

counterpart in England, spawned various manifestations of neo-medievalism.

Whereas neo-medievalism in England had expressed itself primarily in the poetry and prose of the Romantics, and in neo-Gothic architecture and Pre-Raphaelite paint-ing, it found expression most potently in German culture in the form of music. The music historian Susan Treacy evokes the excitement generated by the brilliance of Bee-thoven in the early nineteenth century:

> Try to imagine yourself in Vienna at a marathon concert that included the world premieres of Beethoven's fifth and sixth symphonies, his fourth piano concerto (Op. 58, G major), and his *Fantasia* in C minor (Op. 80, pop-ularly known as the *Choral Fantasy*). These four works truly were premiered at the same concert, on Decem-ber 22, 1808![9]

Apart from these completely new works, which were being performed for the very first time, the concert program that evening also included the *Gloria* and *Sanctus* from Beetho-ven's Mass in C major. Five years later, E. T. A. Hoffmann would write in his 1813 essay "Beethoven's Instrumental Music" that instrumental music "is the most romantic of all arts—one might almost say, the only genuinely roman-tic one—for its sole subject is the infinite".[10] Hoffmann continued that Beethoven's music, in particular, "wakens ... that infinite longing which is the essence of romanti-cism". Such longing is what C. S. Lewis called "joy", an essential characteristic of man's longing for God.

---

[9] Susan Treacy, *The Music of Christendom: A History* (San Francisco: Ignatius Press, 2021), 136.

[10] E. T. A. Hoffman, "Beethoven's Instrumental Music", in *Source Readings in Music History*, ed. Oliver Strunk (New York: W. W. Norton, 1950), 775.

Another great composer of the time was Franz Schubert, whose *Ave Maria* has remained enduringly popular. It was originally composed as a German translation of a song from Sir Walter Scott's narrative poem *The Lady of the Lake*, illustrating the influence of English (and in this case Scottish) Romantic literature on German Romantic music. In Scott's poem, the protagonist is singing to the Blessed Virgin—including the refrain *Ave Maria*—but the words are not those of the Hail Mary prayer.

Perhaps the most controversial figure in nineteenth-century German music is Richard Wagner, who put his incomparable musical gifts at the service of a quasi- or pseudo-pagan devotion to the ancient Norse gods. This apparently anti-Christian stance earned him the admiration of Friedrich Nietzsche, the philosopher of superbia par excellence. Such admiration was terminated unceremoniously when Wagner's final music drama, *Parsifal*, was perceived by Nietzsche as a surrender to Christianity. Although the work is somewhat idiosyncratic theologically, Wagner also seemed to believe that it represented his reconciliation with Christianity, writing to his patron King Ludwig II of Bavaria that "it seems to me as if the making of this work has been entrusted to me in order to uphold to the world its own most profound mystery, the truth of the Christian faith; indeed, even to rekindle this faith."[11]

Another musical giant of this period is Anton Bruckner, who might be considered the Catholic Wagner. Greatly influenced by Wagner, Bruckner's Mass in D minor puts Wagnerian musical innovation at the service of God. The importance and centrality of Bruckner's Catholic faith was emphasized by Susan Treacy:

[11] Quoted in Treacy, *Music of Christendom*, 163.

Though Bruckner is known primarily as a symphonic composer, his sacred music deserves to be better known. Bruckner's Catholic faith shines forth in his liturgical music, from the sublime motets *Ave Maria* and *Os iusti* to his larger sacred choral works. Bruckner's Masses and his *Te Deum* are like vocal symphonies, or as some have commented, his symphonies are rather like "Masses without words".[12]

It would be remiss to omit reference to Italian opera in a survey of all that is beautiful in the nineteenth century. The operas of the earlier part of the century by Rossini and Bellini appear to be preoccupied, if not obsessed, with the tragedy of English history during the reign of the Tudors and Stuarts. Another influence was the Scottish Romantic author Sir Walter Scott. Rossini wrote an operatic adaptation of Scott's *Lady of the Lake*, which, as we have seen, had also inspired Schubert, whereas Donizetti adapted Scott's *Bride of Lammermoor*.

As with Wagner, the greatest of the nineteenth-century Italian composers, Giuseppe Verdi, ended his life with at least a partial rejection of his earlier revolutionary views. After the success of *Aïda* in 1871, he retired from composing opera to compose his famous *Requiem*. This would have been his final word as a composer, and perhaps his artistic last will and testament, if he had not been persuaded to come out of retirement to compose an adaptation of Shakespeare's *Othello*, which includes the beautiful *Ave Maria* sung by the doomed Desdemona, and his final work, *Falstaff*, a comedy inspired by the feckless buffoon who disgraces several of Shakespeare's plays.

We will conclude our brief survey of the beautiful music of the nineteenth century in France, which also

[12] Ibid., 167.

experienced a Catholic revival in the latter half of the century to complement the earlier revival set in motion by Chateaubriand. This period, sometimes referred to as the *Belle Époque*, includes the restoration of Gregorian chant, begun in the 1850s at the Benedictine Abbey of Saint Peter of Solesmes, which continues to enrich the Church liturgically to this day. Perhaps the greatest French composer of this period is Gabriel Fauré, who is best known, and justly, for his wonderful *Requiem*.

Finally, to close our sketch of the nineteenth century, we will offer a panoramic overview of the great paintings that graced this period of Catholic revival.

The first great painter of the century was Francisco de Goya, whose most celebrated paintings illustrate the sheer brutality of the City of Man. His *Colossus* shows a chaotic and possibly demonic presence that darkens the cosmos. Michael Levy conjectures that it may symbolize "the collapse of rationality, perhaps, and the birth of monsters" or possibly "a feeling of despair as the modern world comes painfully into existence".[13] It was painted at around the same time as Mary Shelley was writing *Frankenstein*, which could suggest a sense of angst in the presence of the monsters of scientistic modernity. It is more likely, however, that it is simply a representation of the wickedness of the times in which it was painted. The latter is suggested by the subject of arguably his most famous painting, *3 May 1808*, which shows French soldiers killing defenseless hostages in cold blood.

In England, William Blake's eccentric genius enabled him to write some of the finest poetry of the time and also inspired him to execute some of the finest art. His

---

[13] Michael Levy, *From Giotto to Cézanne: A Concise History of Painting* (London: Thames and Hudson, 1964), 256.

poetry ranged from theologically mystic musings on the symbolism of God's creation of the lamb and the tiger to an Arthurian call to arms in his timeless anthem "Jerusalem". It also inspired him to take up the brush to bring to life, in his own mind's eye, the mystical vision of Dante or Milton. Other great English art of the century, apart from the aforementioned and very important Pre-Raphaelites, was the proto-impressionism of Turner and Constable, which prefigures and prophesies the French impressionist movement of several decades later.

From a Catholic perspective, the most pertinent of the French impressionist paintings are Monet's representations of the façade of Rouen Cathedral illumined by various hues of sunlight, of which the resplendent magnificence of the cathedral in full sunlight is the most striking, suggestive of the sun's placing of a halo on the hallowed edifice.

We will end, however, with Millet's quintessentially timeless masterpiece, *The Angelus*, which shows two peasants, a husband and wife, pausing from the day's labors, at the prompting of the church bells, to pray the Angelus. The painting is not an icon but is beyond iconic in its evocation of the perennial power of prayer. The two peasants are apparently powerless in the presence of worldly wickedness, and yet they have the hidden and silent power of the peasants of the Vendée who rose up in defiance of the colossus of the French Revolution. Even more important, they have the hidden and silent power of the poor peasant girl who knelt in awe of the presence of the apparition of the Blessed Virgin at Lourdes. Most important of all, they have the power of the poor peasant girl who knelt in the presence of an angel in a small town called Nazareth. It was this presence that had overcome the imperial power of the City of Man and, by the grace of God and the miraculous apparition of His mother at Lourdes, had been born anew.

Twentieth Century

Wars of Irreligion

The Good

As we move toward the conclusion of this two-thousand-year survey of the history of Christendom, it would be helpful to look back over the long journey we have already taken.

There are few better ways of capturing the whole landscape of history than through the telescopic lens provided by the great historian Christopher Dawson. Dawson speaks of the six ages of Christendom.[1] The first age began at Pentecost; the second was the age of Constantine in the fourth century and the granting of religious liberty to Christians; the third began with the missionary efforts of St. Gregory the Great in the late sixth century; the fourth was the age of monasticism from the Cluniac revival in the tenth century to the rise of the mendicant orders three hundred years later; the fifth was the Catholic Revival, sometimes called the Counter-Reformation, which arose in response to the Protestant rupture; and the sixth was the age of the strong popes who led the Church's response to the rise of secularist state tyranny.

[1] Christopher Dawson, *The Historic Reality of Christian Culture* (New York: Harper and Bros., 1960), quoted in Alan Schreck, *The Compact History of the Catholic Church* (Ann Arbor, Mich.: Servant Books, 1987), 145.

Much that was good in the twentieth century was the result of the courageous teaching of the popes in the face of anti-Christian revolution, ideological totalitarianism, and irreligious war. Writing in 1987, Church historian Alan Schreck wrote that "every pope of the Catholic Church since the middle of the nineteenth century to the present has been a holy, strong, and gifted leader in his own right."[2] If anything, this is something of an understatement. It could be argued that every pope since Pius VII at the very dawn of the nineteenth century has been a holy, strong, and gifted leader, making the nineteenth and twentieth centuries something of a golden age of the papacy. It is, therefore, the popes who will dominate the discussion of what was especially good in the twentieth century.

The pope at the turn of the century was Leo XIII, whose encyclical *Aeterni Patris*, published in 1879, had laid the foundations for the rise of Neo-Scholasticism and the consequent return of St. Thomas Aquinas as the universally acknowledged preeminent theologian and philosopher in the Church's history. This Thomistic revival would arm the Church with the tools of faithful reason it would need to fight the pernicious secularist dogmas of the twentieth century. Pope Leo's other enduring achievement was his explication of the Church's social teaching in the encyclical *Rerum Novarum*, published in 1891, which gave the definitive Catholic response to socialism and to free market libertarian capitalism, especially in its elucidation of the twin pillars of subsidiarity and solidarity as the only just solution to economic and political injustice. This document was so important in the century that followed that Pius XI issued his own social encyclical (*Quadragesimo Anno*) on the fortieth anniversary of *Rerum Novarum*'s

[2] Schreck, *Compact History of the Church*, 144.

publication, and John Paul II would follow suit with a further encyclical (*Centesimus Annus*) reiterating the Church's teaching on the centenary of its publication.

Following Leo XIII's death in 1903, the saintly Pius X became pope. He is best known to posterity, and quite rightly, for his resolute defense of the Church from the heresy of modernism, or what we might now call "progressivism" within the Church. In essence, Pius X stood firm against those within the Church's hierarchy who wanted the Church to adopt some of the philosophical ideas of the Enlightenment. His stance gained the enthusiastic endorsement of a young English writer, G. K. Chesterton, who denounced the ideas of modernism within the Catholic Church, even though he was not himself yet a Catholic. A popular aphorism ascribed to Chesterton is that "we don't want a church that will move with the world, we want a church that will move the world."[3]

As a means of countering the errors of modernism, Pius X added his own weight behind the Neo-Scholastic movement, buttressing the intellectual life of the Church, and promoted the need for robust catechetical instruction of the faithful. He also restored the Church's musical tradition and encouraged frequent reception of the Blessed Sacrament, as well as lowering the age of First Communion: "The age of discretion, both for Confession and for Holy Communion, is the time when a child begins to reason, that is, about the seventh year, more or less."[4]

Pius X's successor, Benedict XV, was the reigning pontiff during World War I. He deserves to be remembered

[3] Maisie Ward, *Gilbert Keith Chesterton* (New York: Sheed and Ward, 1943), 468.

[4] Sacred Congregation of the Discipline of the Sacraments, Decree on First Communion *Quam Singulari* (August 8, 1910), Papal Encyclicals Online, https://www.papalencyclicals.net/pius10/p10quam.htm.

primarily as the pope who could have saved the world from the horrors of the following world war if his words had been heeded. In August 1917, over a year before the war ended, he proposed a peace plan that was conciliatory in tone and designed to bring both sides to an agreement to end hostilities. The steps he proposed were necessary to end the "useless massacre" that the war had become but also to avert "the recurrence of such conflicts". Addressing national leaders at the conclusion of his peace proposals, he stressed the gravity of the situation and their personal responsibility for the consequence of ignoring the call to peace: "On your decisions depend the rest and joy of countless families, the life of thousands of young people, in short, the happiness of the peoples, whose well-being it is your overriding duty to procure."[5]

At around the same time as the pope was issuing his peace proposal, Blessed Karl of Austria, the emperor of Austria and king of Hungary, was involved in secret negotiations with the Allied Powers aimed at bringing the war to an end. Well may such a holy and peace-loving monarch, a lamb among ravenous warmongering wolves, have been beatified by the Catholic Church.

After the Armistice, the Allied Powers not only ignored Benedict XV's peace proposals; they excluded him from the international peace conference at Versailles, ensuring that his call for reconciliation and justice would not be heard. In the event, the imposition of the egregiously unjust and maliciously vengeful Treaty of Versailles sowed the seeds of the Second World War twenty years later. It was ironic that the refusal of the viciously anticlerical governments of Italy and France to allow the pope to be a part

---

[5] Quoted in Russell Shaw, *Eight Popes and the Crisis of Modernity* (San Francisco: Ignatius Press, 2020), 41.

of the conference at Versailles led to both their countries suffering the evil consequences of a second war that could have been avoided.

The pope who would preside over the Church in the years between the two world wars was Pius XI, who was elected in 1922 and would die in 1939. His encyclical *Divini Illius Magistri*, published in 1929, defended the rights of parents and the Church in education against the encroachments of secularist governments with respect to the schooling of children. In the following year, in *Casti Connubii*, he issued a robust defense of the Church's timeless teaching on marriage, family, and human life. Ironically, it was published in the very year in which the Anglican church surrendered to the culture of contraception at its notorious Lambeth Conference, a retreat from orthodoxy which marked the beginning of the inexorable disintegration of the Anglican Communion. In choosing to move with the world, the Church of England had condemned itself to the worldliness that precedes irrelevance and ultimate self-destruction. A year later, as we have seen, Pius XI confirmed the social teaching enunciated in Leo XIII's *Rerum Novarum* forty years earlier. In the same year, 1931, Pius XI responded to the boasts of Italy's fascist dictator, Benito Mussolini, that "the Church is not sovereign nor is it even free"[6] by insisting on the independence and sovereignty of the Church from state control and criticizing Mussolini's regime for its persecution of Catholics.

Having defied the Italian fascists, Pius XI then turned his attention to the evils of both the Nazis and the communists. In two encyclicals, issued a week apart in 1937, he condemned the Nazi government in Germany for its persecution of Catholics, its racism, and its anti-Semitism,

[6] Ibid., 53.

and for its tribal neo-paganism. In the encyclical against communism, he attacked the evils of Marxism in general and Soviet communism in Russia in particular. "Society is for man and not vice versa," he insisted, condemning communism for reversing this right order.[7] Such was the courage and the brilliance of this great pope that papal historian Eamon Duffy, who is not given to grandiloquence or hyperbole in his judgment of character, was uncharacteristically effusive in his praise: "Always a strong man and energetic pope, in the last years of his pontificate he rose to greatness. The pope of eighteen concordats ceased to be a diplomat, and achieved the status of a prophet."[8]

As Benedict XV had become pope at the dawn of the First World War, Pius XII ascended to the papal throne as the world descended into a second global conflagration. His first encyclical, *Summi Pontificatus*, issued shortly after the war had begun, condemned the Nazi and Soviet invasion of Poland, which had caused Britain to enter the war in Poland's defense, as well as condemning anti-Semitism and totalitarianism.

Although Pius XII was true to the Church's traditional policy of remaining neutral in times of war, he served the Allied cause in secret by serving as a conduit of communication between the British government and German military leaders contemplating a coup to overthrow Hitler. He also passed onto the Allies intelligence he had received about the imminent Nazi invasion of the Netherlands. Then, during his Christmas address in 1942, he was unequivocal in his criticism of the persecution of the Jews in what would later become known as the Holocaust: "The hundreds of

[7] Ibid., 55.
[8] Eamon Duffy, *Saints and Sinners: A History of the Popes* (New Haven: Yale University Press, 2014), 344–45.

thousands of persons who, without any fault on their part, sometimes only because of their nationality or race, have been consigned to death or a slow decline."[9] It is hardly surprising that the Axis Powers were outraged by the pope's words. "Both Mussolini and the German Ambassador, von Ribbentrop, were angered by this speech, and Germany considered that the Pope had abandoned any pretense at neutrality. They felt that Pius had unequivocally condemned Nazi action against the Jews."[10] The courage of the pope's words, considering that he was himself living in the midst of Mussolini's Italy, is a mark of true heroism, and it is likely that he would have said more had it not been for fear that his Christmas message had actually provoked the Nazis to increase the persecution of the Jews in the Netherlands and elsewhere.

After the courageous response of the popes of the first half of the century, the popes of the latter half of the century enjoyed relatively peaceful and uneventful pontificates. For John XXIII, Paul VI, and John Paul II, the war would be fought against the enemies within the Church, especially in the manner in which modernist and progressive theologians abused the authentic teaching of the Second Vatican Council in the name of the so-called "spirit of Vatican II". We will address this struggle in the next section. First, however, we must praise the role of John Paul II in helping to bring down the Soviet Empire.

With respect to John Paul II's place in history, his role in the defeat of Soviet communism is likely to be preeminent. His visit to communist-controlled Poland, his own homeland, in 1979 led to the rise of the Solidarity trade union, which would itself lead to the toppling of Poland's

---

[9] *New York Times*, December 25, 1942.
[10] Duffy, *Saints and Sinners*, 348.

communist regime. This led to a domino effect in which one communist country in Eastern Europe after another was overthrown by anticommunist revolutions. By 1991, the resignation of Mikhail Gorbachev signaled the fall of the Soviet Union itself. Although there were other key players in this political process, including Ronald Reagan, Margaret Thatcher, and the Russian dissident writer Aleksandr Solzhenitsyn, there is no doubt that John Paul II's part in this historical liberation of Europe from the Soviet yoke was crucial.

Before we conclude this discussion of the heroism of the popes in the twentieth century, we should make note of four important encyclicals issued by John Paul II. The first, *Centesimus Annus* (1991), we have already noted. *Veritatis Splendor*, issued in 1993, reiterated the traditional teachings of the Church on fundamental moral principles. *Evangelium Vitae*, published in 1995, was an unequivocal defense of human life in the face of the rise of the culture of death, which reinforced the teaching of Paul VI's earlier encyclical *Humanae Vitae* (1968). Last but emphatically not least, the encyclical *Fides et Ratio*, promulgated in 1998, insisted on the indissoluble marriage of faith and reason, which has ever been the foundation of Christian theology and philosophy.

At the end of the century, Cardinal Ratzinger, the future Pope Benedict XVI, who had been John Paul II's righthand man for almost the entirety of the latter's papacy, was working on his seminal work, *The Spirit of the Liturgy*, presumably with St. John Paul II's blessing, in which he elucidates the definitive principles governing the celebration of the Mass with the brilliance of one of the century's finest minds and one of its greatest theologians.

Although the role of the papacy has necessarily been accentuated, there is no escaping the fact that the holiest event of the century was the series of Marian apparitions at Fatima in Portugal between May and October 1917. It is surely no coincidence that these apparitions occurred in the same months in which the communist revolution was happening in Russia, nor can it be anything but providential that the Bolshevik Revolution in October of that year coincided with the final apparition at Fatima, in which seventy thousand people were present for what has become known as the miracle of the sun. As with the priceless gift of her apparition at Lourdes in the previous century, the Fatima apparitions took place during a time of anti-Catholic persecution. In the midst of the darkest hour, in which the diabolical specter of communism was rising to spread its murderous darkness over the world, the Queen of Heaven comforted her children with the promise of the victory that her Son had already won for those who remain faithful to Him.

Having focused on some truly "holy fathers", we will end with a litany of a few of the holy women who graced the twentieth century, each of whom warrant much more space than we are able to give them: Maria Goretti, Gemma Galgani, Francis Xavier Cabrini, Teresa of the Andes, Faustina Kowalksa, Teresa Benedicta of the Cross, Josephine Bakhita, Katherine Drexel, Gianna Beretta Molla, and Teresa of Calcutta.

The Bad

There have been so many dark centuries in the history of Christendom that one hesitates to call any particular century the darkest of all. Some have been as dark as the twentieth century, but none have been as deadly. In terms of the sheer body count, the twentieth century, with its wars of irreligion and its access to industrialized weapons of mass destruction, is the most murderous in human history. It is almost among the most tyrannous.

World War I was the first great war of the machines in which millions of human persons were butchered by new technology. The British brought the newly invented tank to the fray. The Germans used chemical weapons in the form of mustard gas. Both sides employed the recently discovered flying machines. Barbed wire barred the way through no-man's land, and more efficient and effective machine guns and artillery ensured carnage on a scale beyond the wildest imaginings of previous generations of warmongers. The harsh and hellish reality of this new form of technology-driven "total war" was described by Winston Churchill:

> Neither peoples nor rulers drew the line at any deed which they thought could help them to win. Germany, having let Hell loose, kept well in the van of terror, but she was followed step by step by the desperate and ultimately avenging nations she had assailed. Every outrage against humanity or international law was repaid by reprisals—often of a great scale and of longer duration.... The wounded died between the lines: the dead mouldered into the soil. Merchant ships and neutral ships and hospital ships were sunk on the seas and all on board left to their fate, or killed as they swam. Every effort was made to starve whole nations into submission without regard to age or sex.[11]

By the end of the war, it is estimated that more than eight million combatants had been killed and a further twenty million wounded.[12]

---

[11] Quoted in Shaw, *Eight Popes and the Crisis of Modernity*, 39.

[12] Dennis E. Showalter and John Graham Royde-Smith, "World War I", *Encyclopaedia Britannica*, last updated June 13, 2023, https://www.britannica.com/event/World-War-I/Killed-wounded-and-missing.

Under the cover of the darkness of World War I, with the eyes of the world on the carnage of the battlefields, the Ottoman Turks began the systematic extermination of the Armenian Christians in what has become known as the Armenian Genocide. Between 1915 and 1916, somewhere between six hundred thousand and 1.5 million Armenian civilians—men, women, and children—were killed.

The demonic darkness deepened in October 1917 with the triumph of the communists in the Bolshevik Revolution in Russia. Yet the violence of the revolution was merely a drop in the ocean of blood that the Soviet communists would spill over the next seventy-four years of Red Terror. Under the iron-fisted rule of Lenin, Stalin, and their successors, countless millions of civilians were killed for failing to toe the party line. As with the Reign of Terror after the French Revolution, the sheer scale of the Soviet slaughter illustrates what happens when God is declared to be dead.

Marxism was not confined to Russia, however. On the contrary, its atheistic poison spread throughout the world, intoxicating idealistic youth until they became drunk with bloodlust. In Mexico, in the 1920s, thousands of Catholics were killed by the anti-Catholic regime. A particularly bloodthirsty hater of Catholics was Governor Canabal of the Tabasco province, who boasted that every Catholic church in his jurisdiction had been destroyed. He ordered the destruction of the shrine of Our Lady of Guadalupe, but the miraculous image was saved, being smuggled to Costa Rica until it could be returned.

One hero of the Catholic resistance to the Mexican Revolution was Blessed Miguel Pro, a brave priest who has been described as a real-life Scarlet Pimpernel in his secret ministry to the faithful. When he was finally captured, he was executed. The moment of his death by firing squad was captured on film and in photography by the government to warn of the fate that awaited dissident priests. The plan backfired, however, because the photograph of the priest's martyrdom became a holy card passed from Catholic to Catholic as a token of resistance to the regime. The photograph showed Fr. Pro moments before he was shot, his arms stretched out like the crucified Christ, and with the cry of "Viva Cristo Rey!" ("Long live Christ the King!") on his lips. Far from the photograph serving its propaganda purposes, it was declared illegal for anyone to possess it. Inspired by Miguel Pro's heroism, the people of Mexico rose up in what became known as the Cristero War, reminiscent of the Vendée uprising against the French Revolution.

In the following decade, a communist and anarchist republic in Spain waged war on the Church. Nearly seven thousand priests were murdered, the majority in a brief period between July and December 1936. Most were diocesan priests, among them thirteen bishops, but more than two thousand male religious were also murdered, as were 283 nuns.[13] Unlike the risings in the Vendée and in Mexico, the Catholic nationalist resistance to the Red Terror in Spain led to the Spanish Civil War and the ultimate defeat of the communist tyranny.

In 1939, the year in which the Spanish Civil War ended, World War II began. In the two decades since the previous world war had ended, technology had "progressed" to such a degree that the tools of warfare were more effective and efficient than ever in taking human life. It is estimated that between fifteen and twenty-five million military personnel were killed, twice as many as in the previous war. This was, however, the less gruesome half of the story.

---

[13] Julio de la Cueva, "Religious Persecution, Anticlerical Tradition and Revolution: On Atrocities against the Clergy during the Spanish Civil War", *Journal of Contemporary History* 33, no. 3 (July 1998): 355.

World War II was the first war in human history in which civilians were considered "legitimate" military targets by both sides. It is estimated that as many as forty-five million civilians were killed during the war, many of them by the bombing of cities from the air.[14] This strategy, which had played a minor role in the Spanish Civil War, became a major part of World War II. Instigated by the Nazis as blitzkrieg (lighting war), it was used widely against British cities, especially London. It was, however, adopted by the Allies in vengeance, the anti-Christian doctrine of an eye for an eye being the realpolitik of war. Toward the end of the war, the "carpet bombing" of the German city of Dresden with incendiary bombs created fires in which those who escaped death by the bomb blast itself were burned alive. It is estimated that around twenty-five thousand civilians were killed. What was particularly controversial about the bombing of Dresden is that it was not a center of industry. There were no military targets. It was merely an attack by the U.S. Air Force and the Royal Air Force on unarmed civilians to soften eastern Germany ahead of the Soviet attack which would place half of Europe under communist control.

A few weeks later, six Japanese cities were laid to waste by U.S. bombing raids: Tokyo, Nagoya, Kobe, Osaka, Yokahama, and Kawasaki. Ominously, two cities were spared: Hiroshima and Nagasaki, the latter of which was home to Japan's oldest Catholic community. In August 1945, these two cities became the first cities on which atomic bombs were dropped.

---

[14] National WWII Museum, "Research Starters: Worldwide Deaths in World War II", https://www.nationalww2museum.org/students-teachers /student-resources/research-starters/research-starters-worldwide-deaths-world -war.

Immediately after the war, the process of "decolonization" changed the global political landscape. Beginning with the independence of India and Pakistan from Britain in 1947, the European empires made way for the rule of the weakest nations of the world, especially those in Africa, by global corporations and financial institutions. Thus did one deplorable age of empire and exploitation make way for another, leaving the poorest countries as powerless as ever.

At the same time, the world had transitioned from world war to Cold War. On one side was the Soviet Empire under the control of Moscow; on the other were the NATO nations under the de facto control of Washington, D.C. The ensuing arms race led to the development of nuclear weapons so powerful that the atomic bombs that fell on Nagasaki and Hiroshima seemed almost "medieval" by comparison. This military strategy was known as "mutually assured destruction", or MAD, an acronym that speaks for itself. As for the Soviet Empire, it continued its pathological war on the Church, imprisoning Church leaders for their adherence to the faith: Cardinal Wyszynski in Poland, Cardinal Stepinac in Yugoslavia, Cardinal Beran in Czechoslovakia, and Cardinal Mindszenty in Hungary.

Communism also spread like a murderous cancer throughout other parts of the world. China, Korea, Vietnam, and Cambodia, in particular, fell victim to its doctrine of death. The Chinese communists, under the tyrannous rule of Mao Zedung, would kill even more people than the Soviets. In Cambodia, Pol Pot, leader of the communist Khmer Rouge, oversaw the murder of 1.7 million of his own people before he was deposed.[15]

---

[15] "Genocide in Cambodia," Holocaust Museum Houston, https://hmh.org/library/research/genocide-in-cambodia-guide.

The 1960s saw the sexual revolution, which would reap havoc. To take but one example of a legion that could be offered: In 1950, before the sexual revolution, only 2 percent of British babies were born out of wedlock; by 1998, thirty years or so after the revolution, 38 percent were born outside of marriage.[16] In addition, millions of unborn children have been butchered in the womb, as abortion was legalized and encouraged throughout the "developed" world. In 1968, in the midst of the immoral mayhem and madness of the sexual revolution, Paul VI issued his truly heroic encyclical, *Humanae Vitae*, which was unequivocal in its defense of the procreative purpose of the sexual union. The widespread rebellion against this teaching within the Church laid the foundations for the widespread sexual abuse that would become a pervasive blight by the end of the century. At root, Paul VI was making the necessary connection between chastity and charity. When the former is no longer respected as a necessary virtue, human persons are no longer loved but are treated as objects to be used and abused.

The widespread opposition to *Humanae Vitae* was a symptom of the spirit of doctrinal apostasy that prevailed at the time. This was encapsulated in a homily preached by Paul VI in 1972 in which he saw the demonic dimension of the so-called "spirit of Vatican II", which distorted and perverted the teaching of the Second Vatican Council in the service of modernism and relativism. "Through some fissure," Paul VI lamented, "the smoke of Satan has entered the temple of God."[17] Thankfully and by

---

[16] *The Week* (British Edition), March 17, 2001, quoted in H.W. Crocker III, *Triumph: The Power and the Glory of the Catholic Church* (New York: Three Rivers Press, 2001), 413.

[17] Quoted in Shaw, *Six Popes and the Crisis of Modernity*, 117.

the grace of God, the tide was turned by the election of John Paul II in 1978. The Catholic restoration began during his pontificate, in which he was aided and abetted by Joseph Cardinal Ratzinger, whom he had chosen as his righthand man and trusted confidant. The smoke of Satan might have entered the temple, but the gates of hell would not prevail.

The Beautiful

On January 1, 1900, the first day of the new century, Edward Elgar received a commission to compose a musical setting of John Henry Newman's poem *The Dream of Gerontius*. The result was one of the masterpieces of the twentieth century in which Elgar unites his genius with that of Newman to bring to dramatic life the story of a soul's transit, assisted by its guardian angel, to the cleansing fires of purgatorial love. Another British composer of fine sacred music in the early years of the century was Ralph Vaughan Williams, who is responsible for some of the finest and most popular hymn tunes ever written. Like Elgar, however, he did not restrict himself to sacred music. Elgar's "Pomp and Circumstance" and "Nimrod Variations" have become part of the canon as has Vaughan Williams' sublimely beautiful "Lark Ascending", a setting of a poem of the same name by George Meredith.

Across the Channel in France, the Catholic musical revival was set in motion by St. Pius X's motu proprio on sacred music, *Tra Le Sollecitudini*, issued in 1903, which called for the promotion of Gregorian chant and sacred polyphony in the liturgy. The restoration of the Church's musical tradition would influence the works of three young composers who were, or became, devout

Catholics. These were Maurice Duruflé, Francis Poulenc, and Olivier Messiaen.

Duruflé's *Requiem*, composed in 1947, is resonant throughout with traditional chants from the Requiem Mass. His *Messe "cum jubilo"*, a late work composed in 1966, in the midst of the widespread abandonment of chant and polyphony in the Church's liturgy, remains true to the tradition of chant, in compliance with Pius X's teaching. Music historian Susan Treacy conjectures that "this was Duruflé's way of continuing the Gregorian tradition in the wake of the domination of liturgical music by secular commercial music styles."[18] Francis Poulenc's *Dialogues des Carmélites*, which premièred in 1957, was inspired by the sixteen Carmelite Martyrs of Compiègne, who were guillotined in 1794, during the Reign of Terror following the French Revolution. Olivier Messiaen was preoccupied with the Four Last Things (death, judgment, heaven, and hell), as is evident in works such as *Le banquet céleste* (*The Heavenly Banquet*) and *Quatuor pour la fin du temps* (*Quartet for the End of Time*). "In the increasingly secular twentieth century," writes Susan Treacy, "Messiaen sought to reveal the sublimity, the vastness, the depths, the tenderness, the anguish, the joy, the clarity, and the mystery of Catholicism to a world that did not care to be reminded of its own finiteness and apostasy."[19]

The latter part of the century was dominated by the holy minimalists, especially Henryk Górecki, John Tavener, and Arvo Pärt. Górecki used his gifts in the service of the Catholic resistance to communist tyranny in Poland. His *Miserere* was written in response to the violence used

---

[18] Susan Treacy, *The Music of Christendom: A History* (San Francisco: Ignatius Press, 2021), 207.

[19] Ibid., 209.

by communist militia against members of the Solidarity trade union, and his *Totus Tuus* was composed for John Paul II's third visit to Poland in 1987. According to Susan Treacy, Górecki was "a composer whose numinous music is an antidote to the brutality and ugliness of today's secularized world".[20] Arvo Pärt, as an Estonian, lived in what was then the Soviet Union and suffered accordingly for his Christian faith. His *Credo*, composed in 1968, was banned by the communist authorities. As a student of Gregorian chant and late medieval polyphony, Pärt's decidedly modern minimalism was nonetheless informed by tradition. Again, we will let Dr. Treacy encapsulate the spirit of Arvo Pärt's music:

> In this world of noise pollution there is need for silence, yet many seem not to realize this. Silence is that precious state that allows one to encounter God and to hear His voice. The music of Estonian composer Arvo Pärt is born of such silence, and it bespeaks a vastness that is both an emptiness shorn of all excess and an amplitude containing everything.[21]

For the most part, the twentieth century signaled the disintegration of the visual arts into formless and meaningless abstraction. Expressing nothing but the angst-ridden narcissism of the artist, it ceased to engage with any objective reality beyond the self. Disconnected from reality, it had nothing to say. Having nothing to say, it says nothing. There were a few noble exceptions to this general death wish on the part of the century's artists. Pietro Annigoni was an unabashed realist, influenced and inspired by the masters of the Renaissance, who distanced himself publicly

[20] Ibid., 222.
[21] Ibid., 222–23.

and controversially from the dominant abstraction, modernism, and postmodernism of twentieth-century art. He was commissioned to paint portraits of Queen Elizabeth, Princess Margaret, and other members of the British Royal family, as well as portraits of Pope John XXIII and U.S. presidents John F. Kennedy and Lyndon B. Johnson.

A contemporary of Annigoni who also painted in the realist tradition was the Scottish painter Sir James Gunn. Like Annigoni, he specialized in portraiture and, also like Annigoni, he was commissioned to paint portraits of the British Royal family. His *Conversation Piece at Royal Lodge, Windsor*, painted in 1950, shows King George VI seated at table with his wife, Queen Elizabeth, and his two daughters, the princesses Elizabeth and Margaret, the former of whom would become queen two years later. Another famous "conversation piece" executed by Sir James Gunn is *Conversation Piece: Hilaire Belloc, G. K. Chesterton and Maurice Baring*, which shows the three Catholic writers gathered round a table and concentrating on something that Chesterton is writing. Gunn, who was a convert to the Catholic faith, is buried in the same graveyard in Sussex as Hilaire Belloc.

Perhaps the most famous artist of the century, with the possible exception of Picasso, is Salvador Dali, who was himself a convert to his own quirky form of Catholicism. His return to tradition and the faith was animated by his disgust and disillusionment with the anarchists and communists of the surrealist movement with whom he had collaborated in his youth. Taking the anticommunist side during the civil war in his native Spain, his later work is dominated by religious themes. *The Dream of Christopher Columbus* is triumphalistic in the way in which it depicts the settlers of the New World as being on a crusade to plant the seeds of the faith on pagan ground. His best-known religious work is, however, *Christ of St. John of the Cross*, which shows the crucified Christ, seen from above, which was inspired by a drawing attributed to St. John of the Cross.

Moving from art to architecture and remaining in Spain, the greatest sacred edifice built in the twentieth century is the Basilica of the Sagrada Família in Barcelona, the architect of which, Antoni Gaudi, lived such a holy life that he has become known as "God's architect" amid calls for his beatification. Sagrada Família is as magnificent as it is singular and strange, a masterpiece that breaks with tradition without compromising form or beauty. The interior is as breathtaking as the famous exterior, the columns adopting organic forms that appear as giant trees, as alive as the Gospel and as evocative to readers of *The Lord of the Rings* as the elven magic of Lothlórien.

The reference to *The Lord of the Rings* segues the discussion to the great literature of the twentieth century. As for *The Lord of the Rings* itself, the most popular literary work of the century in terms of sales and most powerful in terms of influence, it was described by its author as "a fundamentally religious and Catholic work".[22] It is indeed a testimony to the Catholic literary revival throughout the world that there is a treasure trove of fundamentally religious and Catholic works from which to choose in a century that constitutes a golden age of Catholic literature.

Apart from Tolkien's success with *The Hobbit* and *The Lord of the Rings*, the works of Tolkien's friend C. S. Lewis would also prove hugely successful globally. Although Lewis was a convert to Anglican Christianity and is not therefore technically a Catholic, his works are essentially

[22] *The Letters of J. R. R. Tolkien*, ed. Humphrey Carpenter (London: George Allen and Unwin, 1981), 172.

orthodox in their portrayal of Christianity. Staying in England, Chesterton and Belloc were giant figures of the Catholic revival in the first third of the century. Their works would inspire many literary converts to the faith, including Evelyn Waugh and Graham Greene.

T. S. Eliot, an American who spent most of his life in London, described himself as a Catholic, a royalist, and a classicist. He would prove to be the most influential poet of the century. Other Americans who were either Catholic or were inspired by Catholicism are Flannery O'Connor, Walker Percy, and Willa Cather, whose *Death Comes for the Archbishop* is masterful historical fiction about the pioneering Catholics who evangelized the American West.

Returning to Europe, there was a Catholic literary revival in France that paralleled the musical revival that we have already discussed. Writers who graced this revival include François Mauriac, Charles Péguy, Léon Bloy, and Georges Bernanos, whose *Diary of a Country Priest* is a classic of Catholic fiction.

The Austrian poet, playwright, and novelist Franz Werfel was not a Catholic, but his wonderful novel, *The Song of Bernadette*, inspired by the Marian apparitions at Lourdes, became an international bestseller that would be adapted as a very successful film, a whole new medium of art that is so rich that it must, of necessity, remain beyond the scope of our present study of history.

The Norwegian novelist and convert Sigrid Undset deservedly won the Nobel Prize in Literature in 1928 for her epic depictions of life in medieval Norway.

Last but not least, and with apologies for the inevitable sins of omission, is another winner of the Nobel Prize in Literature, Aleksandr Solzhenitsyn. This indomitable giant of literature and history exposed the evils of the communist regime in the Soviet Union in a succinctly powerful novella, *One Day in the Life of Ivan Denisovich*, and in weighty historical tomes, such as the three-volume *Gulag Archipelago*. He stands alongside John Paul II, Ronald Reagan, and Margaret Thatcher as a key player in helping to bring down the Soviet Union. A convert from Marxism and atheism to Russian Orthodox Christianity, he epitomized the unbroken spirit of Christendom after twenty centuries of struggle.

It was Solzhenitsyn who said that the battle between good and evil takes place in each individual human heart. This battle in each human heart is the battle at the heart of history. It is the battle between the goodness of the saints and the wickedness of the worldly, of those who accept and embrace goodness, truth, and beauty, and those who make the great refusal, choosing instead the path of pride. There is no final victory for one side or the other within the confines of time. The victory or defeat comes at the end of time that, for each of us, is the end of our own time, the moment of our death. It is with this contemplation of the Last Things, which should always be the first things in our mind, that we will end this journey through three-dimensional history.

EPILOGUE

The End of History

This journey through two millennia of history is not doomed to end with any apocalyptic prophesies about the end times. We do not know the hour when God will bring down the final curtain on history, and it is foolish to waste the little time we are given in idle speculation. The world will end in God's good time, which could be in the next year or the next millennium. When will the world end? God knows when.

On the other hand, we do know that our own world will end at the hour of our death. This is the only end of the world that should concern us. This is the end of the world we keep in mind every time we say the Hail Mary. We know that, for us, this world might end tomorrow, or even today. We know that, for us, it will not end in the next millennium, or indeed the next century. It will happen much sooner.

So much for the end of the world, but what about the end of history?

According to Francis Fukayama, it has happened already. In his international bestseller, *The End of History and the Last Man*, Fukayama argued that history ended with the triumph of liberal democracy following the end of the Cold War and the fall of Soviet communism. According to Fukayama, the whole of humanity, from 1991 onward, has nothing to look forward to in the future but a happier and happier ending.

This is really too foolish to be taken seriously, though this has not stopped millions of people from taking it very seriously indeed. As G.K. Chesterton quipped, when people stop believing in God they do not believe in nothing; they believe in anything.[1]

We will leave such foolishness to be judged by history itself, if indeed it has not already been judged and found absurdly wanting. Instead, we will discuss the end of history, not in terms of *when* it might end but in terms of *what* is its end. What is its purpose? To what end does it serve?

The end of history, its purpose, is to make the will of God manifest in time. History is His story.

The knowledge of history allows us to see and understand the dynamic and the moral of the story. It allows us to see the three threads, the three dimensions, that weave the pattern of the providential design. The purpose of each one of us, as participants in history, is to choose the good and the beautiful and to lay down our lives for them. This is choosing the right side of history.

Time is the battlefield. We must choose to be a warrior in the Church Militant or else, by default, we will choose to be the Judas figure who serves the lord of this world.

Our mortal lives are our tour of duty in the cosmic struggle. Our active service ends when we cross the threshold from time to eternity. In the interim, we are called to struggle as soldiers of Christ in the Church Militant so that we might find our ultimate fulfilment in God's eternal presence in the Church Triumphant. This is the only purpose of history as it is the only purpose of life.

---

[1] There is no record of Chesterton ever having used this specific form of words that is so often attributed to him, though he said many things that sound remarkably similar. If it is not the literal Chesterton, it certainly evokes the spirit of Chesterton.

We will conclude with some words of wisdom from J. R. R. Tolkien, who waxed lyrical and wistful on the perennial presence of evil throughout history:

> I am a Christian, and indeed a Roman Catholic, so that I do not expect "history" to be anything but a "long defeat"—though it contains ... some samples and glimpses of final victory.[2]

In the long defeat of history, in which the bad souls who serve the lord of this world always seem to be in the ascendant, the samples and glimpses of final victory are seen in the presence of God's love in the lives and deaths of the saints and in the creative presence of God's beauty in His creation and in the great works of art that have graced the centuries. These things, the good and the beautiful, point beyond history to the end of history itself. They point beyond the long defeat to the final victory.

The final victory has already been won. It was won by Christ on Calvary and in His Resurrection from the dead. All that we need to do is to keep His victory in mind and the finishing line in sight. The rest, the requiescat, is not history but His Story in all its glory. This is the happy ending that awaits those who fight for the good and lay down their lives for the beautiful. It is the happy ending that is the true beginning of the happy ever after.

[2] *The Letters of J. R. R. Tolkien*, ed. Humphrey Carpenter (London: George Allen and Unwin, 1981), 255.

INDEX

Aachen, Germany, 97, 106–7
Abbey Notre-Dame de Jouarre, 91
Abbey of Lérins, 60, 98
Abbey of Saint-Étienne, Caen, 138
Abbey of Saint-Riquier, 122
Abbey of St. Gall, Switzerland, 94
abortion, 268
Acacius (Patriarch of Constantinople), 63
Adam of Bremen, 130
Adoration in a Wood (Lippi), 188–90
Adrian of Canterbury (saint), 86
Adversus Hereses (Irenaeus), 26, 30–31
Aelred (saint), 141–43
The Aeneid (Virgil), 15
Aeterni Patris (Leo XIII), 255
Africa
    Christianity, 36–38
    colonial conquests, nineteenth century, 245
    Muslim presence, seventh/ eighth centuries, 88, 98
    Roman Empire, 56
    slave trade, 199, 210
    Vandal presence, fifth century, 62
Against Heresies (Irenaeus), 26, 30–31

Agapitus II (pope), 120
Agilbert (saint), 83
Agrippina (empress), 20
Aïda (Verdi), 251
Aidan (saint), 83–84
Alans (barbarian tribe), 61
Alaric (Visigoth leader), 61
Alberic II (secular ruler of Rome), 120–21
Albert the Great (Albertus Magnus, saint), 157–58
Alcuin of York, 93, 96–97
Alexander Severus (emperor), 37, 40
Alexander V (antipope), 183
Alexander VII (pope), 213
Alexandria, Egypt, 88
    massacre (A.D. 215), 40
Alfred Jewel (gold and crystal gem), 115
Alfred the Great (English king), 96, 108–11, 112, 115
Algonquin people, 211
allegory, Christian, 54, 94, 101, 102–3, 123
Alphonsus Liguori (saint), 221
Ambrose (saint), 49, 53–54
Ambrosian chant, 53–54
Americas
    Catholic missions, 209–10
    European conquest of, 198–99
Anastasius I (emperor), 59
The Angelus (Millet), 253

Anglican church, 247, 258
Anglo-Saxon
    art, 113–14
    history, 94. *See also* England
    language, 101, 104, 135–36
    literature, 100–104, 114, 152
    missionaries, 95
Anglo-Saxon Chronicle, 111
Annigoni, Pietro, 271–72
Annunciation (Fra Angelico), 188
Anselm of Canterbury (saint),
    140–41
Anthony of Egypt (saint), 48, 55
Anthony of Padua (saint), 158, 192
anthropos, 8n3, 9
Antioch, Greece, 16, 27, 88, 145
Antonina (wife of Byzantine
    commander), 75–76
Aquinas, Thomas (saint), 157–58,
    161, 163, 175, 255
    poetry and hymns, 163–64
architecture
    Gothic, 162–63
    Gothic Revival, 247
    Romanesque, 122, 138
Arianism, 48, 50–52, 73–74, 78
Aristotle, 58, 140, 157
Arius, 50. *See also* Arianism
Armenia, 37, 64–65
Armenian Genocide, 264
art
    as apologetics, 189
    beauty of, 10
    catacomb, 34–35, 42–45
    fourteenth century, 174–77
    God's presence in, 9
    man, 34–35
    religious, 42–45
    steles, 90–91
    Vikings, 113–15

Renaissance, 188–92
    waning power of, eighteenth
        century, 230–32
Arundel, Thomas, 171
asceticism, 48, 50, 211
Asia Minor, 37
Assumption of the Virgin (El
    Greco), 204
Athanasius (saint), 51, 55
atheism, 224–26, 231, 264
Attila the Hun, 62
Auden, W. H., 45
Augustine of Canterbury (saint),
    93
Augustine of Hippo (saint), 49,
    54, 56–58, 62, 68, 82–83, 94
Augustinian Canons Regular,
    180
Aurelian (emperor), 41
Austen, Jane, 248
Ave Maria (Schubert), 250–51
Ave Maria (twelfth century
    prayer), 153
Averroës, 140
Avicenna, 140
Avignon, France, and papacy,
    167, 173–74, 183
Aztec Empire, 198

Bach, Johann Sebastian, 233
Bacon, Roger, 158
Bakhita, Josephine, 262
The Ballad of the White Horse
    (Chesterton), 109
ballet, 218
The Banquet Scene (in catacomb
    of Priscilla), 35
Baptistery of the Orthodox, 66
Baring, Maurice, 272
Barker, Ernest, 155

Barking Abbey, Essex, 85
Basilica of Saint-Sernin, Toulouse, 138
Basilica of Santa Cecilia, 44–45
Basilica of Sant'Apollinare Nuovo, Ravenna, 78
Basilica of Santa Pudenziana, 66
Basilica of San Vitale, Ravenna, 78
Basilica of the Sagrada Família, Barcelona (Gaudi), 273
Basil the Great (saint), 48, 51
Battle of Agincourt, 171
Battle of Bannockburn, 170
Battle of Belgrade, 182
Battle of Eddington, 109–10
Battle of Hastings, 133. *See also* Norman Conquest (1066)
Battle of Kosovo, 172
Battle of Lepanto, 197–98
Battle of Louvain, 113
Battle of Manzikert, 135
Battle of Ostia, 107
Battle of Roncevaux Pass, 110
Battle of the Milvian Bridge, 47
Bayeux Tapestry, 136
beauty
    of art, 10
    of Christ, 8, 13, 23, 43–44
    and Christian art, 34, 43–44
    Creator/creation, 9–10, 12–13, 67–68, 279
    and Four Last Things, 175
    human love of, 34
    and humility, 12–13
    of the liturgy, 196
    of music, and divine mystery, 44, 232–33
    mystical marriage of love and, 157

    and Renaissance art, 188–91
    revival of and Romanticism, 246
    sacramental, in Eucharist, 23–24
Becket, Thomas (saint), 146–48, 192
Bede the Venerable (saint), 84–86, 93–96, 100–101, 104
Bedouelle, Guy, 64, 72
Beethoven, Ludwig van, 249
Belisarius, Flavius, 75–76
Belle Époque, 252
Bellini, Giovanni, 251
Belloc, Hilaire, 64, 108–9, 111–12, 119, 124, 147–48
Benedict (saint), 60–61, 71
Benedictine revival (tenth century), 87, 118–19
Benedict XV (pope), 256–59
Benedict XVI (pope), 9–10, 153, 187, 261
Beowulf, 101–3, 152, 176
Beran, Cardinal, 267
Berlin Conference, 245
Berlinghieri, Bonaventura, 163
Bernardine of Siena (saint), 180–82
Bernanos, Georges, 274
Bernard of Clairvaux, 141, 144
Bernart de Ventadorn, 150–51
Bernini, Gian Lorenzo, 218–19
Berno (saint), 117–19
Bertan de Born, 151
Bertin (saint), 87
Bertrando, Lawrence (saint), 232
Bible
    Acts of the Apostles, 16–17
    canonization of New Testament, 26

Bible (*continued*)
  Daniel, Book of, 42–43
  John, Gospel of, 11, 16–17,
    115, 125
  Matthew, Gospel of, 16
  synoptic, 16
  translations, 49
  Vulgate, 49
  writing of, 26
Birinus (saint), 83
Birth of Venus (Botticelli), 189
Bismarck, Otto von, 244–45
Black Death, 77, 165, 172–73
Blake, William, 252–53
Blessed Sacrament. *See* Eucharist
Blessed Virgin. *See* Mary
Bloy, Léon, 274
Blunden, Edmund, 45
Bobbio, Lombardy, abbey, 72, 86
Boethius, 73–75, 79–80, 110
Bohemond, 146
Boizot, Claude, 156
Bologna, university, 140
Bolshevik Revolution, 262, 264
Bonaventure (saint), 158
Boniface (saint), 93–96
The Book of Kells, 113–14
The Book of Lindisfarne, 91
The Book of Margery Kempe, 169
Borromeo, Charles (saint), 195,
    196
Bosch, Hieronymus, 55, 150
Bosco, John, 242
Botticelli, Sandro, 189
Bouchard, Gary, 205
Boucher, François, 232
Bride of Lammermoor (Scott), 251
Bridget of Sweden (saint),
    166–67, 173
Bridgettine Order, 166

British Empire, 243, 245–46
British Humanist Association, 231
Britten, Benjamin, 45
Brown, George Mackay, 124–25
Bruckner, Anton, 250–51
Brunelleschi, Filippo, 191
Bruno of Querfurt (saint), 129–30
bubonic plague. *See* Black Death
Bunyan, John, 217
Burgundians, 70, 73
Burial of Count Orgaz (El Greco),
    204
Byrd, William, 205
Byzantine army, 135, 186
Byzantine culture, 137

Cabrini, Francis Xavier, 262
Caedmon, 101
Caedwalla (saint/Wessex king),
    85–86
Calderón de la Barca, Pedro, 217
Caligula (emperor), 19–20
calligraphy, 91. *See also*
    manuscripts
Callistus (pope), 38
Callistus III (pope), 184
Calvin, John, 197, 199
Campion, Edmund (saint), 200,
    205
Canaletto, 232
Canterbury Cathedral, 146–47
"Canticle of Brother Sun"
    (Francis of Assisi), 67, 163
Canute (Scandinavian/English
    king), 131–32
Can vei la lauzeta mover (Bernart
    de Ventadorn), 150–51
capitalism, 255
Cappadocia, Turkey, 48
Cappadocian Fathers, 48, 51

Caracalla (Roman emperor), 40
Caravaggio, 218, 232
Carloman (Frankish ruler), 95
Carmelite order, 201, 208
Carmen Campidoctoris, 137
Carroll, Charles, 222
Carroll, John, 221–22, 239
Carroll-Dulany controversy, 222
Carthage, 38, 41, 88
Casti Connubii (Pius XI), 258
catacomb art, 34–35, 42–45
Catechism of the Catholic Church, 195–96
Cathedral of Saint-Lazare, Burgundy, 149
Cather, Willa, 274
Catherine of Alexandria (saint), 192
Catherine of Aragon (saint), 173
Catherine of Bologna (saint), 191–92
Catherine of Siena (saint), 166, 167, 168, 173
Catherine of Sweden (saint), 167–68
cave painting, 33–34
caves, symbolism of, 33–35
Cecilia (saint), 44–45, 55
Cedd (saint), 84
Celestine I (pope), 59
Celestine V (pope), 158
Celtic Christianity, 71–72, 112–14
Centesimus Annus (John Paul II), 256, 261
Cervantes, Miguel de, 216–17
Cézanne, Paul, 55
Chad (saint), 84
Chanel, Peter, 242
chansons de geste, 151–52

chant
    Ambrosian, 53–54
    Gregorian, 80–81, 91–92, 124, 153, 252, 269–70
    Hildegard of Bingen, 152–53
    liturgical, 53–54
charity, twelfth century revival of, 142–44
Charlemagne, 97–98, 105–7
Charles I (Scottish king), 215
Charles of Anjou, 146
Charles the Great. See Charlemagne
Charles VI (Holy Roman Emperor), 223
Charpentier, Marc-Antoine, 45
Chateaubriand, François-René de, 248, 252
Chaucer, Geoffrey, 45, 136, 177
Chesterton, G.K., 33–34, 35, 42, 87–88, 90, 92, 109–11, 157, 162, 197, 236, 256, 278, 278n1
Chi-Rho (Christian symbol), 34–35
chivalry, 143–44
Christ
    beauty of, 12–13, 23, 43–44
    "consubstantiality" with God, 51
    divine/human natures, 58, 63, 66
    divinity of, 50–51
    Eucharistic presence, 24–25
    humility of, 125
    Infant Jesus, 192
    as New Song, 44
    Sacred Heart of Jesus, 208–9
    Suffering Christ, 179

Christ (*continued*)
  as template of pattern of
    history, 11–12
  triune nature of, 8
  as "the way, and the truth, and
    the life", 23
Christianity
  persecution of early Christians,
    21, 28–29, 34, 36, 41
  spread of early Christianity, 16,
    22–23, 37, 46–47, 129–30
Christ of St. John of the Cross
  (Dali), 273
Christ Unfurled (Meconi), 27
Church
  anti-Christian edicts under
    Diocletian, 41
  apostolic succession, 30–31
  authority of, 27, 59, 134, 237
  blood of martyrs as seed of, 29,
    36, 39, 45
  as Bride of Christ, 39, 45
  Catholic Reformation, 193,
    196
  Catholic Revival (Counter-
    Reformation), 248, 252,
    254
  as City of God, 56–57, 59–60,
    62, 70, 134, 149
  Concordat between Napoleon
    and Pius VII (1801),
    237–38
  conversion in Ireland, 66–67,
    71–72
  conversion of Norsemen
    (Vikings), 124–25, 130
  conversion of pagan kings/
    tribes, 70–73
  conversion of Slavs, ninth
    century, 108

corruption within, tenth
  century, 116–17, 133–34
danger of worldliness, fourth
  century, 50
Doctors of the Church, 94,
  140–41, 153, 167, 207
East/West schism, fifth
  century, 63
ecumenical power of, 57–58
Eucharist as center of worship,
  27–28
faith and reason (*fides et ratio*),
  58, 96, 157, 203, 231
first called "catholic", 27
Great Persecution, 46
growth during third century,
  46
heresy as threat from within,
  29–30
Jubilee Year (1450), 179–80
mendicant orders, 155
missionary evangelization, 37,
  130, 194–95, 209–10
Mother of the faithful/Bride
  of Christ, 38–39
as Mystical Body of Christ,
  45, 65, 179, 193–94, 204,
  219, 236
persecution of early Christians,
  17, 19, 28–29, 38–39
power and authority, 134
six ages of Christendom, 254
Society of Foreign Missions,
  239
and state, fusion of, 106
teaching authority of, 59
third century growth in
  Rome, 37–38
tradition, 92
True Cross, fragments of, 104

Church, Eastern, 63, 133–35, 138, 145, 186, 204. *See also* Great Schism

church and state. *See also* Becket, Thomas (saint)
eighteenth century, 226–27
French Revolution, 228–30
under Charlemagne, 106–7
under Holy Roman Emperor, 122

Churchill, Winston, 263

Church of Cyriakus, Gernrode, Germany, 121–22

Church of San Clemente, Lérida, Spain, 149

Church of the Holy Sepulchre, Jerusalem, 48, 53, 139

Cimabue, 163, 174–75

Cistercian order, 141–43
Trappist reform of, 208

Citeaux, France, monastery, 141

The City of God (Augustine), 54, 56–57, 62, 94

City of God/City of Man, 56–57, 59–60, 62, 65–66, 70, 134, 149, 159, 246

Clairvaux, Cistercian abbey, 141–42

Clare of Assisi, 158

Claret, Anthony Mary, 242

Claudius (emperor), 20

Claver, Peter (saint), 210–11

Clement I (pope/saint), 44

Clement IX (pope), 213

Clement of Alexandria (saint), 44

Clement VI (pope), 167

Clement XIV (pope), 187, 226

Clovis (Frankish king), 64–65, 70, 73

Cluniac revival, 254

Cluny, Abbey, 116–18, 125, 133–34

Coelfrith (Abbot of Wearmouth and Jarrow), 103–4

Cold War, 267

Coleman (monk), 136

Coleridge, Samuel Taylor, 246

Colette (saint), 182

Cologne Cathedral, 122

Colossus (Goya), 252

Columba (saint), 72

Columban (saint), 98

Columbanus (saint), 72, 86, 88, 91

Columbus, Christopher, 187–88

Come, Thou Redeemer of the Earth (Neale), 54

communism, 259
Soviet, 260–61
spread during twentieth century, 267

Confessions (Augustine), 49, 54, 68

Congregation for the Causes of Saints, 187

Congregation of the Most Holy Redeemer, 221

Congregation of the Oratory, 233

Congregation of the Passion of Jesus Christ, 220

The Consolation of Philosophy (Boethius), 73–74, 79

Constable, John, 253

Constans II (emperor), 89

Constantine (emperor), 47–48, 254

Constantine III (emperor), 61

Constantine V (emperor), 99–100

Constantine VI (emperor), 100

Constantinople, Turkey, 73–75,
    77–78
  cultural and theological
      influences from East, 99
  dangers from within, 89, 99
  fall of, fifteenth century, 182,
      185–86
  Great Schism, 135
  sacking of, thirteenth century,
      160
contraception, 258
Conversation Piece (Gunn), 272
*Conversation Piece at Royal Lodge,
    Windsor* (Gunn), 272
Corinth, Greece, 16
Cornelius (pope), 41
Cornelius (Roman centurion),
    17
Coronation of the Virgin (Gaddi),
    163
Cortés, Hernán, 198
Council of Chalcedon (451),
    57–58, 63, 75
Council of Constance (1417),
    183
Council of Constantinople (381),
    51
Council of Ephesus (431), 57–58
Council of Nicaea (325), 51, 57
Council of Trent, 193–96
Counter-Reformation, 193, 254
Crashaw, Richard, 205, 217
Crete, Greece, 16
Crispus (Archbishop of Milan),
    86
Cristero War, Mexico, 265
Crocker, H. W., III (Harry),
    22–23, 88, 135, 184, 186, 196,
    228–29
Cross of St. Cuthbert, 90

Crucifixion
  and final victory, 13–14
  Gero Crucifix, 121–22
  Isenheim altarpiece, 203–4
Crusades, 136, 144–46
  First Crusade, 128, 135, 139,
      144–45
  Second Crusade, 145
  Third Crusade, 145
  Fourth Crusade, 159–61
Crypt of the Veiled Lady (in
    Catacomb of Priscilla), 43
Cuthbert (saint), 86, 91
Cyprian (martyr), 38–39, 41
Cyprus, 16
Cyriakus (saint), 121–22
Cyril (saint), 108, 167
Cyrillic script, 108
Czech nation, 183–84

D'Alembert, Jean Le Rond,
    225–26
Dali, Salvador, 55, 150, 272–73
Damasus I (saint and pope), 49
Damian, Peter, 127
Daniel, Arnaut, 151
Dante, 69, 150, 175–76, 247
  De vulgari eloquentia, 151
Dark Ages, 88, 116
*David Composing the Psalms (Paris
    Psalter)*, 123
David II (Scottish king), 170
Da Vinci, Leonardo, 190–91
Dawson, Christopher, 15–16, 65,
    69–70, 81, 86–87, 95–96, 112,
    128–29, 138, 145–46, 152,
    165–66, 173–74, 176–77, 254
Death Comes for the Archbishop
    (Cather), 274
Decius (emperor), 38, 41

decolonization, twentieth
century, 267
Decretum (Gratian), 141
De doctrina Christiana (Augustine),
54
deism, 225
Demiurge (lesser God), 31
De Musica (Boethius), 79–80
Denis (Portugese king), 168
De Porres, Martin, 210–11
Deposition (Fra Angelico), 188
Descartes, René, 214
Desert Fathers, 48
de Tocqueville, Alexis, 239
De Trinitate (Augustine), 58
De vulgari eloquentia (Dante), 151
The Dialogue of Divine Providence
(St. Catherine), 167
Dialogues des Carmélites
(Poulenc), 270
Diary of a Country Priest
(Bernanos), 274
Díaz de Vivar, Rodrigo (El Cid),
136–37
Dickens, Charles, 158, 248
Didache, 28
Diderot, Denis, 225
Diocletian (emperor), 41, 46
Disputation of the Holy Sacrament
(Raphael), 203
The Divine Comedy (Dante), 69,
151, 175
Divine Liturgy for the Celtic
rites, 115
Divine Office (Liturgy of the
Hours), 118
Divini Illius Magistri (Pius XI),
258
Doctors of the Church, 153, 167,
207, 221

Dominic (saint), 155–58
Dominican Order, 155–58
Donizetti, Gaetano, 251
Donne, John, 205, 217
Don Quixote (Cervantes), 217
Dostoyevsky, Fyodor, 248
*The Dream of Christopher
Columbus* (Dali), 272
The Dream of Gerontius
(Newman), 269
"The Dream of the Rood"
(Anglo-Saxon poem), 103
Drexel, Katherine, 262
Dryden, John, 45, 217
Dublin, Ireland, 111–12
Duccio, 163
Du Fay, Guillaume, 191
Duffy, Eamon, 47, 120, 127, 171,
173, 180, 259
Dunstan (saint), 119, 124
Durham Cathedral, 138
Duro-Europos, Syria, 43
Duruflé, Maurice, 270

Eanswith (saint), 84
Earpwald (Anglian king), 83
Easter, timing of, 84
Eastern Church, 63, 133–35, 138,
145, 186, 204
Eastwood, Clint, 7
Ebionite sect, 33
Eboracum (York), 40, 112
*Ecclesiastical History of the English
People* (Bede), 94, 100–101
Ecstasy of Saint Teresa (Bernini),
218
ecumenical
origin of word, 57
power of Church, 57–58
Edgar (English king), 123

Edict against the Christians
(Diocletian), 46
Edict of Milan, 47, 50, 52
Edmund the Martyr (saint), 177
Edward III (English king), 170
Edward the Confessor (saint),
132–13, 177
Edward VI (English king), 200
Edwin (Northumbrian king),
83
Elagabalus (emperor), 40
El Cid, 136–37
Eleanor of Aquitaine, 150
Elgar, Edward, 269
El Greco, 114, 204–5
Eliot, T.S., 104, 175–76, 274
Elizabeth (English princess/
daughter of George VI), 272
Elizabeth I (English queen), 197,
200, 205, 214–15
Elizabeth II (English queen), 272
Elizabeth of Hungary (saint),
158, 168
Elizabeth of Portugal (saint), 168
Elmham, Thomas, 171
Ely Cathedral, 85
*The End of History and the Last
Man* (Fukuyama), 277–78
England. *See also* Anglo-Saxon
history; Anglo-Saxon
language; Anglo-Saxon
literature
Anglo-Saxon England, demise
of, 132–33, 135–36
British Empire, nineteenth
century, 243, 245
Catholic Emancipation (1829),
247
conversion to Christian
country, 83–84

Elizabethan political climate,
205
English Civil War, 215
and French Revolution
refugees, 238
mission to, 82–83
"Our Lady's Dowry", 170–71,
177–78
patron saints, 177
unification as nation, 110
English language
Middle English, 136
Old English (Anglo-Saxon),
104, 135–36
Old English to Middle
English, transition, 176
English literature, 101–4
English Reformation, 169, 193,
199–200
Enlightenment, 224–25
impact on Church, 256
reactions against, 230, 240,
246
Ephesus, Greece, 16
Erikson, Leif, 125
Erik the Red, 125
Erkenwald (saint), 85
Estonia, 167
Ethelbert of Kent, 65, 71, 82
Ethelburga (saint), 85
Etheldreda (saint), 84–85
Ethelwold (saint), 123
Eucharist, 23–25, 256
holy sacrifice as center of
worship, 27–28
Real Presence of Christ,
162–63
veneration of, 142, 169
Eusebius, 21–22, 28–29, 47
Eustace, Katharine, 218

Evangelium Vitae (John Paul II), 261
The Everlasting Man (Chesterton), 33–35
evil, as dark thread through history, 8–10, 12, 279
excommunication, 30, 63, 99, 107–8, 127, 159, 183, 197, 240
Experiment with an Air Pump (Wright), 232
Expulsion from Paradise (Masaccio), 188

Fabian (pope), 38
Fahan stele, Ireland, 90
faith and reason, 58, 96–97, 140, 157, 203, 231, 261
Falstaff (Verdi), 251
Fara (saint), 87
Farmer, David Hugh, 119
Faroe Islands, 87, 124–25
Fatima, Portugal, Marian apparitions, 262
Fauré, Gabriel, 252
Feast of Our Lady of Victory, 197
Feast of the Sacred Heart of Jesus, 208–9
Felicity (martyr), 36
Felix (saint), 83
fides et ratio (faith and reason), 58, 157, 261
Fides et Ratio (John Paul II), 261
fiery furnace, Book of Daniel, 42–43
First Communion, 256
First Crusade, 128, 135, 139, 144–45
fish, symbolism of, 34
Fisher, John (saint), 199
Flaubert, Gustave, 55

Florence, Italy, 163
    Florence Cathedral, 191
    Medici family, 191
Folquet of Marseilles, 151
Fonte Avellana, monastery, 127
Four Books of Sentences (Lombard), 141
Four Last Things, 149, 175, 235, 270
The Four Men: A Farrago (Belloc), 124
The Four Seasons (Vivaldi), 233
Fourth Crusade, 159–60
Fourth Lateran Council, 154–55
Fra Angelico, 188
France
    Calvinism, 207
    civil wars, sixteenth century, 199
    Clovis, King of the Franks, 64–65
    Franco-Prussian War, 243, 245
    French Revolution, 225–26, 228–30, 236, 238
    Gallicanism, 213, 214
    Thirty Years' War, 212–13
Francis (pope), 187
Francis de Sales (saint), 208
Franciscan Order, 155–57, 180–82
Francis de Sales (saint), 207
Francis of Assisi (saint), 67, 155, 156–57, 163
Francis Xavier, 194–96
Franco-Prussian War, 243, 245
Frankenstein (Shelley), 252
Franks (barbarian tribe), 41, 73
    missionaries to, 97
    See also France
Freemasons, 227

French impressionism, 253
Frisians (Germanic tribe), 95
Froissart, Jean, 170
Fukayama, Francis, 277

Gaddi, Gaddo, 163
Galerius (emperor), 46
Galgani, Gemma, 262
Gall (saint), 87
Gallicanism, 213, 214
Gallic Empire, 40–41
Gaudi, Antoni, 273
Gelasius (pope), 59–60
General Reform Decree, 194
George VI (English king), 272
Gerard of Brogne (saint), 119
Gregory VII (pope), 118–19,
    127–28, 133–34
Germanic tribes, 40, 95
Germany
    Catholic resistance to German
        Empire, nineteenth
        century, 244
    Dresden during World War II,
        266
    imperialism, nineteenth
        century, 243–44
    Kulturkampf, 244
    missions to Germanic tribes,
        eighth century, 95–96
    Nazi government, 258–60
    Peasants' War (1524), 199
    Romanticism, nineteenth
        century, 248–50
Gero (Archbishop of Cologne),
    122
Gero (nobleman), 121–22
Gero Crucifix, 122
Geta (son of Roman emperor),
    40

Gibbon, Edward, 71
Giotto, 163, 174–75
Girl with Chocolate (Liotard), 232
Giustiniani, Giovanni, 186
Glastonbury Abbey, 200
Glorious Revolution, England,
    215
Gnosticism, 30–31
God
    beauty of, 68
    and creativity, 35
    man's longing for, 249
Godfrey of Bouillon, 146
Golgotha, thieves crucified on
    either side of Christ, 12
Gombrich, E.H., 43, 162
The Good, the Bad, and the Ugly
    (film), 7
Gorbachev, Mikhail, 261
Górecki, Henryk, 270–71
Goretti, Maria, 262
Görres, Joseph, 248
Gospel Book of Archbishop Ebbo of
    Reims, 114
The Gospel Book of Charlemagne,
    114
Gospels. See Bible
Gospels of Otto III, 125
Gothic architecture, 162–63
Gothic invasions, 61
Gothic Revival, 247
Goths (barbarian tribe), 41
    assimilation in Italy, 63–64
Gounod, Charles, 45
Goya, Francisco de, 252
Grant, Johan, 186
Gratian, 141
Great Schism, 135, 165, 167,
    173–74, 179, 182–83. See also
    Church, Eastern

Greek culture
  adoption by Romans, 63–64
  classical heritage of, 123–24
  impact of, 69
Greene, Graham, 274
Greenland, 125
Gregorian chant, 80–81, 91–92, 124, 152–53, 252, 269, 271
Gregory III (pope), 99
Gregory IX (pope), 155
Gregory of Nazianzus (saint), 48, 51
Gregory of Nyssa (saint), 48, 51
Gregory of Tours, 64, 73
Gregory the Great (saint/pope), 72, 76–77, 80–83, 93, 108, 254
Gregory the Wonder-Worker (saint), 37
Gregory VI (pope), 126–127, 173
Gregory VII (saint/pope), 118–19, 127–28, 133–35
Gregory X (pope), 155
Gregory XV (pope), 209
Gregory XVI (pope), 240
Grenada, Spain, 187
Grünewald, Matthias, 55, 203–4
Guardi, Francesco, 232
Guido of Siena, 163
Guilday, Peter, 221–22
Gulag Archipelago (Solzhenitsyn), 275
Gulliver's Travels (Swift), 230
Gunn, Sir James, 272
gunpowder, invention of, 172

Hagia Sophia, Constantinople, 74, 77–78, 160
Hamlet (Shakespeare), 216–17
Handel, George Frideric, 45, 233–34

Harald Bluetooth (Danish king), 124–25
Harald Hardradi (Norse king), 136, 136n18
Harding, Stephen (saint), 141
Haydn, Joseph, 45, 234
Hayes, Carlton, 224
Hegel, Georg Wilhelm Friedrich, 214
Helena (saint), 48
Hellmouth manuscript, 150
Henry II (English king), 146–47, 150
Henry IV (Holy Roman Emperor), 127
Henry of Huntingdon, 131–32
Henry V (English king), 171
Henry VIII (English king), 84–85, 133, 193, 199–200, 247
Herbert, George, 205, 217
heresies
  Arianism, 48, 50–52
  Gallicanism, 213–14
  Gnosticism, 30–31
  iconoclasm, 99–100, 132, 169
  Jansenism, 213–14, 221
  John Huss, 182–84
  Marcionism, 31–33
  modernism, 256
  Monophysite heresy, 63, 66, 75, 89
  Monothelitism, 89
  Montanism, 31–33
  Pelagianism, 62–63, 101–2
  as threat to Church, 29–30, 219
hermits, 48
Hessians (Germanic tribe), 95
Hilary of Arles (saint), 60
Hildegard of Bingen (saint), 152–53

Hildesheim Cathedral, 138
"The Hind and the Panther"
    (Dryden), 217
Hippo, seige of, 62
Hiroshima, Japan, 266–67
Historia Francorum (Gregory of
    Tours), 73
Historia Roderici, 137
history
    Christ as template of pattern
        of, 11–12
    end of, 277–79
    Eucharistic presence,
        importance of, 25
    of human creativity, 35
    patterns of, 8–9, 11–13
    six ages of Christendom, 254
    three dimensions of, 9, 11–14,
        278
    worded into being by God, 11
*The History of the Rise and Fall of
    the Roman Empire* (Gibbon),
    71
Hitda (abbess), 137
Hitler, Adolf, 259
The Hobbit (Tolkien), 273
Hoffmann, E. T. A., 249
Holocaust, 259–60
Holy Communion. *See* Eucharist
Holy Land
    conquered by Muslims, 98–99,
        135
    seizure in seventh century,
        88–89
Holy League, 197–98
Holy Roman Empire, 105, 112,
    121, 199
    Ottonian dynasty, 122–23
    and secularism, eighteenth
        century, 227–28

War of the Austrian
        Succession, 223–24
    See also Charlemagne
Homer, 69, 152, 175
homo superbus, 8–9
homo viator, 8–9
Honorius (emperor), 61
Honorius (saint), 83–84
Honorius III (pope), 155
Honorius of Canterbury (pope),
    101
Hopkins, Gerard Manley, 35,
    205, 248
Huguenots, 209
Hughes, Philip, 30–31, 33, 37–38,
    93, 98–100, 106, 113, 213
Hugo, Victor, 248
Humanae Vitae (Paul VI), 261, 268
humility and beauty, 12–13
Hundred Years' War, 167, 172,
    184
Hungary, 129–30
    invasions by Islamic Turks, 182
Hunyadi, John, 182
Huron people, 211
Huss, John, 182–84
Hyacinth (saint), 232

Iceland, 125, 130–31
ichthys (fish symbol), 34–35
iconoclasm, heresy of, 99–100,
    169
iconography
    The Book of Kells, 113–14
    Byzantine influence on Russia,
        137–38
    Gero Crucifix, 122
    icon of Christ Pantocrator, St.
        Catherine's Monastery, 78
    Vladimir Madonna, 137

Ignatius of Antioch (saint), 27–28
illuminated manuscripts, 113–15
   The Book of Lindisfarne, 91–92
   Vienna *Genesis*, 78
images, removal of by Muslims, 99
The Imitation of Christ (Thomas à Kempis), 179
Immaculate Conception, 241
Impressionism, 253
India, 194–95
   independence of, 267
Indigenous peoples, North America, 210–11
injustice, economic and political, 255–56
Innocent I (saint/pope), 59, 66
Innocent III (pope), 154–56, 159
Innocent V (pope), 155
Innocent X (pope), 213
Innocent XI (pope), 209, 214
Inquisition, 154, 159, 161
Introduction to the Devout Life (Francis de Sales), 207
Iona, Scotland, abbey, 72
Ireland
   Irish missionaries, 87, 90, 98
   Irish monks, influence of, 84
   Norse raids, 111–12
Irenaeus (saint), 26, 30–31
Irene (empress), 100
Iroquois people, 211–12
Isenheim altarpiece, 203–4
Islam
   attack on Otranto, 186–87
   conflict with Christianity, fourteenth century, 172
   conquest of Holy Land, 98–100
   fall of Constantinople, 185–86
   loss of Iberian Peninsula, 187–88
   Muslim invasion of Italy, ninth century, 111
   Saracens, 98–99, 107, 111
   seizure of Holy Land, seventh century, 88–89
   tenth century, 116
   threats to Rome, tenth century, 120
   threat to Western world, 197
Italy
   Gothic rulers, fifth century, 61–64
   invaded by Muslims, ninth century, 111
   Mussolini, 258, 260
   opera, nineteenth century, 251
   unification, nineteenth century, 244–45

James I (English king), 215, 217
James II (English king), 215
Jansen, Cornelius, 213
Jansenism, 213–14, 218, 221
Janson, H. W., 78
Japan, atomic bombs dropped on, 266
Jarrett, Bede, 143
Jeanne de Chantal (saint), 207–8
Jehovah's Witnesses, 32
Jennens, Charles, 234
Jerome (saint), 49, 51, 61–62, 192
Jerusalem, 123, 135, 139, 145, 159
   heavenly Jerusalem, 149
   destruction of, 21–23
   seizure in seventh century, 88
"Jerusalem" (Blake), 253

Jesuit Order (Society of Jesus),
    194–95, 211–12
  Jesuit martyrs: 200, 205, 210,
    211
  reestablishment of (1814), 239
  suppression of, eighteenth
    century, 226–27
Jews. *See* Judaism
Joan of Arc (saint), 184–85
John (English king), 154–55
John Chrysostom (saint), 48–49
John Duns Scotus, 158
John Eudes (saint), 208
John I (pope), 74–75, 77
John III (Portugese king), 194
John of Capistrano (saint),
    180–82, 192
John of the Cross (saint), 201–2,
    205, 208, 273
John Paul II (pope), 167, 188,
    196, 204,256, 260–61, 269,
    271, 275
Johnson, Lyndon B., 272
John the Baptist (saint), 177
John the Evangelist (saint), 16, 28
John X (pope), 120
John XI (pope), 120
John XII (pope), 121
John XXIII (pope), 260, 272
Jonson, Ben, 233
Jordani, Catacomb of, 42
Joseph II (Holy Roman
    Emperor), 227
Josephus, 22
Jubilee Year (1450), 179–80, 181
Judaism
  Jewish revolts, 21–22
  Jews as Chosen People, 31
  persecution and Holocaust,
    259–60

Judas Iscariot, 29
Julian of Norwich, 168–69
Julian the Apostate (emperor),
    52
Julius Caesar (Shakespeare), 216
Julius II (pope), 203
Junipero Serra (saint), 221
Junius Bassus, 53
Justin (emperor), 73
Justinian I (Byzantine emperor),
    75–78
"just war", 143–44

Kant, Immanuel, 225
Karl (Austrian emperor), 257
Kempe, Margery, 168–69
Kennedy, John F., 272
Khmer Rouge, 267
Kiev, 129–30, 137–38
Kilian (saint), 87
King Harald's Saga (Norse epic),
    136
King Lear (Shakespeare), 131,
    216–17
knighthood, 143–44
Knox, Ronald, 156, 184–85,
    241, 242
Kowalksa, Faustina, 262

Lactantius, 47
The Lady of the Lake (Scott), 250,
    251
Lambeth Conference, 258
Langland, William, 176–77
Langton, Stephen, 155
Läpple, Alfred, 71, 208
Las Navas de Tolosa, Spain, 161
Last Supper (Da Vinci), 191
Lateran Palace, 89
Latvia, 167

Lauda Sion Salvatorem (Thomas Aquinas), 164
Lawrence (saint), 66
Le banquet céleste (Messiaen), 270
Leif Erikson, 125
Lenin, Vladimir, 264
Leoghaire (Irish king), 66
Leo III (emperor), 99
Leo III (pope), 105–6
Leo IV (pope), 100, 107
Leo IX (pope), 127, 132
Leonardo da Vinci, 190–91
Leone, Sergio, 7
Leonine Wall, 107
Leo the Great (pope), 59, 62, 108
Leo VI (pope), 120
Leo VII (pope), 120
Leo XII (pope), 239
Leo XIII (pope), 94, 255, 258
"Lepanto" (Chesterton), 197
Levote, Francesca, 187
Levy, Michael, 230–31, 252
Lewis, C.S., 249, 273–74
Liber Scivias (Hildegard of Bingen), 152
Life of Constantine (Eusebius), 47
Liguori, Alphonsus (saint), 221
Lindau Gospels, 114–15
Lindisfarne (English island), 84, 111
Line, Anne (saint), 215–16
Liotard, Jean-Étienne, 232
Lippi, Fra Filippo, 188–89, 190
Litany of Loreto, 197–98, 228
Liturgy, 84, 162, 227–28
    Gregorian chant, 81
    liturgical chant, 53–54
    sacred polyphony, 269–70
Liturgy of the Hours (Divine Office), 118

Locke, John, 225
Logic (Aristotle), 140
Lollards, 183–84
Lombard, Peter, 141
Lombards (barbarian tribe), 72
    Lombard kingdom, 86–87
The Lord of the Rings (Tolkien), 273
L'Orfeo (Monteverdi), 218
Lorsch Gospel Book, 114
Lothair (king of Lorraine), 107–8
Louis (saint), 146
Louis (son of Charlemagne), 106–7
Louis de Montfort (saint), 220
Louise de Marillac (saint), 208
Louis II (emperor), 108
Louis IX (French king), 158
Louis XIV (French king), 209, 214, 218
Lourdes, 253, 274
Loyola, Ignatius (saint), 194–95
Lucca, Italy, 163
Ludwig II (Bavarian king), 250
Luithar Gospels, 123
Luke (saint), 16–17, 114
Luther, Martin, 31, 193, 197, 199, 203
Luxeuil, Burgundy, abbey, 72, 98
Lyrical Ballads (Wordsworth & Coleridge), 246

Macbeth (Shakespeare), 133, 216–17
MAD (mutually assured destruction), 267
Madonna and Child (Cimabue), 163, 174–75
Madonna and Child (Masaccio), 188

Madonna of the Carnation (Da Vinci), 190

Magna Carta, 154–55

Magnus IV (Swedish king), 166–67

Magyars, 116, 129

Manson, Aelfric, 96–97

manuscripts
  copying of, 97
  illumination of, 78, 91–92, 114–15, 123, 150
  manuscript paintings, 137

Manzoni, Alessandro, 248

Mao Zedung, 267

Marcion
  dualistic misreading of Gospel, 31
  revised version of New Testament, 31–33

Marcus Postumous, 40–41

Margaret (English princess), 272

Margaret Mary Alocoque (saint), 209

Margaret the Barefooted (saint), 168

Maria Theresa (empress), 223–24, 227

Marie Antionette (French queen), 224, 228

Mark (saint), 114

Marozia (matriarch), 120

Martel, Charles, 95, 98

Martindale, C. C., 19

Martin I (saint/pope), 89

Martin of Tours (saint), 49

Martin V (pope), 183

martyrdom, 89–90
  Asian and Ugandan martyrs, 242

blood of martyrs as seed of Church, 29, 39

Catholics in Japan, 211

French Revolution, 229

Jesuit missionaries, 200, 205, 210, 211

Miguel Pro, 264–65

Otranto Martyrs, 187

persecution of saints, sixteenth century, 200–202

under reign of Septimus Severus, 36

second century, 28–29

St. Anne Line, 215–16

St. Cecilia, 44–45

St. Ignatius, 27

SS. Peter and Paul, 21

third century, 36

Thomas Becket, 147–48

Tudor Terror, England, 200–201

Martyrdom of St. Sebastian (Pollaiuolo), 189

Marxism, 259, 264

Mary
  Blessed Virgin, 57–58
  devotion to, 169–71
  heart of, 208
  Marian apparitions, 169–70, 262, 274
  Mother of Christ/God-bearer, 57–58
  role in salvation, 241
  Sorrows of Mary, 179
  visions of St. Bernadette, 241

Maryland, United States, 221–22

Mary Magdalene (saint), 192

Mary Tudor, 215, 224

Masaccio, 188

Masonic secret societies, 239–40

Mass in B Minor (Bach), 233
materialism, 230, 240
Matthew (saint), 114
Matthew, Gervase, 93–94
Mauriac, François, 274
McInerny, Ralph, 158
Meconi, Fr. David Vincent, 27, 39
Medici, Piero de', 191
Mellitus (Bishop), 83
The Merchant of Venice (Shakespeare), 79–80, 216, 217
Messe "cum jubilo" (Duruflé), 270
Messiaen, Olivier, 270
Messiah (Handel), 233–34
Metaphysical poets, 217
Methodius (saint), 108, 167
Metz, France, 90–91, 172
Mexico
   anti-Catholic regimes, twentieth century, 264–65
   Cristero War, 265
   missionaries to, 198, 221
Michelangelo, 55, 203, 218
Millet, Jean-François, 253
Milton, John, 217
Mindszenty, Cardinal, 267
The Miracle of Bolsena (Raphael), 203
miracles, 84, 181, 212, 241, 262
   Cuthbert and Adrian, 86
   Ethelreda and Ethelburga, 85
Mirari Vos (Gregory XVI), 240
Miserere (Górecki), 270–71
Missionaries, 60, 83, 93, 130, 194
   to the Americas, 209–11
   Irish missionaries, 87, 90

   to Germanic tribes in eighth century, 95–96
   to Mexico, 198, 221–22
   Society of Foreign Missions, 239
   third century, 37
Moczar, Diane, 105–6, 126, 128
modernism, 268–69
   ecclesiastical, 256
Mohammed, 88
Mohawk people, 211
Möhler, Johann Adam, 248
Moissac, France, priory of Saint-Pierre, 149
Molière, 217–18
Molla, Gianna Beretta, 262
monasticism
   Benedictine, 71
   foundations of, 48–49
   iconography, 78
   in Ireland, 71–72
   monastic communities, 92
   monk, origin of word, 48
Monet, Claude, 253
Monophysite heresy, 63, 75
Monothelitism, 89
Montanism, 32–33
Monte Cassino, monastery of St. Benedict, 71
Monteverdi, Claudio, 218
morality plays, 153
Moral Theology (Liguori), 221
More, Thomas (saint), 199
Moscow, St. Basil's Cathedral, 204
Moses, 78
Mozart, Wolfgang Amadeus, 234–35
Munch, Edvard, 188
Mura (saint), 90

music. *See also* chant
  chansons de geste, 151–52
  chant/polyphony, 204, 269–71
  harmony, 79–80, 153
  Hildegard of Bingen, 152–53
  inspiration for composers, 45
  liturgical, 53–54, 251, 270
  musical notation, 92
  pictorialism, 233
  polyphony, 204–5
  prayers, 153
  reform of church music,
    sixteenth century, 196
  Romantic movement, 233
  rooted in Greek philosophy,
    79
  sacred vs. pagan, 44
  St. Cecilia as patron saint,
    44–45
  troubadours, 150–52
musica humana, 79
musica instrumentalis, 79–80
musica mundana, 79–80
Muslims. *See* Islam
Mussolini, Benito, 258, 260

Nagasaki, Japan, 266–67
Napoleon, 230, 236–39, 243, 246
narcissism and twentieth century
  art, 271
nationalism, secular, 228, 242–43
NATO nations, 267
Nazi Party, 258–60
  blitzkrieg, 266
Neale, John Mason, 54
Nebuchadnezzar II, 43
neo-medievalism, 247, 249
Neoplatonists, 58, 140
Neo-Scholasticism, 255–56
Neri, Philip (saint), 195, 233

Nero (emperor), 19–21
Neumann, John, 242
Newfoundland, 125
Newman, John Henry, 87, 242,
  247–48, 269
"New Song", Christ as, 44
Nicene Creed, 51
Nicholas I (Nicholas the Great)
  (pope), 107–8
Nicholas V (pope), 180
Nietzsche, Friedrich, 250
"Nimrod Variations" (Elgar), 269
Nobel Prize in Literature,
  274–75
Norman Conquest (1066), 119,
  132–33, 135–36
Norsemen (Vikings), 111–13,
  116, 124–25, 130, 136
Northern Rebellion, England,
  200
Norway, missionaries to, 130
Notker the Stammerer, 94
Novatian of Rome, 41–42
novels, golden age of, nineteenth
  century, 248
nuclear arms
  arms race during Cold War,
    267
  used in World War II, 266

O'Connor, Flannery, 274
Oderisi da Gubbio, 175
Odo of Cluny, 120
Ognissanti Madonna (Giotto), 174
Olaf (Norwegian king), 130
Old English (Anglo-Saxon), 101,
  104, 135–36, 176
Omer (saint), 87
"On a Dark Night" (St. John of
  the Cross), 202

*One Day in the Life of Ivan
    Denisovich* (Solzhenitsyn), 275
Opellius Macrinus (emperor), 40
opera, nineteenth century, 251
Order of Reformed Cistercians of
    Our Lady of La Trappe, 208
Order of the Visitation, 207–8
Ordo virtutum (Hildegard of
    Bingen), 153
Origen (theological scholar),
    37–38
Original Sin, 62–63, 213, 241
Orkney Islands, 124–25
O Salutaris Hostia (Thomas
    Aquinas), 163
Ostrogoths (Germanic tribe),
    63, 73
Oswald (Northumbrian king/
    saint), 84
Othello (Shakespeare), 216, 217
Othello (Verdi), 251
Otranto, Italy, 186–87
Otranto Martyrs, 187
Otto I (Holy Roman Emperor),
    121
Otto II (Holy Roman Emperor),
    121, 129
Otto III (Holy Roman
    Emperor), 121, 123, 128–29
Ottoman Empire, 172, 186, 197,
    264
Ottonian dynasty, 121–23
Ouen (saint), 87
Our Lady of Guadalupe, 198, 264
Oxford, university, 140
Oxford Movement, 247–48

Pachomius (saint), 48
pagan gods/practices, 38, 52
Pakistan, independence of, 267

Palestrina, Giovanni Pierluigi da,
    196, 204
Pange Lingua (Thomas Aquinas),
    163
Papacy
    doctrinal understanding of,
        foundations, 49
    golden age of, 255
    papal authority, 49, 106–8
    prestige and power, eleventh
        century, 126–27, 128–29
    rival popes in Avignon, 167,
        173
    saeculum obscurum (dark
        century), 120–21
    secular influences, eighteenth
        century, 226
    "three pope" period, fifteenth
        century, 182–83
    See also names of specific popes
Papal Basilica of St. Paul Outside
    the Walls, 53
Paris, university establishment
    (1150), 140
Paris Psalter, 123
Parsifal (Wagner), 250
Pärt, Arvo, 45, 270, 271
Pascal, Blaise, 217–18
Paschal I (pope), 45
Paschal II (pope), 118, 128
Passionist Order, 220
Patrick (saint), 60, 66, 71
Paul (saint), 15–16
    escape from prison, 17
    execution of, 18–19
    exile of, 17
    Letter to the Hebrews, 62
    trials and suffering, 17–18
Paul III (pope), 194
Paul of Bernried, 128

Paul of the Cross (saint), 220
Paul VI (pope), 167, 260, 261, 268
Peada (Mercian king), 83
Peasants' Revolt (1381), 170, 177
Peasants' War (1524), 199
Péguy, Charles, 274
Pelagianism, 62–63, 101–3
Pelagius, 62, 101
Penda (Mercian king), 85
Pensées (Pascal), 218
Pentecost, 254
Pepin (king of Franks), 95
Percy, Walker, 274
Perpetua (martyr), 36, 40
Peter (saint), 59
    execution of, 18–19
    First Letter, 17
    and foundations of Church, 49
    significant role in early Church, 16–17
Petrarch, 176
Philibert (saint), 87
Philip II (Spanish king), 201
Philip the Arab (emperor), 37
philosophy
    Descartes and modern philosophy, 214
    revival of, twelfth century, 140–41
    theology, and, 58, 69, 261
Physics (Aristotle), 140
Piazzetta, Giovanni Battista, 232
pictorialism, 233
Pietà (Botticelli), 189
Pietà (Michelangelo), 218
Pilgrimage of Grace, 200
pilgrimages
    Holy Land, 144–45
    pilgrim culture, eleventh century, 138–39

Rome, Jubilee Year (1450), 179–80
    St. Brigid to Rome, 166
    St. Helena to Holy Land, 48
    twelfth century, 148–49
    Walsingham, England, 133, 169–71
pilgrim man (*homo viator*), 8–9
Pisa, Italy, 138 163
Pius V (saint/pope), 196–98, 209
Pius VI (pope), 230
Pius VII (pope), 237, 239, 255
    held captive (1808–1814), 238
Pius VIII (pope), 239–40
Pius IX (pope), 167, 240–41, 244–45
Pius X (pope), 256, 269
Pius XI (pope), 255, 258
Pius XII (pope), 167, 259–60
plague, 77, 172–73
Plato, 8n3, 58, 79
Poema de Mio Cid, 136–37
poetic man (*anthropos*), 9
poetry
    Anglo-Saxon, 101–4
    Dante, 175–76
    fourteenth century, 163–64
    inspiration for poets, 45
    vernacular poetry and troubadours, 150–51
Poland, Solidarity trade union, 259–61, 270–71
Pollaiuolo, Antonio, 189
Pol Pot, 267
Polycarp (saint), 28
polyphony, 204–5. *See also* music
"Pomp and Circumstance" (Elgar), 269
Poor Clare nuns, 168, 191–92
Pope, Alexander, 45

Popular History of the Catholic Church (Hughes), 100
Postgate, Nicholas, 216
Poulenc, Francis, 270
Pre-Raphaelites, 189, 247, 253
pride, as dark thread in history, 10
Primaldi, Antonio, 187
Primavera (Botticelli), 189
Priscilla, catacomb of, 35, 42
    Crypt of the Veiled Lady, 43
Pro, Miguel, 264–65
Probus (emperor), 41
progressivism, ecclesiastical, 256
Protestantism, 31–32
    combating, 197
    Marcionist "church" and Gospel purity, 32
    Protestant Reformation, 183, 193, 199
proud man (*homo superbus*), 9
Prussia, 243–44. *See also* Germany
Pudentiana (saint), 66
Pugin, Augustus, 247
Purcell, Henry, 45
Pythagoras, 79

Quadragesimo Anno (Pius XI), 255
Quatour pour la fin du temps (Messiaen), 270

Raphael, 203
Ratzinger, Joseph Cardinal (Pope Benedict XVI), 9–10, 24–25, 261, 269
Ravenna, Italy, 65–66, 78–79, 99
Reagan, Ronald, 261, 275
Reccared I (Visigoth king), 71
Reclining Girl (Boucher), 232
Redemptorists, 221

Reformation, 193–94, 199
Reign of Terror, French Revolution, 228–30, 246–47, 270
relativism, 183, 268
Rembrandt van Rijn, 218
Remigius (Bishop of Reims), 64
Renaissance, 174–76
    Renaissance artists, 188–91
Requiem (Duruflé), 270
Requiem (Fauré), 252
Requiem (Mozart), 235
Requiem (Verdi), 251
Rerum Novarum (Leo XIII), 255–56, 258
Revelations of Divine Love (Julian of Norwich), 169
revolutions
    age of, nineteenth century, 246
    anticommunist, Eastern Europe, 261
    Bolshevik Revolution, 264, 264
    French Revolution, 224–30, 238–40, 246–47, 264
    Glorious Revolution, 215
    Sexual Revolution, 268
Richard II (English king), 170, 177
Richeldis de Faverches, 133
Rievaulx, Yorkshire, abbey, 141–42
Robert of Molesme, 141
Robert the Bruce, 170
Roland, 110
Roman Empire
    adoption of Greek culture, 63–64
    collapse of, 56, 61–62
    and Western culture, 69–70

Romanesque style
  architecture, 122, 138
  sculpture, 149
Romania, 37
Romanticism, 246–47
  German, nineteenth century,
    248–50
Romaric (saint), 87
Rome
  called "Babylon", 17
  catacombs, 34–35
  climate of treachery, first
    century, 20–21
  early spread of Christianity, 16
  as Eternal City, 15–16
  threats from Islam, 120
Romeo and Juliet (Shakespeare), 216
Rosarium Metricum (St. Catherine
  of Bologna), 192
Rose of Lima (saint), 211
Rossini, Gioachino, 251
Rouen Cathedral, 253
Rousseau, Jean-Jacques, 226
Rubens, Peter Paul, 218
"The Ruin" (Anglo-Saxon
  poem), 103
Rule of St. Benedict, 71, 117, 141
Russia, 37
  as center of Eastern
    Christianity, 204
  Conversion of Russia, 130
  Russian art, eleventh century,
    137–38
  See also Soviet Union
Ruthwell Cross, Scotland, 103–4

sacramentary, 115
sacraments
  and beauty, 23
  deepening and renewal,
    nineteenth century, 240–41

Sacred Congregation of the
  Propogation of the Faith,
    209–10
Sacred Heart of Jesus, 208–9
saeculum obscurum (dark century),
    120–21
Sagrada Família, Basilica of,
  Barcelona (Gaudi), 273
Saint Matthew Passion (Bach), 233
Saint Peter of Solesmes,
  Benedictine Abbey, 252
saints
  folk tales and legends, 124
  goodness of, 10
  patron saints of Europe, 167
  persecution of, 200–202
  veneration of, 139
  women, fourteenth century,
    166
  See also specific names of saints
Saint-Savin-sur-Gartempe,
  Benedictine Abbey, 149
salvation, mystery of
  Handel's Messiah, 234
  Mary's role, 241
Salve Regina, 153
Sandoval, Alfonso de, 210
Sant'Ambrogio Basilica, Milan,
    138
Santiago de Compostela, 148–49
Santiago de Compostela
  Cathedral, Galicia, 138
Santi Quattro Coronati, church,
    128
Saracens, 98–99, 106, 111. See
  also Islam
Saxons (Germanic tribe), 95
Scandinavian Vikings, 124. See
  also Norsemen (Vikings)
Scarlatti, Alessandro, 45
Schlegel, Friedrich, 248

scholarship
  eighth century, 96–97
  monasteries in British Isles,
    112
  seventh century, 86
Scholasticism, 157, 175
The School of Athens (Raphael),
  203
Schreck, Alan, 121, 135, 144–46,
  154, 159, 161, 164, 255
Schubert, Franz, 250
scientism, reactions against, 230,
  246
Scott, Sir Walter, 250, 251
The Scream (Munch), 188
"The Seafarer" (Anglo-Saxon
  poem), 103
Second Coming of Christ, 32
Second Crusade, 145
Second Vatican Council, 260,
  268–69
The Secret of Mary (St. Louis de
  Montfort), 220
The Secret of the Rosary (St. Louis
  de Montfort), 220
secularism
  secularism vs. faith, 148
  secularist revolutions (1848),
    240
  secular nationalism, 228
  tyranny of, 254
Segna di Bonaventura, 163
Senior, John, 81
Septimus Severus (emperor), 36,
  39–40
Sergius (pope), 86
Seton, Elizabeth Anne, 242
*Seven Spiritual Weapons Necessary
  for Spiritual Warfare* (St.
  Catherine of Bologna), 192
sexual revolution, 268

Shakespeare, William, 69, 79–80,
  205–6, 206n12, 216–17, 251
Shannon, Christopher, 211
Shelley, Mary, 252
Shetland Islands, 124–25
Siege of Metz, 172
Siena, Italy, 163
Sigismund (Burgundian king), 70
Silverius (pope), 75–76
simony, 127
Sir Gawain and the Green Knight,
  176–77
Sisters of Charity, 208
Sistine Chapel, 203
Sixtus II (pope), 38
Slattery, William J., 97
slavery, 210–11
  slave trade, 199
  United States Civil War, 243
Smithsonian History Year by Year,
  224–25
socialism, 255
Society of Foreign Missions,
  239
Society of Jesus. *See* Jesuit Order
  (Society of Jesus)
sola fide, 183
sola scriptura, 183
Solidarity trade union, Poland,
  260–61, 271
Solzhenitsyn, Aleksandr, 202,
  261, 274–75
The Song of Bernadette (Werfel),
  274
The Song of Roland (French
  medieval epic), 110, 151–52
Sophocles, 69
Soubirous, Bernadette (saint),
  241
Southwell, Robert (saint), 200,
  205, 217

Soviet Union, 259, 260–61, 267
  Bolshevik Revolution and
    Red Terror, 264
  dissolution of, 275
  Solzhenitsyn, 274–75
Spain
  Islamic vs. Christian control,
    161
  Spanish Civil War, twentieth
    century, 265
Speculum Caritatis (Aelred), 142–43
Spenser, Edmund, 205
Speyer Cathedral, 138
The Spirit of the Liturgy (Benedict
  XVI), 261
"Spiritual Canticle" (St. John of
  the Cross), 202
Stalin, Joseph, 264
St. Basil's Cathedral, Moscow, 204
St. Catherine's Monastery,
  Egypt, 78
Stein, Edith, 167
steles, 90–91
Stephen (saint/Hungarian king),
  129
Stephen, Sir James, 127–28
Stephen II (pope), 95
Stephen VII (pope), 120
Stepinac, Cardinal, 267
St. Foy in Majesty statue, 139
St. Gall monastery, Switzerland,
  115
St. Mark's Basilica, Venice, 138
Stolberg, Friedrich Leopold, 248
The Story of Art (Gombrich), 162
Stowe Missal, 115
St. Patrick's Breastplate, 66
St. Paul's Cathedral, London, 83
St. Peter's Basilica, Rome,
  52–53, 218–19

Stradivari, Antonio, 232–33
St. Sophia Cathedral, Kiev,
  137–38
Sturluson, Snorri, 136
Suetonius, 20
Sueves (barbarian tribe), 61, 71
Summa Theologica (Thomas
  Aquinas), 158
Summi Pontificatus (Pius XII), 259
Swift, Jonathan, 230
Sylvester I (pope), 53
Sylvester II (pope), 129
symbolism
  of fish, 34
  images of apostles, 114
  of pilgrimages, 149
Synod of Benevento, 128
Synod of Whitby, 83, 84
Syria, 37, 43

Tacitus, 20–21, 33
A Tale of Two Cities (Dickens),
  158
Tallis, Thomas, 205
Tantum Ergo (Thomas Aquinas),
  163
Tatian, 33
Tavener, John, 270
technology, adoption of, 240
Te Deum (hymn), 54, 251
Tekakwitha, Kateri (saint),
  211–12
The Temptation of Saint Anthony
  (Flaubert), 55
Ten Dates Every Catholic Should
  Know (Moczar), 126
Teresa Benedicta of the Cross
  (saint), 167, 262
Teresa of Ávila (saint), 167, 201,
  208, 217

Teresa of Calcutta, 262
Teresa of the Andes, 262
Tertullian, 29, 32–33, 39
Thatcher, Margaret, 261, 275
Theodora (empress), 75
Theodoric the Great, 63, 73–75, 78
Theodotians, 30
Theotokos (God-bearer), 57–58
Thérèse of Lisieux, 242
Thessalonica, Greece, 16
Theutberga, 107–8
Third Crusade, 145
The Thirteenth, Greatest of Centuries (Walsh), 164
Thirty Years' War, 212–13
Thomas à Kempis, 179
Thomistic revival, 255. *See also* Aquinas, Thomas (saint)
3 May 1808 (Goya), 252
The Three Men in the Fiery Furnace (in Catacomb of Priscilla), 42–43
Tiberius Caesar (emperor), 19
Tolkien, J. R. R., 25, 101, 273, 279
Tolstoy, Leo, 248
Totus Tuus (Górecki), 271
Tra Le Sollecitudini (Pius X), 269
translation
    of Aristotle into Latin, 140
    of Scripture, 183
    into Slavic languages, 108
    Vulgate, 49
Trappists, 208
Trastevere, Basilica of Santa Cecilia, 44–45
Travancore, India, 194–95
Treacy, Susan, 80, 153, 218, 234, 249–51, 270–71

Treatise on the Love of God (Francis de Sales), 207
Treaty of Aix-la-Chapelle, 223
Treaty of Versailles, 257–58
Tridentine Catechism, 196
Tridentine Reformation, 194, 203
Trinity, 51
    De Trinitate (Augustine), 58
Trojan War, 15
troubadours, 150–52
Troy, 15
True Devotion to Mary (St. Louis de Montfort), 220
Tudor Terror, England, 200–201
Tunisia, 245
Turner, J. M. W., 253

Ubi Primum (Pius IX), 241
Ugolino di Nerio, 163
Undset, Sigrid, 274
United States
    Catholicism in nineteenth century, 239
    Catholics in Maryland, 221–22
    Civil War, 243
universities, foundation of, twelfth century, 140
"Upon the Image of Death" (Southwell), 217
Urban I (pope), 45
Urban II (pope), 118, 128, 135, 145
Urban VI (pope), 167, 173

Valentinus, 33
Valerian, 44
Valery (saint), 87
Vandals (barbarian tribe), 61, 62
Vasari, Giorgio, 174

Vatican Hill, 107

Vatican II. *See* Second Vatican Council

Vaughan Williams, Ralph, 269

Vega, Lope de, 217

Velazquez, Diego, 218

Vendée, rising, 237, 253

Veni redemptor gentium (hymn), 54

Verbum Supernum Prodiens (Thomas Aquinas), 163

Verdi, Giuseppe, 251

Veritatis Splendor (John Paul II), 261

Versailles, palace, storming of, 228

Verus (emperor), 28

Vianney, Jean-Marie, 242

Victor (pope), 29–30

Victoria (English queen), 245–46

Victoria, Tomás Luis de, 204

Victor III (pope), 128

Vienna, Turkish Siege (1683), 209

Vienna Genesis (illuminated manuscripts), 78

Vienne, France, persecution of Christians, 28–29

Vigilius (pope), 75–76

Vikings (Norsemen), 111–13, 116, 124–25, 136

Villani, Giovanni, 174

Vincent (saint), 232

Vincent de Paul (saint), 207–8

Vincent of Saragossa (saint), 66

Vinland (Brown), 124–25

Vinland, North America, 125

violins, 232–33

Virgil, 15, 69, 175

Virgin Mary, 57–58. *See also* Mary

Virgin of the Rocks (Da Vinci), 190

Visigoths (barbarian tribe), 61, 71, 73

visions, mystical, 132, 152, 166, 169, 209

Visitation Order, 209

Vivaldi, Antonio, 233

Vladimir (saint), 129–30

Vladimir Madonna, 137

Voltaire, 226

von Ribbentrop, Joachim, 260

Voss, Johann, 180

Vulgate, 49

Wagner, Richard, 250

Walburga (saint), 137

Walpole, Henry, 205

Walsh, James J., 164

Walsingham, England, 133, 169–71

"The Wanderer" (Anglo-Saxon poem), 103

Wandrille (saint), 87

warfare
    civilians as targets, 264, 266
    industrialized weapons, twentieth century, 262–63, 265–66
    introduction of cannon and gunpowder, 172
    "just war", 143–44

War of the Austrian Succession, 223

Waugh, Evelyn, 274

Wayne, John, 7

Way of the Cross (Liguori), 221

"weird", origins of word, 8n2

Werfel, Franz, 274

Western Hemisphere, European conquest of, 198–99

Westminster Abbey, 132
Whitby Abbey, 101
Whiting, Richard, 200
Wild West, myth of, 7
Wilfrid (saint), 86
Wilhelm I (Prussian emperor), 243, 246
William of Ockham, 183
William the Pious (Duke of Aquitaine), 116–18
Wilton Diptych, 170, 177–78
Winchester Cathedral, 123
Winchester Psalter, 150

Windesheim, Netherlands, 180
Wordsworth, William, 246
World War I, 256–58, 263–64
World War II, 259, 265–66
Wright, Joseph, 232
Wulstan (saint), 136
Wycliffe, John, 183
Wyszynski, Cardinal, 267

York (Eboracum), 112

Zadar, Croatia, 159